DEVELOPING HELPING SKILLS

DEVELOPING HELPING SKILLS

A Step-by-Step Approach

Valerie Nash Chang
Indiana University

Sheryn T. Scott
Azusa Pacific University

Carol L. Decker
Indiana University

BROOKS/COLE
CENGAGE Learning™

Australia · Brazil · Canada · Mexico · Singapore · Spain · United Kingdom · United States

BROOKS/COLE
CENGAGE Learning

Developing Helping Skills:
A Step-by-Step Approach
Valerie Chang, Sheryn Scott, Carol Decker

Development Editor: Tangelique Williams

Assistant Editor: Stephanie Rue

Editorial Assistant: Caitlin Cox

Technology Project Manager: Andrew Keay

Marketing Manager: Karin Sandberg

Marketing Assistant: Ting Jiang Yap

Marketing Communications Manager:
Shemika Britt

Project Manager, Editorial Production:
Christy Krueger

Creative Director: Rob Hugel

Art Director: Caryl Gorska

Print Buyer: Judy Inouye

Permissions Editor: Mardell Glinski Schultz

Production Service: Matrix Productions

Copy Editor: Janet Tilden

Cover Designer: Brenda Duke

Cover Image: Mick Tarel/Getty Images

Compositor: International Typesetting
and Composition

For product information and technology assistance,
contact us at
**Cengage Learning Academic Resource Center,
1-800-423-0563**
For permission to use material from this text or product,
submit all requests online at **cengage.com/permissions**.
Further permissions questions can be e-mailed to
permissionrequest@cengage.com.

Library of Congress Control Number: 2007933301

Student Edition with DVD:

ISBN-13: 978-0-495-09258-2
ISBN-10: 0-495-09258-4

Student Edition:

ISBN-13: 978-0-495-59568-7
ISBN-10: 0-495-59568-3

Brooks/Cole
10 Davis Drive
Belmont, CA 94002-3098
USA

Cengage Learning is a leading provider of customized learning solutions with office locations around the globe, including Singapore, the United Kingdom, Australia, Mexico, Brazil, and Japan. Locate your local office at **international.cengage.com/region**.

Cengage Learning products are represented in Canada by Nelson Education, Ltd.

For your course and learning solutions, visit **academic.cengage.com**.

Purchase any of our products at your local college store or at our preferred online store **www.ichapters.com**.

Printed in Canada
4 5 6 7 11 10

To our clients, our students, our families, and our friends: we have learned so much from each of you.

CONTENTS

OVERVIEW OF THE CASES

Case Title	Brief Description
Jill Asks for Help	Young, Caucasian woman who is depressed after the breakup of a relationship
Additional Cases on the Instructors' Website	
Bill: Are You Saying She's Going to Die?	Middle-aged, Chinese American male with ALS living in a nursing home where his mother also resides
John: Where Do I Fit In?	Mexican-American junior high age boy who is being teased by his peers
Buddy Returns Home	Rural, white, family whose 16-year-old son is being returned home after five years in residential treatment
The 10th Street Community Comes Together	Mixed-race lower socioeconomic class community looking for ways to improve their community
Tony: I Just Don't Know	African American family who are initiating court-ordered home-based services for their 12-year-old son with truancy and delinquency problems

Reading Assignment	Case Material	
Chapters 4, 5, and 6: Core interpersonal qualities, basic interpersonal skills, and opening and closing a session	Part 1: Basic intake information	page 79
Chapters 7 and 8: Expressing understanding, using questions to explore	Part 2: Material from the first meeting with client	page 106
Chapters 9 and 10: Seeking clarification and further understanding, assessing readiness and motivation	Part 3: Additional material about case situation	page 134
Chapters 11 and 12: Identifying key problems or challenges and establishing goals	Part 4: Goal-setting information	page 172
Chapter 13: Taking action	Part 5: Information about action or treatment	page 200
Chapter 14: Evaluating progress and ending	Part 6: Planning for evaluation and ending	page 216
	Part 7: Evaluation and ending	page 220

CONTRIBUTING AUTHORS

TEXT

CASES

PREFACE

A tremendous amount of information is available regarding techniques for working with specific systems such as organizations, families, or groups, but fewer texts explore the overarching skills, knowledge, and processes that are essential to working with any system. This text is designed to fill that gap by focusing on skills that can be used in working with systems of all sizes. Our premise is that beginning practitioners need to master foundational information and demonstrate understanding, appropriate use of self, and professional tasks and skills before moving to advanced approaches or system-specific knowledge and skills.

The chapters in this book have been organized into five sections: I. Foundation; II. Building Relationships; III. Exploring and Assessing with Clients; IV. Defining the Focus of Work; and V. Doing the Work, Evaluating, and Ending the Work. The chapters in Section I cover practitioner information and tasks related to the importance of self-understanding, major ways of perceiving self and others, and understanding professional relationships, roles, ethics, and legal obligations. In most educational programs there will be additional courses that cover in-depth information related to cultural competency and diversity, ethics, and theoretical models. The chapters in Sections II through V describe skills and qualities used by practitioners and strengths and resources contributed by clients. Each chapter provides ample opportunities for students to practice the skills described.

This text was written with two main goals in mind. The first is to provide fundamental knowledge about professional relationships, basic perspectives, and the change process to students who are preparing for careers in the fields of social work, psychology, educational counseling, counseling, marriage and family therapy, pastoral counseling, human services, and related helping professions. The second goal of the book is to provide students with opportunities to learn the basic practice skills necessary to work effectively with all sizes of client systems. In order to achieve these goals, the following teaching-learning system is recommended.

TEACHING-LEARNING SYSTEM

Becoming a competent practitioner requires that students learn not only the foundational practice knowledge but also how to approach cases as an experienced practitioner. It involves appropriate use of the skills and tasks necessary to work effectively with clients. The learning system presented in this book provides information and practice to help students become competent, self-reflective professionals, able to evaluate their practice and identify strengths and areas for growth related to skill development and knowledge acquisition.

Achieving competency requires multiple methods of learning. Although each person learns in his or her own unique way, we have found active learning methods to be useful, effective, and popular with undergraduate and graduate students. This teaching-learning system involves the following learning methods:

Reading about information related to professional practice and the skills and tasks needed to work effectively with clients;
Thinking and writing about ideas related to the concepts that are discussed;
Watching and discussing a DVD demonstration of appropriate use of the skill;
Working with cases to apply knowledge and skills to specific situations;
Practicing the skills in a simulated interview;
Evaluating the use of the skills immediately after practicing them.

READING

As each new concept, skill, or task is introduced, students read about how the knowledge or skill is applied with different system sizes including individuals, families, groups, and larger systems.

THINKING AND WRITING

Homework exercises are provided following the introduction of each new concept. The homework exercises invite students to think about the concepts and skills presented and to write about and actively work with new concepts. In many homework exercises students are encouraged to reflect on how the concept is related to their own life experiences. Additional information about ways to use the exercises and grade the homework is available on the website for instructors who are using this text.

WATCHING AND DISCUSSING

This text is accompanied by a DVD demonstrating the use of many of the skills. Following the introduction of a group of new skills, students can watch a practitioner using the skills with an individual, a support group, and/or a family. Exercises for each section of the DVD include asking students to name the skills being used, to identify other skills that might be used, and to evaluate the practitioner's use of skills. Further discussion of exercises is provided on the instructors' website. Transcripts of the client-practitioner interaction are provided on the instructors' website and on the students' website.

WORKING WITH CASES

Problem-based learning is an educational system in which students work with the complexities of real cases. For many students, information and skills learned in class do not transfer to real-world practice (Koerin, Harrigan, & Reeves, 1990; Vayda & Bogo, 1991). One way to help students with this transfer of knowledge and skills is by providing opportunities for them to work on real-life cases. Thinking through the complexity of working with cases based on actual practice situations helps students learn to think like professionals (Wolfer & Scales, 2005). Using a modified problem-based learning system, each case is presented in seven sections with accompanying questions for students to consider. Each section provides additional information and questions for students to answer. The first case section includes the intake level of information. The second section builds on information from the first meeting. The third section provides additional information on the problems being addressed. The fourth section focuses on goals. The fifth section describes the action phase of the work. The sixth and seventh sections cover evaluating and ending the professional relationship. To maximize student participation and learning, we suggest having students form groups to work on the cases. Students should answer all the questions individually prior to coming together with their group to discuss the answers. The final step is for the group to present and/or write their answers to each question.

The example case provided in the book can be used in class to demonstrate how to work with the cases. Several other cases with a variety of clients and client situations are available on the instructors' website, and more cases will be added. These cases have been selected because they include numerous topics and issues to invite discussion and learning. Providing the case information on the instructors' website allows instructors to select any or all of the cases for classroom use and to present the case information sequentially. We recommend using a modified problem-based learning approach that simulates real practice by giving students a section of case information at a time. Students who have used this modified problem-based learning method have reported that working with cases required them to think about how to apply theory to practice, prepared them to work with clients, and helped them to feel confident about their readiness to work with clients. The instructors' website also includes information about this modified problem-based learning method and suggests ways to use the cases to enhance student learning.

PRACTICING AND EVALUATING

The next aspect of the learning system involves using practice exercises to develop students' ability to apply their knowledge of appropriate practice tasks and skills. In the practice exercises, each student works in a group of three or more people who take turns playing the roles of practitioner, client, and peer supervisor. Each practice exercise includes specific directions for the person in the role of client, practitioner, and peer supervisor and is followed by a simple evaluation tool to be completed by the peer supervisor and practitioner.

As students practice new skills, it is important for them to be able to evaluate their competency. This book includes an evaluation system that has been tested and shown to be valid (Pike, Bennett, & Chang, 2004). Undergraduate and graduate students as well as agency supervisors have been able to quickly learn and use this system. After teaching the students basic information about the importance of immediate feedback and evaluation as well as how to use this simple evaluation system, instructors have found that the most effective way of using this evaluation system is to move from one small group to another to assist students who are acting as peer supervisors and to offer additional evaluative comments for the students who are in the role of practitioner. Later in the course, instructors may require students to do videotaped interviews that are evaluated both by the student and by the instructor. Additional information related to using the evaluation system is available on the instructors' website. When the students move on to practicum or internship placements, they can assess the quality of their work with clients by using the same evaluation system. If their supervisors have been trained to use this evaluation system, it will be simple for students and their supervisors to set specific goals for improvement. Using this evaluation system in class and/or in field settings is an excellent way to measure and demonstrate skill competency.

The evaluation system introduced in this book provides students with immediate feedback about their use of skills and their demonstration of core interpersonal qualities. Immediate feedback is a central part of this learning system. After each practice session, three things happen: (1) the person in the client role gives feedback about whether or not he or she felt understood and thought there was a respectful connection with the practitioner, (2) the practitioner identifies his or her perceived strengths and weaknesses, and (3) the peer supervisor gives the practitioner feedback on the use of skills. In the role of peer supervisor, students learn to constructively evaluate both the use of skills and the demonstration of core interpersonal qualities and to give constructive feedback to others. Guidelines for making these judgments are provided so that beginning practitioners can learn to accurately evaluate skills and recognize strengths and limitations. Learning to evaluate self and others is essential to professional growth. Without the use of behavioral descriptors in evaluating themselves, beginning practitioners are not likely to be aware of their mistakes and to correct and learn from their errors (Kruger & Dunning, 1999).

Using this learning system, students focus on one group of skills at a time. After mastering one group of skills, students move on to the next discrete group of skills. Each new group of skills builds on the previously practiced skills. With each practice session, students repeat the previously practiced skills and begin to learn new skills. As students improve their ability to use skills, they receive positive feedback and experience increasing confidence in their ability to use the practiced skills. The many students who have used this approach to learning practice skills report that they learned a great deal from being in each role. Using this book and education system, students can gain a sense of competency in the use of the basic knowledge, tasks, and skills necessary to effectively facilitate the change process.

After developing an adequate repertoire of basic interviewing skills, students can move on to more advanced skills, develop a personal style or ways to more fully include their unique ways of relating in the process, and learn to use skills effectively with a wide variety of clients in many different situations. As these basic skills become automatic, students will be able to focus more completely on the process with clients. Their ability to be empathic, warm, respectful, and genuine will increase as they develop greater confidence in their mastery of the basic skills.

Ultimately, our goal is that each student will become an effective, reflective practitioner who uses self-evaluation, learns from mistakes and successes, and is continuously improving.

A FEW WORDS ABOUT LANGUAGE

Although we believe that there are no right ways to deal with the challenges of language, we value clarity. Therefore, we will explain the language decisions that we have made. We have chosen to use the word *practitioner* in reference to helping professionals from all backgrounds (e.g., counseling, psychology, social work, pastoral care, nursing, marriage and family therapy, and so on). We use gender-specific pronouns when that seems appropriate but otherwise use *s/he* to designate a person. When referring to clients who may be individuals, families, groups, or organizations, we specify a particular system size if that designation is needed; otherwise we use the word *client* to refer to the many system sizes. We use the word *group* to refer to a task group (people working on a project), a support group (people whose goal is to support and encourage each other), and a counseling group (people who are helping each other to make life changes). Finally, we have chosen to use the word *counseling* when referring to the many activities engaged in by practitioners when working to facilitate change with individuals, families, and groups.

ACKNOWLEDGMENTS

We want to thank all of those who have contributed to our work: clients, students, teachers, and colleagues at Indiana University School of Social Work and Azusa Pacific University, Department of Graduate Psychology, our families, our friends, the reviewers, editors, and all of the many other people who have contributed to this project.

We are grateful to each person at Cengage Learning who helped and encouraged us at each step of this process. Lisa Gebo, our first editor, suggested that we write a practice book that would meet the needs of several disciplines. Her suggestions and ideas helped us through the beginning phases of creating the plans for the book. Alma Dea Michelena, the next editor, met with us and facilitated thinking through the plans for the DVD. The high standards and wonderful support of Dan Alpert, the next editor, assisted us through some challenging times. Tangelique Williams, Development Editor, certainly deserves her title. She helped us develop every part of the book. There have been many others at Cengage who have provided support along the way, including Tracy Stuart, Senior Custom Editor, who has been very patient and helpful in creating custom editions of the book; Marcus Boggs, Publisher; Julie Aquilar, Technology Project Manager; and Stephanie Rue, Assistant Editor. Aaron Downey, Project Editor at Matrix Productions, has been terrific to work with during the production phase of this project. Janet Tilden, Copy Editor, has done a wonderful job of improving every page of this text.

We also want to thank each of the many outside reviewers who spent hours reading and thinking about this book. They gave us many wonderful suggestions for improving the book. They are:

Peggy Adams
Bowling Green State

Nick Alenkin
California State University, Los Angeles

Julie Birkenmaier
Saint Louis University

Linda L. Black
University of Northern Colorado

Everett Blakely
University of Michigan, Flint

Scott Burcham
Arkansas State University

Mary Byrne
Salem State College

Mikal Crawford
Frostburg State University

Adele Crudden
Mississippi State University

Sister Nancy DeCesare
Chestnut Hill College

Becky Donaghy
Jefferson Community College

John Elhai
University of South Dakota

Karen Faehling
University of Nevada, Reno

Jerold Gold
Adelphi University

Heather M. Helm
University of Northern Colorado

Roxanne A. Howes
Sitting Bull College

Patricia Karwoski
Northern Michigan University

Barbara Lipinski
California Lutheran University

Sandra A. Lopez
University of Houston

Wade Luquet
Gwynedd-Mercy College

Tina Maschi
Monmouth University

Rosilyn Meisel
Ohio State University

John P. Mellein
Western Michigan University

Bonni Raab
Dominican College of Blauvelt

Jeanette Roberts
Illinois State University

Cassandra E. Simon
The University of Alabama

James E. Smith
University of Wyoming

Dee Stokes-Barclift
Jacksonville State University

Debra L. Stout
California State University, Fullerton

Roberta Suber
California State University Northridge

June Williams
Southeastern Louisiana University

We are grateful to all the people who helped with the production of the DVD. Our Production Director, Steve Stiles, and his production staff were wonderful. Thanks to Bob Decker who provided the "settings" for our DVD. Of course, the film could not have been made without the participation of the volunteers who were in the film, including Misha Bennett, Karen Butterworth, Rochelle Cohen, Barbara Furlow, Carolyn Gentle-Genitty, Eddie Johnson, Jeremy Johnson, Joseph Johnson, Nicholas Johnson, Gina Kammerer, Lisa Lewis, Christy Meyer, and Justine Sherwood. For reasons of confidentiality, actual clients were not used; however, the individuals in the DVD were playing the roles of real clients that we know. None of the roles were scripted. The practitioners were responding to the challenges presented.

This book would not have been written if we had not had the opportunity to work with many clients and students. From our clients we learned about what really is effective. From our students we learned what methods of teaching they find most helpful in their journey to becoming competent practitioners.

We have been fortunate to have had the assistance of many contributing authors, including Kathy Lay, Sabrina Williamson, Carol Hostetter, Alice Fok, Lynne Fisher, Susan Charlesworth, Phyllis Shea, and Carolyn Gentle-Genitty. In addition, Alice Folk, Diane Puchbauer, Lauren Adelchanow, and Jennifer Costillo offered editorial expertise that helped to make the text and the test bank questions more readable.

FROM VALERIE CHANG

I want to particularly thank my family and friends who have been supportive, understanding, and very patient through all the challenges of writing this book. Special thanks go to my parents, Ava and Howard Nash, who not only told me "you can do it" but also believed that I could do whatever I decided to do.

FROM SHERYN SCOTT

There are many students, friends, and family members who sacrificed time so that I could work on this text. I particularly want to thank my daughters, Ali Borden, who, having gone through the process of writing a book, was always encouraging me that there was an end point to the work and Kara Russ, who provided wonderful grand-children as a necessary distraction to the hard complexities of writing a book. No part of my participation in the project could have happened without the patient support of my husband, Larry Hixon, who put up with my absences and helped to see that the household ran when I was immersed in meeting one deadline or another.

FROM CAROL DECKER

I want to thank my husband for his support throughout the writing and rewriting process and all of the patient "teachers" I have had over the years of my life.

FOUNDATION

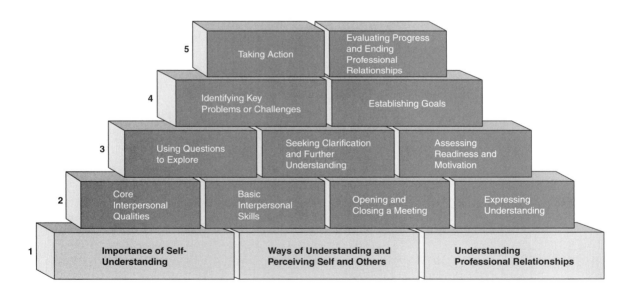

5 Taking Action — Evaluating Progress and Ending Professional Relationships

4 Identifying Key Problems or Challenges — Establishing Goals

3 Using Questions to Explore — Seeking Clarification and Further Understanding — Assessing Readiness and Motivation

2 Core Interpersonal Qualities — Basic Interpersonal Skills — Opening and Closing a Meeting — Expressing Understanding

1 Importance of Self-Understanding — Ways of Understanding and Perceiving Self and Others — Understanding Professional Relationships

If the authors of this book could give you just one thing, it would be the desire to be the very best practitioner you can be. As is true in any profession, becoming a skilled practitioner takes energy, perseverance, dedication, and time. However, this effort will bring many rewards and will enhance your ability to assist your clients as you grow and develop as a practitioner. There is satisfaction in seeing individuals developing self-esteem, families working together, communities finding a renewed sense of purpose, and organizations building a culture of acceptance and encouragement.

To become a competent and effective practitioner, you'll need to acquire an array of new skills and knowledge. Developing this knowledge base can be compared to building a wall. Beginning with the foundational information covered in Chapters 1 through 3, each chapter is an essential building block that adds to your development as a practitioner. Chapter 1, Importance of Self-Understanding, provides information and exercises that will help you understand stress management, personal styles of coping, and the influences of family, culture, gender, race, class, religion, and spirituality on each person's view of the world. Because all practitioners use themselves to help others, self-understanding is vital. Chapter 2, Ways of Understanding and Perceiving Self and Others, focuses on basic perspectives including constructivism, resiliency, empowerment, strengths, and ecological influences. Each of these perspectives influences our perceptions of and actions toward ourselves and others. Thoughtfully choosing an appropriate perspective is a critical aspect of professional practice. After acquiring this foundational knowledge, you will be ready to begin learning processes and skills for working effectively with clients. Chapter 3, Understanding Professional Relationships, deals with the complex issue of developing professional relationships and understanding the ethical and legal obligations that govern professional work. Also addressed are the differences between functioning as a practitioner in a professional relationship and functioning as a friend, parent, or partner in a personal relationship.

IMPORTANCE OF SELF-UNDERSTANDING

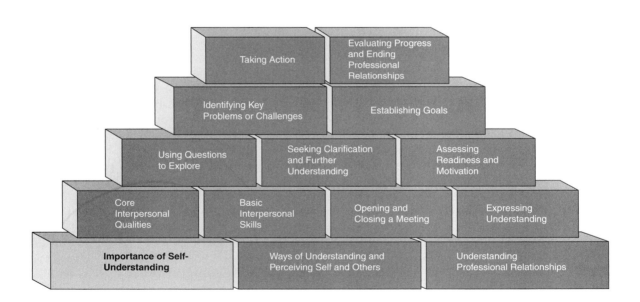

CHAPTER 1

Taking Action

Evaluating Progress and Ending Professional Relationships

Identifying Key Problems or Challenges

Establishing Goals

Using Questions to Explore

Seeking Clarification and Further Understanding

Assessing Readiness and Motivation

Core Interpersonal Qualities

Basic Interpersonal Skills

Opening and Closing a Meeting

Expressing Understanding

Importance of Self-Understanding

Ways of Understanding and Perceiving Self and Others

Understanding Professional Relationships

In this chapter you will learn about the following topics:

Practitioner Tasks:
- Understanding the influences of culture, race, ethnicity, gender, sexual orientation, family of origin, spirituality, stresses and demands, and your view of self and others

INFLUENCES ON PERSONAL DEVELOPMENT

Personal experiences, capacities, physical abilities and challenges, privileges, and limitations influence each person's development. As we grow and develop our self-concept, we absorb and are influenced by culture, race and ethnicity, gender and sexual orientation, family, and spiritual beliefs and norms. Our task as practitioners is to understand how these beliefs about the way life is or should be are often viewed as the "truth" rather than just one way of looking at a situation. Some viewpoints may be engrained so deeply that other perspectives can seem not only different but wrong. For example, in one therapeutic group, a client who experienced a difficult childhood believed that the world was a dangerous place. She often felt scared that something frightening might happen in her neighborhood. Other members of her group told her they experienced her neighborhood as a very safe place to live, but she wasn't able to see it that way herself. Our perception of what is true depends on the beliefs we hold.

As a practitioner, understanding and accepting yourself is an essential step toward understanding others (Hill & Lent, 2006). Thus, developing self-understanding is a particularly important process in the journey to becoming a competent practitioner (Williams, Hurley, O'Brien, & DeGregorio, 2003). Self-understanding can be gained by reading and taking classes, receiving competent supervision, being in personal therapy, and setting aside time for self-reflection. When you are in the position of helping another, your own life experiences and decisions will influence the types of interventions you choose and the way that you perceive your client. In this chapter, basic information related to understanding yourself and others will be covered. Pay particular attention to areas you have found to be most important to your self-identity and aspects you may not have considered before.

The way you see the world has been influenced by the family you grew up in, the culture you inhabit, and the way you have made sense of the events of your life. Our beliefs tend to affect how we think about ourselves, others, and the world. For example, a woman who was teased a lot during childhood learned to perceive herself as inadequate. As an adult, she believes she is only capable of obtaining a low-level job despite her college degree. She believes others will not take her seriously and will see her as inadequate.

HOMEWORK EXERCISE 1.1 | UNDERSTANDING YOUR PERSONAL BELIEF SYSTEM

It is important to recognize the beliefs that have established your views of yourself, others, and the world. A cultural belief that was once common was "A penny saved is a penny earned." What truisms about money did you learn in your family? Perhaps you received messages about how to behave, such as "If you don't go to church, you'll go to hell," "Cleanliness is next to Godliness," "If you don't work hard, you won't succeed," and "We don't associate with certain kinds of people." Can you

HOMEWORK EXERCISE 1.1 | UNDERSTANDING YOUR PERSONAL BELIEF SYSTEM *continued*

recall other adages that you were raised with? You may have absorbed beliefs about human nature such as "You should be independent and take care of yourself; being beholden to others is wrong," "You can't trust men, they just want one thing," "Working hard is the way to succeed," "Poor people are just lazy," "Beggars can't be choosers," or "It is best to be cautious around others because you can't count on them." Write down what you believe about yourself, others, the world, success, money, and relationships. These beliefs will reflect your values, your reactions to life experiences, your culture, and other factors.

THE INFLUENCE OF CULTURE, RACE, AND ETHNICITY

It is important for practitioners to understand their own cultural beliefs and to be aware of the ways in which these beliefs influence their behavior and expectations of others (Roysircar, 2004). Although the terms *race, culture,* and *ethnicity* are often used interchangeably, they are defined differently. *Race* refers to a group of people characterized by specific physical characteristics that differentiate them from other groups of people (Tseng, 2001). *Ethnicity* refers to a group of people distinguished by a shared history, culture, beliefs, values, and behaviors (Tseng, 2001). In contrast, *culture* is defined as the customary beliefs, social forms, and behavior patterns of a racial, religious, or social group. In this section, we will be discussing how our culture affects our beliefs and values.

Our culture teaches us our language, behaviors, rules, and ways of understanding others. It provides us a framework of assumptions or premises for understanding the world and communicating that understanding to others. From our socialization within our culture, we develop a personal belief system that influences our behavior, our expectations of others, and our standards for what is right and wrong. We may not always recognize the assumptions underlying our behavior, but they are always there and always important. Members of the dominant culture may have difficulty identifying the influence of their own culture because it has been accepted as the norm.

One aspect of cultural influence is that members of the dominant culture are granted unearned privileges that they perceive as "normal" and "expected." These may be awarded based on race, gender, class, physical ability, sexual orientation, or age. *White privilege* is an institutionalized set of benefits granted to those who resemble the people in power in a culture's institutions (Kendall, 2001). People of color (a description that includes anyone who perceives himself or herself as non-white) do not receive these privileges. These benefits include greater access to power and resources than people of color, the ability to make decisions that affect everyone without taking others into account, and the ability to discount the experiences of individuals of color (Kendall). These often unidentified assumptions influence our perceptions of our clients and their experiences. Being aware of the privileges granted to members of the dominant group and the related disadvantages of members of minority groups can help you understand the experiences of both the dominant group and minority groups.

HOMEWORK EXERCISE 1.2 | WHITE PRIVILEGE

Make a list of at least five benefits that members of the dominant group have simply because of their race.

Culture has a strong influence on the roles that are seen as appropriate for particular persons. These may be age-related roles, such as beliefs about the proper behavior of children toward parents, teachers, and society in general. As you watch children and parents interact, how do your beliefs about the role of children affect your opinion of the behavior you see? People hold many gender-related beliefs about work, dress, and other aspects of behavior, some of which are seen as appropriate for women and others for men. As you become more aware of your own personal belief system, you can begin to see similarities and differences among diverse cultures and recognize how these beliefs can influence your reaction to the behavior of others. Increased awareness of your own personal belief system and the ways it differs from those of other cultures, or even the culture you were raised in, is vital to your development as a practitioner.

Practitioners need to become particularly aware of other important beliefs that are based in culture (Kim, Ng, & Ahn, 2005). These include cultural differences in attitudes regarding independence and autonomy, patterns of communication (verbal and nonverbal), family boundaries and responsibilities, and the expression of emotions. For example, in many Asian societies, adult children are expected to provide shelter and care for their elderly parents. In some cultures, parents and other family members expect to be involved in decisions made by adult children, such as whom to marry and how money is spent.

Communication patterns include the appropriateness and timing of eye contact, the directness with which a person comes to the point of a discussion, personal space when one converses, and even facial expressions. For example, in Western society, direct eye contact is considered polite and appropriate. However, in some cultural groups, this is considered rude. In some societies, business is discussed only after a period of social exchanges unrelated to the purpose of the meeting. In addition, smiling may represent feelings of discomfort, distress, sadness, or anger, rather than happiness (Tseng, 2001).

Although it is important to understand our own personal belief system, it is equally important to develop an understanding of the cultures of our clients (Carter, 2003; Daniel, Roysircar, & Abeles, 2004). We need to become familiar with the culture and political history of clients who differ from ourselves. Cultural influences occur at a variety of levels, including interpretations of life events, the nature of life stressors, and preferred coping mechanisms (Tseng, 2001). The level of acculturation of immigrants is also a consideration, as is their ability to communicate in the local language. People who are the first generation in a new country tend to be greatly influenced by their culture of origin. The children of these first-generation immigrants have grown up in the new country and often feel torn between the culture of their parents and the culture of their friends. Some clients have come to your community as refugees, or perhaps their parents were refugees. This history can have a profound effect on their relationship to you as their practitioner. Cultural knowledge is helpful in developing a relationship with clients as well as providing insight into the family and community influences on their values, concerns, and decisions. Becoming truly culturally competent or fluent enough in the multiple cultural nuances to work effectively with people from different cultures is a lifetime task, but as a practitioner you should become knowledgeable about the cultures of your clients.

HOMEWORK EXERCISE 1.3 | Y<small>OUR</small> C<small>ULTURAL</small> B<small>ELIEFS</small>

When did you first realize that your family belonged to a certain group of people (e.g., African-American, Caucasian-American, Mexican-American, Asian-American, Irish-American, Euro-American, etc.)? Was your family aware of being the same as or different from others? How were differences dealt with in your family?

What are some recent experiences that have deepened your awareness of other cultures? What kind of experiences do you think would be helpful in developing your awareness of how other cultures might influence a person or group seeking help?

T<small>HE</small> I<small>NFLUENCE OF</small> G<small>ENDER</small>

A number of factors influence who and what we are. One of the most important in our society is gender. From the first moment that a woman knows she is pregnant, the question she will ponder and be asked most frequently is the baby's sex. Whether it is guessed at or determined by medical procedures, this knowledge influences how the baby's movements are interpreted and will affect how others treat the baby from the moment of birth. The social context of the mother will suggest that certain behaviors are male or female.

Our sex is determined by biology, and most of us are born with a clear indication of what sex we are. Growing out of a social context, gender pertains to what we assume is true or will be true of someone who is biologically female or male. Gender includes societal beliefs, stereotypes, and engrained views about the fundamental nature of boys and girls, women and men. These considerations are culturally based and crucial to doing effective work with clients of diverse backgrounds.

Gender bias in counseling comes through the use of unexamined assumptions. For example, separation of the client's concerns from the context in which they occur can cause the practitioner to blame the victim of domestic violence. Such a practitioner may remark, "I don't understand why she didn't leave." This is a way of condemning the individual involved instead of making an effort to understand her circumstances. A focus on family of origin dynamics to explain a client's current problems may lead to blaming the mother for negative behaviors or problems rather than seeing the many other factors that influence clients. The use of gender stereotypes as the standard for defining adaptive or healthy behavior and good psychological functioning may lead the practitioner to define dependency in men as bad and sadness in women as more acceptable than anger (Gilbert & Scher, 1999; Plant, Hyde, Keltner, & Devine, 2000; Seelau & Seelau, 2005). Practitioners who believe in the importance of equal relationships between men and women might be inclined to encourage female clients to be more assertive or independent with their partners than they might choose to be, or feel that they are allowed to be by their cultural values.

It will be important for you to be aware of gender as an integral aspect of counseling and mental health services. Beyond your own stereotypes, it will be important to consider other aspects such as personal space and touch, facial expressiveness, emotional expressiveness, and your experience of yourself and your gender in your interaction with clients. You will need to be responsive and aware if a client moves closer or farther from you and how you interpret these actions as a woman or a man. Some clients will show few emotions, and you will have to discern if this has to do with messages about how their gender is supposed to express feelings. Some clients may find you distant or unexpressive of feelings if you have been trained to avoid showing emotions. Age, gender expectations, and cultural values influence how much or little touching is a part of relationships.

HOMEWORK EXERCISE 1.4 | GENDER INFLUENCES

Imagine that you are working with a person who is concerned about moving away from his or her family of origin. How would you respond if your client is a Middle Eastern woman of 22? How would you respond if he is a man of 30? What about a 45-year-old woman who had been the caretaker of her daughter's children? If you are not currently living with your family of origin, what were the circumstances of your moving away? If you have not moved away, what are the cultural or family rules that support staying there?

When you are walking through a mall, studying at school, or spending time with your family, imagine that you are a member of the opposite sex. What would your body feel like? How would you interact differently with those around you? How do you imagine others might behave differently toward you?

THE INFLUENCE OF SEXUAL ORIENTATION

Sexual orientation is another powerful determinant of who we are and how we respond to others. Embedded in our sexual orientation are societal beliefs, stereotypes, and views about relational and sexual expression—all rooted in a cultural context. Recent research suggests that our sexual orientation is at least partially determined by biology (Appleby & Anastas, 1998; James, 2005; Rahman & Wilson, 2003). Many experience their sexual orientation as a natural developmental process in which they are encouraged and supported throughout their psycho-social-sexual development regardless of whether they are heterosexual, lesbian, or gay. Others identify their sexual orientation or "come out" later in life due to various factors involving family, religious, or cultural prohibitions about recognizing or acknowledging homosexual feelings.

The coming-out process is sometimes complicated by social and cultural constraints created by heterosexism and/or homophobia. Heterosexism is a belief that male-female sexuality is the only natural, normal, or moral mode of sexual behavior (Mohr, 2003). Regardless of the orientation of the practitioner, heterosexism and homophobia may be operational in his or her worldview. It is institutionalized in most systems and manifests in cultural behaviors and norms (Appleby & Anastas, 1998; Morrow & Messinger, 2006).

In a culture dominated by heterosexuality, it is nearly impossible to escape heterosexual bias about others. A key factor in becoming effective practitioners is developing critical awareness of societal heterosexism and how we are influenced by it. Reflection for self-understanding is critical if we are to be effective practitioners with individuals and families from all social and cultural backgrounds.

Homophobia, an individualized fear of homosexuals, is believed to be the result of heterosexism (Appleby & Anastas, 1998; Morrow & Messinger, 2006). Behaviors associated with homophobia have manifested in a broad range of oppressive acts from covert to verbal aggression and violence (Tully, 2000). Effective practitioners are aware of the impact of heterosexism and homophobia on themselves and others (Murphy & Rawlings, 2002).

The helping professions are not immune to the influence of heterosexism and homophobia. Examples of heterosexism by practitioners include forms constructed for intake purposes that reflect only heterosexual relationships, exclusive definitions of family, agency policies that do not honor alternative partnership/family constructions, stereotyping of lesbians and gay clients, and jokes told by colleagues. Awareness of our own heterosexism and perhaps homophobia will help us to work more effectively with clients from diverse backgrounds. Attending to our bias is a lifelong learning process that will result in skillful and respectful interactions with clients.

HOMEWORK EXERCISE 1.5 | SEXUAL ORIENTATION INFLUENCES

What is your sexual orientation? When were you first aware of your own sexual orientation? How did you express your awareness? Whom did you tell? These questions and answers may seem unimportant or even trivial if you are heterosexual. However, lack of awareness of being part of the majority culture can influence how heterosexuals relate to those who are not part of the majority. To gain insight about the difficulties experienced by those not in the majority, imagine that you are working with a person who desires to come out as gay or lesbian. Perhaps the person has lived many years as a presumed heterosexual. Perhaps s/he has been or is married. How would you respond? Suppose the individual wanted a family session to assist in the coming-out process. What are your personal strengths as a practitioner to help facilitate his or her coming out? What challenges come to your mind? What attitudes and beliefs in yourself should be enhanced, developed, or challenged in order to facilitate working with clients whose sexual orientation differs from your own?

THE INFLUENCE OF FAMILY OF ORIGIN

Family experiences have an important and sustained influence on our worldview. Even the way *family* is defined differs from one culture to another. Therefore, it is important to understand how we have been affected by our own family in our own culture in order to recognize that these experiences are personal and not assume the same meanings and experiences are true for those we serve (Nichols & Schwartz, 2006).

There are a number of groups of people who are called "family" beyond the Euro-American traditional family consisting of a father, a mother, and two children, preferably one of each sex. Today a family could comprise two gay parents and their adopted or biological children. It could include stepparents, grandparents, aunts, uncles, or other extended family members. Some families have only one parent in the home, with the other parent being completely absent from the children's lives. Other children are being raised by two different families formed when their parents divorced and re-married (Goldenberg & Goldenberg, 1998; Jones, 2003). Family also can be a couple without children or individuals living alone or with their parents throughout their adulthood. Depending on the practitioner's family of origin and the client's family of origin, expectations for what a *family* is or should be will vary greatly and influence how they see one another.

In addition to recognizing different types of families, practitioners should understand the developmental stages families go through (Carter & McGoldrick, 1999; O'Brien, 2005). A traditional nuclear family is formed when a man and a woman marry. At this life stage they are involved in setting up their own patterns and ways of living that will likely influence future development of their family. Stressors may include pressure from in-laws, decisions related to money management, and finding ways to mesh views of "how things should be done." It is likely that both partners will be working outside the home at least until children arrive. Obviously this could be a more difficult transition if the partners are gay or lesbian and cannot formalize their relationship with marriage but still see themselves as a family.

With the addition of children, the family enters a new stage of development with the potential for new types of stressors. If both parents are working, stressors might include making childcare arrangements, dealing with illness, dividing household chores, and deciding where the family will live. If one parent is not working outside the home, then there are usually more financial stresses and new role definitions to be negotiated. In a single-parent family, concerns related to financial, childcare, and self-care issues can be even greater. The period during which children are living in the home can be one of the most stressful times for a couple or for anyone raising children, be they single parents, grandparents, older siblings, or foster parents. Couples who cannot have children or choose not to have children often experience societal pressure to defend or explain their lack of a child. Social pressure to have children can be very stressful for these couples.

As children grow through adolescence, they challenge the family's way of functioning. As adolescents more clearly define their own personalities, the family must make a number of adjustments. These adjustments can be difficult, depending on the amount of support the parent(s) have from others and the flexibility of the family system. When children leave home (a stage that varies from one culture to another), parents may experience the loneliness of an empty nest along with greater freedom and increased opportunities for personal growth.

With many adults today living well into their 80s in good or relatively good health, many families will experience an extended-retirement phase. The manner in which families experience this life stage depends on the status of family members' health, finances, and relationships. If good health, stable finances, and supportive relationships are present, then the aging process is likely to go more smoothly. For some, the adjustment to retirement can be difficult if it is forced or undesired. For others, it may be a time of fulfillment. At each family life stage, the family must be able to cope with the multiple changes that come with the next period of life. How well they adapt to each stage depends on the resources of each family system.

Practitioners are influenced not only by the patterns of their family of origin, but also by their own developmental stage. If practitioners have young children to care for, are approaching retirement, or are dealing with aging parents, these stressors will affect their own functioning. The stressors that affect all families will affect you as a practitioner. Awareness of your own stage in the life cycle and that of your family is essential.

There are a number of different types of family systems or ways that members of a family interact with each other (Goldenberg & Goldenberg, 1998; O'Brien, 2005). Families form repetitive patterns, or systems, over time. A family system may be open or closed. A closed system tends to exist in relative isolation, with communication taking place primarily between members. Family members are suspicious of outsiders and dependent on each other. Families within a closed system avoid change and hold onto their established traditions and values.

By contrast, families with an open system are characterized by willingness to assimilate new information and to engage in ongoing interactions with their environment. Members are free to move in and out of transactions with each other and with people outside the family. The family has no single correct way of doing things. As the family matures, changes are tolerated, supported, and celebrated.

Most families have characteristics of both closed and open systems. If the closed aspects of the system become rigid, then the family will become increasingly stressed. For example, an adolescent might want to radically change his hairstyle or hair color, but to do so would violate the way a family thinks individuals ought to look. Such a violation might cause considerable tension and fighting in a family with a rigid system. If, after a death or divorce, the members of an open family system do not bond together without the missing family member, the family system may be too open. The feeling of being a family may be lost if the mother was the central figure that tied it together and she dies, leaving the father and children unsure how to function in her absence.

HOMEWORK EXERCISE 1.6 | YOUR FAMILY

Interview a member of your extended family. Ask for information about your father's or mother's family going back at least two generations. Learn where members of your family came from, the cultural background of family members, struggles that individuals faced, health problems and causes of death, and quality of familial relationships (strong relationships, separations and problematic relationships, and divorce). Think about how the family's relationship patterns, ethnicity, struggles, and illnesses have affected you. Write a brief description of the ways you see your family background influencing the manner in which you relate to others today.

THE INFLUENCE OF SPIRITUALITY

Although you may not consider yourself to be a spiritual or religious person, many of your clients will be influenced by spiritual or religious beliefs and training. Just as gender, culture, age, ethnicity, and other factors can influence the therapeutic relationship between a practitioner and a client, so can the spiritual or religious beliefs held by either party. Just as humans are physical creatures with psychological and social dimensions, most people believe we also have a spiritual aspect.

Spirituality can be understood as an individual's relationship with God or any Ultimate Power (including nature, sacred texts, etc.) that influences his or her mission or purpose in life (Hodge, 2005). Fundamentally, spirituality is how each of us "makes meaning" out of the events that occur in our lives. Our spirituality also shapes how we see ourselves and how we participate in the lives of others and in the world around us. Religion can be understood to be the communal behaviors (prayer, fasting, celebration of certain holy days, etc.) that are the result of people of similar beliefs coming together to practice these beliefs (Hodge, 2005). Someone can correctly consider himself or herself to be a "spiritual person" but not necessarily a "religious person."

You may already have some awareness of the ways in which your spiritual beliefs may affect your work with clients (Prest, Russel, & D'sousa, 1999). For example, your beliefs (and possibly your religious practices) may shape your understanding about when life begins, and this understanding will influence your views on abortion and birth control. Similarly, your beliefs may shape your understanding about life at the other end of the spectrum, and this understanding will influence your beliefs about euthanasia, suicide, and the death penalty. When practitioners work with a pregnant teen or a person dying of cancer, their spiritual beliefs may influence the way they relate to a client. Depending on the client and the setting in which help is being provided, these beliefs may be a help to building and maintaining rapport with a client. However, there are times when a practitioner's own beliefs may be a barrier to the work s/he does with clients.

At this point, you may also have a beginning sense of how a client's spiritual beliefs influence his or her behavior and the helping process (Carlson, Kirkpatrick, & Hecker, 2002; Hagedorn, 2005). For example, a woman who believes that the institution of marriage is an everlasting commitment may not be willing to leave an abusive partner. Parents who believe in a Higher Power as the ultimate physical healer may not seek traditional medical care for a child who is seriously ill. You will have clients who, in the midst of a crisis, cope unbelievably well. They believe that their ability to cope is an extension of their spiritual faith, which teaches that they will not be tested beyond what they can bear.

Just as a practitioner's beliefs can be an asset or a barrier in his or her work with clients, spirituality can be a source of strength for some clients if it helps them make meaning out of their struggles and achieve their goals, while for other clients it may hinder progress toward goals. What is most important in working with clients is to honor diversity in spiritual beliefs just as we honor diversity in other areas (Constantine, Lewis, Conner, & Sanchez, 2000). Spirituality is also an essential factor to explore during your initial sessions with clients. As competent practitioners, we must recognize the value of our beliefs and how they motivate our work while making certain that our personal understandings and interpretations do not hinder the helping process or infringe upon the rights of clients to make their own decisions.

HOMEWORK EXERCISE 1.7 | RELIGION OR SPIRITUALITY

If you were involved with organized religion as a child, what was your religion? How have your ideas of religion changed since then? What factors led to the changes that you have made in your religious beliefs? Do you consider your religion to be a source of strength? What are some of the values that you have learned from your religion? Has your religious background influenced your desire to become a practitioner?

If you do not consider yourself religious and do not have a spiritual practice, how do you imagine you will feel working with a client who has a strong faith background?

If you consider yourself a spiritual person, how do you define your relationship to God or a Higher Power? In what ways is this relationship supportive to you or limiting to you?

THE INFLUENCE OF STRESS AND DEMANDS

Because the stress and demands on professional practitioners are continuous and numerous, taking care of yourself is essential. Responsible self-care is interdependent with good practice (Cozolino, 2004). Self-care means being aware of the stressors in your private life as well as those in your professional life. It is important to be aware of your own limits and select the clients you work with accordingly. Maintaining a sense of perspective is also necessary. As noted by Cozolino, this involves noticing whether you are living vicariously through your clients, are getting enough support outside your work, are following your passions, and are doing what you want to be doing. Helping others can be tedious, grueling, and demanding. You are constantly forced to face your own problems and differentiate them from those of your clients. To manage the stress involved in your professional life, it is important to take every opportunity to understand yourself as thoroughly as possible. As you become aware of problems in your life that you can't resolve on your own, you should consider seeking help from professional practitioners.

Remember that in the helping relationship, you are the instrument. Just as a musical instrument must be cared for and kept in tune, so you must keep yourself in top form in order to be the best helper you can be. The factors that influenced your decision to become a practitioner will often affect how you take care of yourself. Many people who choose the helping professions learned early in life to work hard, to keep peace in the family, or to take care of a parent or sibling. They may have learned to put their needs on hold while attending to the needs of others. By the time they are adults they may not even be fully aware of what they need. This *other-centeredness* can eventually lead to burnout unless you learn to attend to your own needs.

Burnout has been defined as a syndrome involving "increasing discouragement and emotional and physical exhaustion" (Dewees, 2006, p. 316). Burnout is not uncommon for practitioners who must handle large caseloads and/or deal with difficulties related to managed care, who have little external support, and/or who are working with involuntary clients or with emotionally charged situations such as abused children and elders (Dewees, 2006; Rupert & Morgan, 2005). Some ways to avoid burnout are to ensure that you have a life outside of the office, to monitor your stress level, to periodically evaluate your goals and priorities, to attend professional conferences, to develop hobbies, and to attend to your spiritual growth. Learning to take good care of yourself is essential (Skovholt, 2001). Start now to build a healthy lifestyle. Many students think that they need to put off self-care until they graduate because they erroneously believe that they will be less busy then. This is rarely the case. Life keeps on being busy. How you handle the stress of school will likely be the same pattern you will follow after you graduate. Learn to relax, breathe, eat well, participate in physical activities, and set aside time for recreation with your family and friends.

Another stress that many practitioners experience is secondary traumatic stress. This stress occurs when practitioners are working with clients who are in a great deal of emotional or physical pain. For example, when practitioners find themselves helping a community group where many children have been killed as a result of gang violence or when they work with someone whose marital partner died as a result of an automobile accident in which the client was driving, it may create feelings that seem overwhelming. Dealing with loss of this magnitude can make practitioners feel as if they have been traumatized themselves. Secondary traumatic stress is an even greater risk for practitioners if the traumatic events experienced by their clients are in some way similar to their own life experiences. If your client's traumas or problems are similar to your own, it is important to carefully evaluate with your supervisor whether it will be in the client's best interest for you to be the practitioner. Even when you believe you have fully worked through the issues or trauma, you may still discover unresolved wounds as you work with the client. Another challenge is thinking that you understand your client because his or her trauma seems so similar to what you experienced. Your experience may help you to understand your client's situation, but it is important to remember that your client's experiences and feelings will be unique.

HOMEWORK EXERCISE 1.8 | INFLUENCE OF STRESS AND DEMANDS

Make a list of all the stressful events in your life in the last year. Remember that positive events such as going on vacation, moving to a nicer apartment, or getting married may be just as stressful as negative events such as being in a car accident, getting sick, receiving a low grade, or not having enough money to pay your bills. Positive and negative events add extra demands to your life. Now put a number between 1 and 10 after each stressful event. A 10 would be something very stressful that had a big impact on your life, such as the death of a family member, and a 1 would be something not very stressful, such as a minor illness. Add up your stress points. Now think about how you react when there is too much stress in your life. Some people become more accident prone, some are more irritable, some withdraw, and some are more likely to get sick. Finally, in what ways have you successfully reduced the effects of stress in your life?

THE INFLUENCE OF YOUR VIEW OF SELF AND OTHERS

All the areas that we have discussed in this chapter influence your view of yourself and others. It is important for you to consider each of these influences and to know yourself well. As a professional practitioner, knowing who you are will allow you to clearly differentiate what is true for you from what is true for your clients. Self-knowledge tends to grow over time. As you work with clients, you will learn more about your uniqueness and become aware of beliefs and values that you did not know you had. One of the joys and challenges of professional practitioners is to always be developing and changing.

Lastly, developing the character strengths and virtues recommended by Peterson and Seligman (2004) will stand you in good stead for the entirety of your career. These strengths and virtues are wisdom and knowledge (creativity, curiosity, open-mindedness, love of learning, perspective); courage (bravery, persistence, integrity, vitality); humanity (love, kindness, social intelligence); justice (citizenship, fairness, leadership); temperance (forgiveness and mercy, modesty and humility, prudence, self-regulation); and transcendence (appreciation of beauty and excellence, gratitude, hope, humor, spirituality).

HOMEWORK EXERCISE 1.9 | SELF-UNDERSTANDING

Write a description of yourself, including characteristics such as age, racial or ethnic identity, spiritual beliefs, sexual orientation, gender, family of origin, values, worldview, and current or past stressors that affect your life. Highlight those aspects that seem most important to you at this time.

Now make a list of strengths you value most in others. Who are the people you have admired most? Have they had the virtues and strengths proposed by Peterson and Seligman? Which strengths are you in the process of developing?

EXPECTED COMPETENCIES

In this chapter you have learned about several aspects vital to thinking and acting as a practitioner.

You should now be able to:

- Identify some of the influences of your religion or spiritual beliefs, culture, sexual orientation, gender, and family beliefs and norms on your attitudes and behavior.

- Identify several risks of burnout for practitioners and ways to minimize these risks.

CHAPTER 2

WAYS OF UNDERSTANDING AND PERCEIVING SELF AND OTHERS

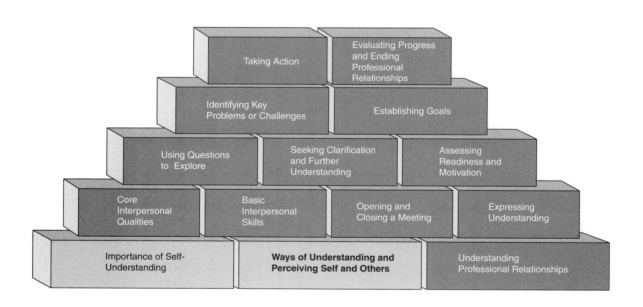

In this chapter you will learn about the following topics:

Practitioner Tasks:
- Applying knowledge of constructivist, strengths, resilience, empowerment, ecological, and dual perspectives to better understand yourself and your clients

A second task that is important as you build the foundation for becoming a competent practitioner is developing an awareness of the many ways we can understand our world. In the last chapter, you learned that our worldview is determined by factors such as our cultural background; our level of self-understanding; and what we have learned about ourselves, others, and the world. It is even influenced by how we are feeling at any given moment. If you aren't feeling well, have a headache, or are tired, you might not notice positive things like flowers blooming or the sun shining. Our perception of other people is determined in part by the lenses we are using to view those people. In the past, helping professionals often viewed the world through a problem-solving lens. Using this lens is important for professionals as they try to understand the difficulties that their clients are experiencing, but it should be only *one* of several perspectives the practitioner uses to view a situation.

In this chapter we will discuss six ways of perceiving self and others: constructivist, strengths, resilience, empowerment, ecological, and dual perspectives. At the end of the chapter, Table 2.2 summarizes practitioner strategies, concepts, and the assumptions of each theory.

THE CONSTRUCTIVIST PERSPECTIVE

DEFINING THE CONSTRUCTIVIST PERSPECTIVE

Constructivism, as explained in the pioneering work of George Kelly (1955/1991), is a perspective that identifies how individuals describe their experience in terms of *personal constructs*. A personal construct is an explanation of an event or series of events that eventually becomes the lens through which the individual sees the world. A personal construct can include decisions about life ("It's hard"), other people ("They are helpful"), and how to behave ("You should be responsible"). These constructs are developed as individuals interpret their experiences. Constructivists propose that people test their personal constructs by noting how well the constructs predict life circumstances and then using their experiences to revise these constructs (if needed). For example, if you thought you weren't very intelligent and then found yourself succeeding in college coursework, you might revise your beliefs about yourself ("I am really smart after all!") or you might revise your construct about college ("College isn't really as difficult as I was led to believe. Anyone can succeed in college if they work hard enough, even if they aren't smart."). Most of us know someone who appears to be thin or at least is not overweight (our construct) but who is always on a diet because his or her construct is "I am fat." According to constructivism, each individual is a personal scientist who is continually testing his or her constructions. These constructions or decisions might be broad, such as "Work before play" or more specific, such as "My mother is a safe person."

PERSONAL AND SOCIAL CONSTRUCTS

The idea of the *self* is viewed as a constructed concept (Burr, Vutt, & Epting, 1997; Thompson, 2006). Our sense of self is developed over time and is based on the way we perceive ourselves. Some of the firmest constructs of the self are developed in childhood and often are difficult to change because people experience these ideas as *truth* about themselves. Some constructs may be quite limiting, such as beliefs that "I am a stupid person" or "I need to be perfect to be loved." Childhood experiences also lead to the development of constructs about others and the world. These constructs might be that "Others are helpful" or "The world is a dangerous place."

Gergen (2006) and Stam (1998) emphasize the importance of social and cultural factors in the construction of individual reality. Gergen contended that there are as many realities as there are cultures, contexts, and ways of communicating. Social constructivists focus on how relationships, language, and context influence an individual's or a group's interpretation of self, others, and the world. Personality, like the idea of a self, is considered a socially constructed idea (Burr, 1995; Gergen, 2006; Hosking, 2005; Stular, 1998; Thompson, 2006; Williams & Thornton, 1998). Personality includes the qualities, traits, characteristics, and behavior patterns that distinguish each individual. Culture strongly influences whether the words used to describe someone's personality are seen as positive or negative. For example, *assertive, strong,* and *independent* generally are viewed as positive descriptions of women today, but in the past and in other cultures, these descriptions would have been considered negative. The ways in which people are identified, talked about, and treated all have an influence on their personality.

Language is an important factor in this process of making meaning of experiences, since the ways that people talk about themselves and their world influence their perceptions. In English there is one word for snow, but the Aleuts have a number of different words for snow. Those who speak English may not even notice aspects of snow that an Aleut would see as significant because the English language limits their ability to recognize and denote differences.

In every culture some ways of accounting for behavior become more dominant or valued while others are suppressed. Historically, Western cultures have valued individualism whereas many other cultures have favored more familial and communal relationships over individualism. This emphasis on individualism can lead practitioners steeped in the Western traditions to perceive families from other cultures as enmeshed even though closer relationships are normative behavior within those non-Western cultures. Family sleeping patterns, forms of discipline, and awareness and expressions of feelings are all examples of behaviors in which cultural values are demonstrated. People from one culture may not even notice certain behaviors that those from other cultures or groups see as primary.

Even though constructivists acknowledge that social factors play an important part in shaping people's views of themselves and the world, the individual person is still seen as the prime source of his or her own constructs (Raskin, 2001). Constructivists do not believe people are programmed by parents, society, or others. Rather, individuals decide who they are and how they will make sense of their world. The individual interprets every event and experience that happens to him or her, and it is this interpretation or construct that influences the person's beliefs and behavior. For example, if a mother has serious problems and cannot be counted on to be nurturing or supportive, her daughter might grow up believing that "The only person you can really count on is yourself." Another person might put a completely different meaning on those childhood experiences and grow up believing that "I am unlovable." In many cases people are not aware of their personal constructs and believe that their understanding of themselves, others, and the world is the only correct interpretation.

HOMEWORK EXERCISE 2.1 | PERSONAL CONSTRUCTS

Think of several people you know whose personal constructs do not fit your view of reality. What are your hunches about how they might have developed these constructs? List five of your own constructs or those of your parents. What factors have influenced the development of your personal constructs?

All people are constructivists in the sense that they are active and intentional agents in their own lives. They make meaning out of the events and experiences they have. If you grow up in a neighborhood where violence is the way to solve problems, then you may decide that trying to negotiate disagreements would be a waste of time. People live their lives in a web of meaning that they have woven (Mahoney, 2003).

HOMEWORK EXERCISE 2.2 | YOUR CONSTRUCTS OF SELF, OTHERS, AND THE WORLD

Think of a time when your life was going well or you were satisfied. Reflect on that time and write down the ideas you held about yourself. Complete the sentence "I am..." with several descriptive words. Based on your view of others at that same time, complete the sentence "They are..." with several words describing your perceptions of other people. Finally, complete the sentence "The world is..." with several descriptive words. That is one set of constructs or beliefs that you have about yourself, others, and the world.

Now remember a time when you felt depressed, discouraged, sick, exhausted, and/or basically miserable. Think about that time and do the same exercise, completing the sentences, "I am..."; "They are..."; and "The world is...". These statements are another set of constructs or beliefs that you have about yourself, others, and the world.

The constructs you just recorded are true for you. Someone else might perceive you, others, or the world quite differently. Who would be right? If you answered that both perceptions would be right, you are correct. Each person's construction of reality is true for that person.

APPLYING THE CONSTRUCTIVIST PERSPECTIVE

Using a constructivist perspective helps practitioners remember that their view of the world may be different from their client's view. Practitioners may think a problem is caused by physical illness, stress and demands, oppressive cultural factors, etc., but their clients may have a completely different view. For example, a client may attribute his alcoholism to his lack of willpower and the practitioner may see alcoholism as a disease.

As practitioners work with clients they will see constructs such as "You can't trust others," which may be based on past experiences (e.g., people of color may have had negative encounters in the dominant culture). Groups may develop constructs such as "We can't make a difference in our community." In each of these cases the practitioner will be working with the clients to find out if there are exceptions to their experiences that might challenge their current construction of reality and to identify ways the construct may be causing problems for the clients.

Another basic belief of constructivism is that there is no totally correct way of conceptualizing an event (Benson et al., 2003; Hayes & Oppenheim, 1997). This means that no individual, culture, or region of the world has a right to define their way as the way things *should* be. If a construct is unsatisfying, the individual is free to creatively develop another meaning for the event or experience. Practitioners using a constructivist perspective often work with clients to help them identify existing constructs and develop new constructs.

Problems arise when individual constructs for two people in a relationship are very different. For example, a couple seeking help to improve their relationship may need to recognize that each partner conceptualizes the issues differently depending on his or her own personal constructs. The practitioner might encourage the husband to understand the wife's interest in her job as a sign of her intelligence and willingness to contribute financially to the family rather than as a sign of her lack of interest in him or her belief that he isn't a good provider. The practitioner might encourage the wife to see the husband's desire for more time together as a compliment rather than a demand.

The constructivist perspective is useful to practitioners as they work to understand the worldviews or constructs of individuals, groups, and community organizations. The constructivist perspective encourages active involvement, hope, belief in the possibility of making changes, and participation of individuals and communities in their own unfolding (Snyder & Lopez, 2001). When people recognize that they construct their own reality or when they perceive themselves as able to have a positive influence in their lives, they feel more able to make changes and to have an impact on their world. Clients and practitioners can then collaborate to weave new meanings and possibilities for the future. These new choices contribute to differences in their lives and the lives of those to whom they are connected. Constructivists propose that change will happen when constricting personal constructs or decisions are opened up to embrace new ideas and behavioral possibilities (Newton, 2006; Sexton & Griffin, 1997).

HOMEWORK EXERCISE 2.3	IDENTIFYING CONSTRUCTS

As you listen to others this week, see if you can identify their personal constructs. What do they believe about the world, themselves, and others? How do you think these constructs might enhance or inhibit their lives? Reflect on how your personal constructs have led you to where you are today.

THE STRENGTHS PERSPECTIVE

DEFINING THE STRENGTHS PERSPECTIVE

Another useful perspective for practitioners is the *strengths perspective*. A strength may be defined as "any psychological process that consistently enables a person to think and act so as to yield benefits to himself or herself and society" (McCullough & Snyder, 2000, p. 3). Strengths are sometimes developed as people struggle to overcome difficulties, traumas, oppression, disappointments, and adversity. Strengths are also related to personal qualities or virtues that are admired, such as intelligence, common sense, patience, loyalty, sense of humor, commitment, responsibility, warmth, flexibility, friendliness, generosity, and many other qualities. Developed and under-developed talents are also strengths. These strengths would include such things as being a musician, a writer, a poet, a good cook, a car mechanic, a carpenter, a vocalist, or a painter (Saleebey, 2002c). As we all know, every person has untouched "mental, physical, emotional, social, and spiritual abilities" (Weick, Rapp, Sullivan, & Kisthardt, 1989, p. 352). These undeveloped capacities can be a source of power and hope (Weick & Chamberlain, 1996).

Families have strengths, just as individuals do. For example, a family's major strength may be an ability to stay together and support each other through challenges and trauma. Other family strengths include encouraging each other, helping each other, loving and caring for each other, accepting each other, and standing up for each other. Even very troubled families usually can identify good times when they were supportive to each other and had more fun together.

Communities, groups, and organizations also have strengths. Many organizations are identified as being *family-friendly* places to work because they have strengths such as on-site child care, opportunities to work from home, time off for family emergencies, and other supportive services that make it easier for parents to be effective on the job and at home. Groups may have strengths such as being effective, efficient, supportive, cooperative, focused, accepting, and fun.

Saleebey (2002a) stated that "focusing and building on client strengths . . . is an imperative" in order to demonstrate values related to "equality, respect for the dignity of the individual, inclusiveness and diversity and the search for maximum autonomy" (p. 264). Whether we are working with individuals, couples, families, groups, or organizations, it is valuable to look for their strengths, to identify their resources (including such areas as money, social support, adequate housing, education, past experiences, etc.), and to invite clients to focus on possibilities for the future.

APPLYING THE STRENGTHS PERSPECTIVE

Using a strengths perspective, practitioners begin by gaining a full understanding of the challenges and struggles their clients are experiencing. As the practitioner listens to clients discuss problems, s/he also pays attention to the strengths and abilities the clients have used in dealing with the problems. Instead of focusing exclusively on deficits, problems, and weaknesses in clients, strengths-perspective practitioners also focus on their clients' strength, capacity, and potential (Wong, 2006). Focusing exclusively on problems tends to invite people to feel hopeless and discouraged. When clients are feeling discouraged, it may be helpful to assist them to identify past successes, however small, and to begin to look at the qualities and strengths that helped them achieve those successes. Using a strengths perspective, practitioners focus on what is right with clients instead of what is wrong with them. They openly admire and show respect for the strengths of their clients. In working with groups, neighborhoods, or organizations, practitioners using a system called Appreciative Inquiry (Hammond, 1998) ask about, focus on, and recognize or appreciate the strengths in the teams or groups with whom they work. The practitioner might talk about a time when "the team/group performed really well," "went beyond what was expected," and/or "put forth extra effort" (Hammond, 1998, p. 34). The practitioner might ask about positive behavior or outcomes.

- What did each of you do in order to produce such a thorough report?
- What are your ideas about what your team is doing in order to work so effectively and cooperatively together?
- This organization seems to be very concerned about the well-being of employees. I wonder how this level of concern developed?

Appreciative Inquiry is another variation on the strengths perspective. In Chapters 6 and 7 we discuss additional ways to apply the strengths perspective.

HOMEWORK EXERCISE 2.4 | STRENGTHS

Find a partner and discuss accomplishments in your life before you were five years old. For each accomplishment allow some time to explore the strengths necessary to achieve that accomplishment. For example, during your first five years of life you probably learned to walk, talk, and perhaps tie your shoes. What capacities do you believe made these successes possible? Move to the next five years of your life when you may have mastered skills such as riding a bicycle, reading, writing, and doing arithmetic. List some of the strengths necessary to master each of these very complex skills.

Now discuss an experience you have had in which someone saw and identified a strength in you that previously had been outside of your awareness. How did that experience affect you? As you were growing up, was it more common for people to identify your strengths or your weaknesses? What impact do you believe that positive or negative emphasis has had on your life?

Since language so powerfully affects our thinking, some authors suggest that using the language of challenges is more positive than talking about problems (Bennet, Wolin, & Reiss, 1987; Hubble & Miller, 2004; Wolin, 1999, 2003). The authors of this text agree that using the word *challenges* is better than using the word *problems*. Challenges are usually experienced as something that can be overcome and may represent an opportunity for growth. Problems, on the other hand, may be experienced as negative and more difficult to change.

Incorporated into the strengths perspective is the belief that everyone has the capacity to develop new resources, to make positive changes, and to use his or her competencies to solve problems. Using the strengths perspective, it is the practitioner's job to invite clients to discover, think about, and figure out how to use their strengths. The past and present are explored to identify strengths and capacities. When clients talk about problems and difficulties from the past, practitioners can help them focus on how they coped with the challenges. Working from a strengths perspective, practitioners often ask clients what they learned from past challenges. Research has shown a significant correlation between a strengths-based approach and client improvement (Lopez & Magyar-Moe, 2006; Rapp, Siegal, Li, & Saha, 1998; Wolin, 2003).

Using a strengths perspective, practitioners explore client competencies, capacities, abilities, and resources and then focus on future possibilities. Practitioners might ask clients to talk about what they do well, what they have taught another person, what they would like to accomplish in the next year, and/or what their wishes or dreams are. By expressing interest in clients' hopes, dreams, and goals, and by focusing on competence and future possibilities, the practitioner heightens clients' belief in the possibility of change (Cheavens, Feldman, Woodward, & Snyder, 2006; Saleebey, 2002b; Wolin, 1999).

HOMEWORK EXERCISE 2.5 | STRENGTHS AND CHALLENGES

Think of a challenging time in your life or the life of your family. What strengths did you or members of your family develop as you coped with the challenge? What did you learn about yourself, others, and the world from that experience?

THE RESILIENCE PERSPECTIVE

DEFINING THE RESILIENCE PERSPECTIVE

Another important perspective is *resilience*, or the ability to recover from challenges. One of the factors influencing the construction of our worldview is our adaptive ability in times of stress. Sources of stress include family and relationship problems, serious health issues, work and financial difficulties, community violence, and fears of terrorism.

The abilities or qualities that help individuals and groups respond effectively to these stressors are many and varied. Resilience is developed from resources that exist within the individual, family, racial or cultural group, spiritual beliefs, and society at large. One of the practitioner's tasks is to access and build upon the resilience of the individuals or groups s/he is serving. Another task is to teach and help develop qualities that increase resilience, such as the following:

- having a positive outlook on life;
- trusting that others can be of help;
- seeing a mistake as feedback rather than failure;
- focusing on the present rather than the past or future;
- having the determination to hang on even when life seems too hard.

Encouraging the feeling of hope can increase resilience as well. Just the thought that things could get better can give clients enough hope to help them persevere for a little longer.

Early research on resilience conducted by Garmezy and Rutter (1983) focused on qualities that helped children to survive and thrive despite living with parents suffering from schizophrenia. Since then a number of conceptual models have been proposed to describe the dynamic relationship between risk, protective factors, personal attributes, and adaptive functioning (Middlemiss, 2005; Ungar, 2004; Yakin & McMahon, 2003; Zimmerman & Arunkumar, 1994). Some of these models are introduced below and summarized in Table 2.1.

RESILIENCE MODELS

In the Compensatory Model, resilience factors neutralize exposure to risk. For example, imagine a young girl whose family has moved frequently, but instead of feeling uprooted she has high self-esteem as a result of knowing that she can adapt to new situations. Higher self-esteem helps the child develop a greater sense of

TABLE 2.1 | CONCEPTUAL MODELS OF RESILIENCE

Model	Mechanisms of Resilience	Example
Compensatory Model[a]	Neutralizes exposure to risk	Higher self-esteem helps a child develop a sense of competence despite the stressors involved with repeated moves.
Challenge Model[b]	Stress (if not excessive) enhances a sense of competence.	The stress from ethnic marginalization helps people develop confidence in their ability to cope with difficult situations.
Protective Models[c]	Resilience factors moderate the effect of exposure to stress and modify responses to the stress.	A Native American youth who has both a strong cultural identity and high self-esteem will be less likely to engage in substance abuse.

[a]Christiansen & Evans, 2005; Hollister-Wagner, Foshee, & Jackson, 2001; Masten, Best, & Garmezy, 1991.
[b]Christiansen & Evans, 2005; Harrison et al., 1990; Hollister-Wagner et al., 2001.
[c]Christiansen & Evans, 2005; Hollister-Wagner et al., 2001; Zimmerman, Ramirez, Washienko, Walter, & Dryer, 1994.

competency as she copes with new stressful situations (Christiansen & Evans, 2005; Hollister-Wagner, Foshee, & Jackson, 2001; Masten, Best, & Garmezy, 1990).

In the Challenge Model, stress is treated as an enhancer of competence, as long as the degree of stress is not excessive. For example, the stress involved with ethnic marginalization has led many people to develop a sense of confidence in their ability to cope with difficult situations (Christiansen & Evans, 2005; Hollister-Wagner et al., 2001). As an additional example, children who have learned how to survive in a poor learning environment in school may develop the capacity to seek out other resources to support their learning. Later, they may apply the same persistence in the work world to find resources to support their career development.

Protective Models identify factors that have a moderating effect on exposure to risk and responses to the stressor. One factor may increase the effect of another. For example, when a Native American youth has both a strong cultural identity and high self-esteem, these qualities augment each other as a predictor of avoiding substance use (Christiansen & Evans, 2005; Hollister-Wagner et al., 2001; Zimmerman, Ramirez, Washienko, Walter, & Dryer, 1994). When the youth experiences himself or herself as valued and valuable and also has a sense of pride in his or her heritage, this combination may deter him or her from using drugs or alcohol to escape the difficulties encountered by Native Americans in our society.

Many protective factors play a role in developing and sustaining resilience, including: individual and family characteristics, the school or work environment, and community support. When practitioners address issues with individuals, groups, or community organizations, they are looking for factors that enhance the resilience of that population. As you might guess from your own experience, research has shown that social support enhances resilience in stressful situations (Colemena & Ganong, 2002; Rodger & Rose, 2002; Watson, T. T., 2003; Wolkow & Ferguson, 2001).

Gabarino and colleagues (1992) found that four categories of factors characterize resilient children:

1. *Individual factors*—Child's developmental level, cognitive competence, experiences of self-efficacy, temperamental characteristics (sociability, good-naturedness, goal orientation, activity, few feeding or sleeping problems), self-esteem, valuing of others, ability to adapt and shape the environment to deal successfully with pressures.
2. *Family factors*—Stable emotional relationship with at least one parent or support person who encourages and models constructive coping, parenting figure accessible in times of stress, and close relationship with other family members.
3. *School factors*—An open, supportive educational climate, teachers who provide emotional support, encourage self-esteem and promote competence, a stable and structured environment, positive role models, and educational stimulation.
4. *Community factors*—Friends and neighbors who are supportive and promote competence, close friends who are supportive, activities that offer self-efficacy to families.

HOMEWORK EXERCISE 2.6 | RESILIENCE

Think about yourself from the perspective of resilience. What individual, family, school, and community factors support your resilience?

Think about a stressful time in your life. What abilities did you use to recover? What abilities do you want to develop that would make you a more resilient person?

Qualities that contribute to resilience are somewhat culturally determined. Therefore, it is important to understand how cultural experiences influence the ways in which people cope with stress. For example, connection, cultural adaptation, spirituality, generativity, and creativity are particularly important to people of color. They are more likely than the dominant white population to endorse a worldview that promotes both individual and collective resilience. Forming strong social and emotional connections with others, embracing a group identity, and valuing community welfare are important. Connection emphasizes intergenerational relationships that may transcend death (Brave Heart, 2003; Tan & Dong, 1999), especially in some Eastern cultures where ancestors are venerated.

Spirituality also predicts resilience. People of color have traditionally been spiritually oriented, and spirituality enhances their cultural resilience (Banerjee & Pyles, 2004; Brodsky, 1999; Gregory, 2002; Littrell & Beck, 1999). Belief systems help people cope with stress by addressing questions about the meaning of life, loss of hope, victimization, and demoralization. The Bible that was used to support slavery also brought hope for a better life after death to many slaves.

When working to build resilience with people of color, it is important to support their ethnic identity; community and extended family ties; positive meaning-making constructs and spirituality; traditional knowledge and ceremonies; and use of storytelling, creativity, and humor. Given the ways various groups respond to trauma, it is easy to see why many governmental interventions based upon individualistic resilience factors have met with limited success. Examples include programs that address post-traumatic stress disorder. The Veterans Administration initially attempted interventions with individuals. Veterans themselves formed groups that proved to be more effective. Sometimes more traditional healing methods such as the sweat lodge of some of the Native American peoples have been found effective as well.

APPLYING THE RESILIENCE PERSPECTIVE

As practitioners work with their clients, they can encourage the building and further development of resilience factors. Although it is helpful if children are raised with multiple sources of support, resilience skills can be taught and developed later in life. People can be taught to set goals, to support each other, to be creative in finding resources, to identify positive aspects in their lives, and so on.

It is important to be aware that people of color may turn to sources of support in times of stress that are different from those of the majority culture. Although much of the research historically has focused on individual traits (Davis, 2001; Gordon, 1995), more recent research has noted that culture, ethnicity, and environment play key roles in the manifestation of resilience in individuals and communities, particularly among people of color (Clauss-Ehlers, 2004). Experiences involving racism, trauma, oppression, immigration, and poverty have led members of minority groups to develop a heightened sense of connectivity, including social ties, belief systems, and community supports (Dudley-Grant, Mendez, & Zinn, 2000). When a group or individuals feel attacked or persecuted from outside, they turn to people like themselves for support. On occasion this may be isolating, but often it is helpful in both surviving and developing more powerful and effective ways to fight oppression. The Civil Rights Movement and the Montgomery Bus Boycott are well-known examples of members of a persecuted group working closely together to bring about change.

THE EMPOWERMENT PERSPECTIVE

DEFINING THE EMPOWERMENT PERSPECTIVE

Empowerment has internal and external components. The *internal component,* or psychological empowerment, involves a sense of control over our motivations, cognition, and personality (Rappaport, 1985; Siegall & Gardner, 2000), and a belief that we can competently make decisions, solve problems, achieve goals, and have a significant impact on our environment. For members of oppressed groups, empowerment has been described as the development of the aptitudes, strengths, and sense of power or competence necessary to be recognized as equal (Littrell & Beck, 1999; Miller, 2004; Nash, 2005; Rose, 2005). The *external component* of empowerment includes the tangible knowledge, competencies, skills, information, opportunities, and resources that allow a person to take action and to actively advocate change (Cheung et al., 2005).

Empowerment is a process as well as an outcome (Hardina, 2005; Miley, O'Melia, & DuBois, 2004). When new abilities are learned through life experiences (rather than from advice offered by an "expert"), the process of using the new competencies results in an increased sense of personal empowerment (Lyons, Smuts, & Stephens, 2001; Rappaport, 1981). Research shows a direct correlation between levels of participation and empowerment (Cheung et al., 2005; Zimmerman, 1990; Zimmerman & Rappaport, 1988). For example, the more involved or active a person is in a challenging project, the more likely it is that s/he will experience an increased sense of empowerment. Think of a group in which you have participated. If you participated in the group's activities, you would gain more of a sense of empowerment or competency than those who remained passive and uninvolved. As a sense of empowerment increases, individuals take more responsibility for actively improving the quality of their lives and of the environment (Miley et al., 2004). The outcome of this process is a sense of competency, personal power (psychological empowerment), and life satisfaction (Cheung et al., 2005) that is supported by having the skills, knowledge, and competencies necessary to actively solve problems and advocate for change.

APPLYING THE EMPOWERMENT PERSPECTIVE

Using an empowerment perspective, practitioners focus on the internal and external components of empowerment (Cheung et al., 2005). No matter what system size the practitioner is working with (individuals through whole organizations), using an empowerment perspective allows clients to develop a sense of power and competency as they experience using their skills and knowledge in new and challenging ways and realize that they are able to accomplish difficult tasks. Practitioners who see it as their job to fix their clients are not working from an empowerment perspective because it is not possible to simply give someone a sense of power or empowerment. Practitioners who use an empowerment perspective relate to clients as partners and recognize that clients are the experts on their situation, their challenges, their strengths and capacities, their choice of what they will work on, their timing and pace, their goals, and their preferred way to work. In these client-practitioner partnerships, practitioners bring professional expertise and resources, and clients provide personal expertise and the energy for change. For example, practitioners can provide resources such as a space to meet, observations, information, and a supportive climate that can be useful as people begin the journey toward empowerment (Hardina, 2005; Simon, 1994).

Practitioners can also help people discover their strengths, identify their goals, and develop a plan to reach their goals. This type of collaborative work allows clients to accept responsibility for change and therefore experience a greater sense of empowerment. It can be particularly empowering for clients to work in a group because they will have the opportunity to help and support others, to take on tasks that might seem too challenging for any one person, to share experiences and competencies with others, to learn from others, to develop skills with others, and to get feedback from numerous people (Cheung et al., 2005; Dodd & Gutierrez, 1990; Home, 1999; Lee, 2001).

HOMEWORK EXERCISE 2.7 | UNDERSTANDING EMPOWERMENT

Identify at least one experience that has been empowering to you. This might be an experience in which you took on some task, problem, or challenge that initially seemed very difficult, demanding, and/or complicated to you. It might be something you had never done before or maybe something that you feared you could not do. This experience might be something you did alone or with other people. In what ways did dealing with this situation enhance your sense of personal competence? What competencies and/or strengths did you acquire as you dealt with this situation? In retrospect, would you have been better off if someone had intervened and just fixed it for you?

THE ECOLOGICAL PERSPECTIVE

DEFINING THE ECOLOGICAL PERSPECTIVE

The ecological perspective is a useful view for those involved in helping others (Dishion & Stormshak, 2007; Germain & Gitterman, 1995; Ungar, 2002). Derived from concepts of biological ecology, this framework enables practitioners and clients to think about the reciprocal relationships between people and their environment. Practitioners strive to understand the interconnected personal, environmental, and cultural factors involved in clients' situations. When you think of client behavior in terms of a cause-and-effect relationship between variables, these additional aspects are left out. While cause-and-effect linear thinking may be useful to explain simple phenomena, it is inadequate to explain the more complex human phenomena seen by practitioners (Ungar, 2002). An ecological perspective is less concerned with cause and effect and more concerned with the transactions that occur between people and their environments. For example, cause and effect might predict that a mother who applies new techniques in disciplining her little girl might see fewer tantrums. In contrast, the ecological perspective would also consider the changes in the mother's sense of competency and willingness to learn new skills. This might also be extended to the child viewing her mother as more strong and confident as a parent, which then results in continued influences back and forth from the interactions between the mother and child. These transactions are defined as interactions that are reciprocal processes used by people to shape their environments while they are in turn being shaped by their environments over time (Dishion & Stormshak, 2007; Germain & Gitterman, 1995).

ECOLOGICAL PERSPECTIVE CONCEPTS

The ecological perspective (Germain and Gitterman, 1995; Wolski, 2004) has three important components: person-environment fit, adaptations, and life stressors.

Person-environment fit refers to how well a person's (or group's) needs, goals, and rights mesh with the traits and functioning of the physical and social environment (Miley et al., 2004; Wolski, 2004). Cultural and historical contexts are important aspects of this fit. Understanding the individual perceptions of this fit requires knowledge of cultural influences on beliefs such as roles and social norms. Historical contexts include individual experiences and societal change. All of these factors will affect the quality of the person-environment fit. Although open to change at all times, the fit can range from unfavorable to favorable. When the fit is at least minimally adequate, adaptation leads to continued development and a satisfying social functioning. This development in turn sustains or improves the environment. There is a reciprocal exchange in which each aspect of the situation continues to provide feedback and promote changes in the individual's development, health, and social functioning. If the exchanges are generally negative, both the individual and the environment are likely to experience detrimental effects. One example of person-environment exchange is the manner in which unmarried teen pregnancies are handled in various communities. When teen pregnancy is judged as *bad* and stigmatized by the environment (i.e., the community), the young mother may not be supported in learning how to provide adequate nurturing for her baby. If the family, community, and/or schools provide a supportive atmosphere, the young mother and her baby have a much better chance of doing well.

Adaptations are the processes people use to sustain or raise the level of fit between themselves and their environment. These changes are ongoing and include cognitive, behavioral, and sensory-perceptual changes. Adaptations can be actions to change the environment (such as leaving an abusive relationship), changes within the individual (such as learning new parenting skills), or both. When these changes occur, the cycle of adaptation continues in response. Thus, adaptation is ongoing and never-ending, with the purpose of achieving the best fit between the individual and his or her situation.

Life stressors are issues that are perceived as exceeding personal and environmental resources available to manage them. These stressors can include social or developmental transitions, traumatic events, or anything that changes the existing person-environment fit. The same situation can be perceived as a life stressor by some individuals and as a challenge by others. While a stressor might be seen as presenting the possibility of serious harm, loss, and the feeling of danger, it can also be seen as a challenge and viewed as an opportunity for growth that can lead to positive feelings of anticipated mastery (Lazarus & Folkman, 1984; Perkins, Crim, Silberman, & Brown, 2004). Poverty and oppression can be life stressors in themselves and can also affect an individual's ability to manage the impact of other life issues. For example, a house fire is a devastating blow, yet an individual's reactions to such an event are tempered by his or her characteristics and resources to deal with the problems that result from such an event. It is natural to have a feeling of loss in such a situation, yet some individuals also see it as an opportunity to make changes in their environment. This is only possible when sufficient resources are available. If a family is unable to re-create an adequate home environment due to lack of resources, they cannot move beyond their feelings of loss and disruption, resulting in high levels of stress.

When high levels of stress continue over a period of time, this may cause emotional and/or psychological disturbances such as feelings of guilt, anxiety, depression, anger, fear, or helplessness. These feelings are often accompanied by diminished self-esteem, relatedness, self-direction, and sense of competence (DeLongis & Holtzman, 2005; Sassaroli & Ruggiero, 2005). Coping strategies are behaviors that are used to manage stress. These can involve managing negative emotional responses to stress and using problem-solving strategies to decrease the levels of stress. Successful coping also depends on individual and environmental resources. Successful coping serves to decrease the misfit between people and their environments. It also improves levels of relatedness, self-esteem, competence, and self-direction.

APPLYING THE ECOLOGICAL PERSPECTIVE

In the ecological perspective, behaviors are not seen as dysfunctional or maladaptive. If behaviors are viewed as adaptations to improve the goodness of fit between internal needs and the environment, how can these behaviors be considered maladaptive? There are behaviors that are unacceptable and have negative consequences, but all behaviors make sense in context. For example, a teenager who carries a gun around the neighborhood may be engaging in undesirable (and unlawful) behavior, but if that teenager's friend was recently killed in a gun violence incident, his decision to have a gun would be somewhat more understandable.

Because behaviors do not occur in isolation, they must be viewed as having multiple dimensions with internal and environmental demands occurring simultaneously. Thus, a behavior that is appropriate in one situation, such as a boy playfully pushing and shoving other children at the local park, is not at all appropriate in another situation such as a classroom setting. Such behavior on the playground may increase the boy's status among his peers, but the same behavior in the classroom may cause him to be labeled *antisocial* and a *behavior problem*. Focusing on the interactions within a peer group may lead to the conclusion that rather than being antisocial, the child actually is socially adept.

Problems arise when challenges occur in unresponsive environments. Returning to the boy who pushes and shoves in the classroom, an environment that nurtures and supports students will provide the opportunity for growth and understanding, improving the goodness of fit. In contrast, if the boy is harshly required to adapt through punishment and humiliation, his behavior may become more unacceptable and have an impact on all his interactions in the school environment, causing him to harbor a negative attitude toward school.

How we work with people and their situations is based on our perception of human behavior. Viewing clients from an ecological perspective helps us understand how they have developed their strengths and vulnerabilities and influences what we do to support growth and change in clients. The ecological perspective emphasizes a focus on the strengths people demonstrate in response to a difficult situation or environment. We are challenged to build on the strengths that clients already possess. Thus, a strengths perspective is essential for the ecological perspective in work with clients.

HOMEWORK EXERCISE 2.8 | ECOLOGICAL PERSPECTIVE

Reflect on your life experiences using an ecological perspective. What are some ways that you have adapted to your environment? Identify at least five ways you adapted to your family of origin, to your friends, to the challenges in your life.

How does your environment affect your thinking, actions, and feelings? For example, if you had to drive in rush hour traffic today, that might have caused you to feel stressed, to think negative thoughts about the other drivers, and to act in more aggressive or competitive ways than usual.

Identify the five to ten most stressful events that have happened to you in the last year. What coping strategies did you use as you dealt with those stresses?

Think of a time when you felt pulled between responding to your needs and wants and responding to the expectations in your environment. For example, some college students live with their family. Frequently, the student's need to study or be with friends conflicts with the family's need for attention.

Imagine that you are working with a city neighborhood that has traditionally been mostly

HOMEWORK EXERCISE 2.8 | ECOLOGICAL PERSPECTIVE *continued*

African-Americans but recently has included a number of immigrants from Somalia. Think about the challenges these new immigrants may be facing, such as adapting to a new country, a new culture, a new city, and a new neighborhood. What other challenges might they be facing? In what ways do you think their environment may not be a good fit for them?

The ecological perspective is useful in working with groups as well as individuals (Conyne & Bemak, 2004). Kurt Lewin (1952) suggested that using the *force field* perspective in considering possible barriers to the achievement of group goals is a helpful way to gain a better understanding of how these goals might be achieved. Lewin posited that groups are more than the sum of the members who come together for a project. Instead, the group is an integration of the members, which suggests that a group possesses a unique structure, unique goals, and a unique relation to other groups. Each group has a need that is linked to unfulfilled group goals, and from this need, tension is produced. This tension provides the impetus to energize the group to take action to meet this need. Similar to the poor fit between a person and his or her environment, the group is committed to working to achieve a better fit with its environment. An example of this quest for a better fit is the battle for women's right to vote during the early twentieth century. As women began to see themselves as a disenfranchised group with particular needs and discovered ways they could contribute to the environment and government, they fought for their right to be recognized as valued and contributing members of society.

Extending Lewin's (1952) force field perspective, Brueggemann (2001) described barriers and benefits groups face in achieving their goals. Barriers to achieving goals, called *restraining forces,* are the disadvantages and costs involved with each action taken to fulfill the identified need. Examples of restraining forces include limited time, money, and manpower. *Compelling forces*, the advantages or benefits of taking action, include an increased quantity and quality of services and greater effectiveness in meeting the group's needs. For example, a group from a poor community might consider building a large park in an area of substandard housing. To achieve this goal, the group would need to purchase the homes and lots in a full block, requiring thousands of dollars (restraining force). The group might also consider the compelling forces for creating this park, such as having a place for recreation and improving the appeal of the area housing. When the restraining forces and the compelling forces are carefully identified, the group can then identify the actors or persons, groups, or organizations to enlist in influencing the forces and altering their strength. This process should provide a solution with a good chance of achieving the goal. Recalling the example of women's right to vote, there were many restraining forces (threats to those in power) as well as compelling forces (expansion of human rights and potential benefits of the important input women had to offer) that led to the passage of laws granting women the right to vote.

TABLE 2.2 | THEORIES OF HUMAN BEHAVIOR

Theory/perspective	Practitioner strategies	Concepts	Assumptions of Theory
Constructivism	Help clients identify existing constructs and develop new ones.	Practitioners need to be aware that the worldview of clients may be very different from their own.	Individuals describe experiences in terms of personal constructs—explanations of events that become the lens through which they see the world.
Strengths	Start with past successes and look at the qualities and strengths through which the client was able to achieve these successes. Explore client competencies, capacities, abilities, and resources and focus on future possibilities.	Everyone has the capacity to develop new resources, to make positive changes, and to use their competencies to solve problems. Problems are described as challenges, since challenges can be seen as opportunities for growth.	Every person has undiscovered or forgotten abilities.
Resilience	Identify, access, and build upon resilience strengths of the individual or group. Teach and help develop qualities that increase resilience.	Resilience qualities include: A positive outlook on life. Seeing a mistake as feedback, not failure. Trust that others can be of help. Focus on the present rather than the past or future. The willingness to prevail even when it seems too difficult to go on.	Resources in the individual, family, racial/cultural group, spiritual beliefs, and society enable one to adapt in times of stress.
Empowerment	Recognize that clients are the experts about their own particular situation, challenges, strengths, what they would like to change, the timing and pace, and their preferred way of working. Practitioners and clients are partners working together.	Empowerment has internal and external components. Internal components involve a sense of control over one's motivation, cognition, and personality, and a belief that one can make effective decisions, solve problems, achieve goals, and have an impact on one's environment. External components include knowledge, competencies, skills, information, opportunities, and resources that allow one to take action and actively advocate for change.	Empowerment results from using competencies in a setting where new abilities are learned through life experience, rather than from advice provided by "experts."

Ecological Perspective	Help clients recognize the barriers to achievement of goals. Help clients think about the advantages and disadvantages of various solutions in making decisions about how to achieve these goals.	Person-environment fit refers to the fit between individual needs, goals, and rights and the traits and functioning of the physical and social environment. Adaptation is the result of processes to sustain or raise the "fit" between people and their environment. Life stressors are the result of issues perceived as exceeding personal and environmental resources available to manage them. Behaviors are not seen as maladaptive, but as attempts to improve the person-environment fit.	Humans are both influenced and influence their environment, and human behavior must be viewed in terms of the interactions between people and their environment.
Dual perspective	Consider how the dominant society might influence clients' beliefs, sense of competence, and ability to make changes in their lives. In keeping with this idea of dealing with two views of reality, practitioners need to work to increase their awareness of the influences of racism, prejudice, and stereotypes.	Those who differ from the majority racially, in sexual orientation, disability, etc., will be viewed in terms of that difference rather than as individuals. To understand the client's worldview, practitioners must view interactions from the dual perspective.	When people are born outside the dominant societal group, they exist in two worlds of reality—the nurturing world of their own societal group and the sustaining group in which they must be educated, make a living, and deal with the economic and political realities of life.

THE DUAL PERSPECTIVE

DEFINING THE DUAL PERSPECTIVE

Most of us who are involved in the helping professions benefit from one type of privilege or another in our lives, whether it is due to our race, gender, social class, sexual orientation, religion, or abilities. Being a member of the dominant group in at least one of these areas makes it challenging for us to truly empathize with members of a marginalized group and understand their perspectives on life. When we can feel what it means to be in the marginalized group, we are more likely to recognize the unjust power structures in our society and to be aware of the privileges from which we may have benefited in our lives. Below is an experiential exercise that can lead you to a place of reflection, self-awareness, and open-mindedness regarding what it is like to be on the receiving end of racism in our society. An exercise such as this one should be optional. If you would like to try the guided imagery, ask a trusted friend or colleague to slowly read the following statement while you close your eyes and reflect:

> *Imagine that you are exactly who you are, but the world around you has changed. As you look around your campus, you see that the vast majority of students are African-American. The majority of your professors are African-American. When you look at your state government, the governor and lieutenant governor are African-American. The majority of people in the statehouse are African-American. Looking beyond your state, to Washington, DC, you see that the president of the United States is African-American, as is the vice president. The vast majority of people in the House of Representatives and in the Senate are African-American. Of the nine Supreme Court justices, eight are African-American. Coming back to your community, you decide to apply for a job, and the business owners and the people taking applications are almost all African-American. You decide you need a loan, and the bank tellers and loan officers are African-American. You need to rent an apartment, and the landlords you meet with are African-American. You drive on the highway and realize you have started to speed—sirens flash, and the police officer who comes to your car is African-American. You decide to fight the ticket, so you go to court and the judge is African-American. You go grocery shopping, and almost all the employees are African-American. If you are not African-American, you have a hard time finding hair products for yourself—you might find them within a small section marked "ethnic." And while you are looking for that section, you might feel that people are watching you closely in the store to see if you shoplift. Take a moment more and look around this world, and just notice what you feel and what you are aware of. Then return your attention to the present.*

If you are an African-American student, you have lived the experience of being a minority and you do not need to do this exercise. Consider sharing some of your life experiences with other students who have not experienced being in the minority.

After doing the exercise, you may have many feelings. Students may react in different ways, depending on their backgrounds and life experiences. Some may have an *aha* moment in which they suddenly empathize with African-Americans in our society, while others may feel that they could live comfortably in the world described by the guided imagery. Occasionally, students will say, "I just couldn't get into it," which is understandable. Allowing yourself to participate fully in guided imagery, especially in a public setting, can feel like an emotional risk. Whatever your reaction to this exercise, it will be helpful to find a safe person with whom to share your thoughts and feelings.

After completing the exercise, it can be useful to imagine it again with a different twist: imagine that the dominant group in the world is women, or people with a homosexual orientation. The world would look very different to most of us.

What is happening in this guided imagery? It is a concrete way to understand the concept of the *Dual Perspective*. Dr. Leon Chestang (1972) created this concept to explain the two worlds experienced by a person born outside of society's dominant group. He describes life for a typical African-American boy: his family is part of the nurturing world, the world where he is known as a unique individual and is loved for who he is. This world might contain not just his family, but also his neighborhood, including local stores, parks, and the church his family attends. Eventually, however, he must venture outside the nurturing world into the sustaining world—the world in which he will be educated, earn a living, and deal with the economic and political realities of life. In the sustaining world, he is more likely to be seen as *an African-American male,* not as a unique individual. Therefore, he must develop two views of reality—that is, a dual perspective. He must constantly evaluate disappointments in life, such as not being selected for a job, to determine whether they are based on his qualifications or on racism from the dominant culture. He must constantly shift between his *home culture* and the dominant culture to choose acceptable behavior in each situation.

After understanding Chestang's dual-perspective concept based on race, the next step is to apply the same concept to someone who is gay or lesbian. If the boy in our example is gay, chances are he is born into a world that does not understand and accept him. He must then create his own nurturing world as he grows up—not an easy feat in a heterosexist society. Similarly, you may apply this approach to a girl born into a family that is not female-affirming. She might always be reminded that she is a second-class citizen. You may also consider social class as another area in which there are profound cultural differences, the discussion of which is almost taboo in our society. It is also useful to consider the perspective of a child who has a disability, whether the disability is present at birth or acquired through a life-changing event.

APPLYING THE DUAL PERSPECTIVE

It is important for practitioners to recognize that life is viewed differently by people in marginalized groups. When practitioners consider the Dual Perspective, they are able to better understand how our culture maintains the dominant group's power by objectifying the "other." When working with clients from a minority group, it is important for the practitioner to be aware of the day-to-day challenges these clients face and to keep in mind that their clients are living in two worlds, the nurturing world and the sustaining world. Minority clients must continually go back and forth between these worlds.

EXPECTED COMPETENCIES

In this chapter, you have learned about several perspectives that can help you better understand how you and your clients think, feel, and make choices.

You should now be able to:

- Give an example of how a personal construct might influence a decision.

- Compare and contrast a strengths perspective with a deficit-focused view.
- Define *empowerment*.
- Describe how the ecological perspective would provide a broader view of a client.
- Give two examples of how the dual perspective provides a deeper understanding of a marginalized group of people.

CHAPTER 3

UNDERSTANDING PROFESSIONAL RELATIONSHIPS

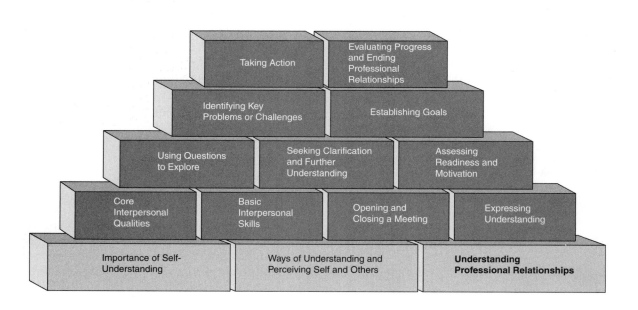

In this chapter, you will learn about the following topics:

Practitioner Tasks:
- Understanding professional roles and responsibilities including ethics, values, and legal obligations

As you develop your knowledge and skills as a professional, you will see that, as in many learning situations, one piece of information, task, or skill builds upon the foundation of the previous information in a building-block fashion. Without a solid foundation, a building or a relationship may not last or serve its purpose. No amount of knowledge and skill will make a difference if practitioners are not able to establish effective relationships with their clients. In this chapter you will learn the key elements of professional relationships.

PROFESSIONAL RELATIONSHIPS

To be a competent practitioner, you will need to know how to form solid professional relationships. The professional relationship between a practitioner and client is different from other types of relationships you have experienced in the past. Relationships are formed in a number of ways, and each type (parent/child, husband/wife, friend/friend, and teacher/mentor) has its own qualities and either stated or unstated rules about how each person should behave. Some relationships involve people who might be seen as equals, such as a husband and wife, and others involve people who have different levels of responsibility and control, as a parent and child. When people establish new relationships, there is a tendency to try to fit them into a pattern similar to an established relationship. Therefore, clients sometimes begin by treating the relationship with the practitioner as the same as a relationship with a friend or with an authority figure such as a parent or the school principal. It is up to the practitioner to explain the nature of a professional relationship

Although various kinds of relationships have some qualities in common, there are also distinct differences. Some of these differences involve who has the most power (based on authority or expertise) and/or responsibility for the relationship, whether it involves a payment for services, how often you meet and for how long, and whether there is mutual sharing of personal information. Some relationships have unique meeting locations. For example, teachers and students generally meet in classrooms whereas doctors and patients usually meet in offices, clinics, or hospitals. Practitioners often meet with clients in the practitioners' office; however, meetings sometimes occur in the client's home, at a community center, or in an agency conference room.

Table 3.1 on the next page compares the characteristics of several types of relationships.

Relationships between practitioners and clients are unique in a number of ways. Although the practitioner is responsible for structuring the relationship and for making it work as effectively as possible, the relationship is also collaborative in many ways (Kottler, 2003). For example, the client and the practitioner will agree on times to meet and collaborate on the focus of meetings. One of the key differences you may have noticed when you have worked with a professional (doctor, lawyer, therapist, etc.) is that the conversations are much more goal-oriented than they are in most personal relationships. One of the challenges of being apractitioner is to keep

TABLE 3.1 | CHARACTERISTICS OF DIFFERENT TYPES OF RELATIONSHIPS

	Friendship	Parent/Child	Husband/Wife	Practitioner/Client
Information sharing	Both directions	Depends on the circumstance of the interaction.	Free flow in both directions is often expected.	Much less information about the practitioner available than client.
Responsibilities	More or less equal	Parent has more than child: teaching, socializing, helping child solve problems, etc.	Varies by culture, but generally shared.	Practitioner has the responsibility to fulfill all agreements with client and to problem-solve with client.
Financial commitment	Little or none	High when child is still a dependent.	Depends on the culture, age, accepted responsibilities for each role.	Practitioner is paid for time by client/insurer/ government/agency, etc.
Length of relationship	Mutually determined	Usually only ended by death.	Depends on desire of each person.	Determined by the goals or agreements established by practitioner and client. When goals are accomplished, relationship ends.
Time spent together	Mutually determined	Considerable	Considerable	Practitioner determines with client.
Availability	Mutually determined	All the time	Much of the time	Scheduled between practitioner and client.

the interaction focused toward finding solutions for the stated problems. Relationships between clients and practitioners should be purposeful. It is all too easy to slip into a social conversation in which there is little sense of accomplishment at the end of the meeting. If the client wants to chat about the weather, the practitioner might join the conversation briefly but should bring the meeting back to the identified purposes. Practitioners also have responsibility for monitoring the emotional side of the relationship. If there is tension, anger, sexual attraction, hurt, or other feelings, the practitioner needs to decide how to address the issues related to these feelings.

Relationships between clients and practitioners are time-limited. Sometimes the practitioner and client agree in the beginning that they will work together for a certain period of time. When the goals are achieved, the relationship ends. Sometimes, though, the relationship is limited by financial considerations. A neighborhood group may want a practitioner to help them create plans to improve their neighborhood, but they only have a limited amount of money to pay for services. The relationship may have to be concluded when the financial resources are depleted, unless other arrangements are made.

The relationship between the practitioner and client is not an equal one. There is an imbalance of power or authority. Practitioners' authority comes from their knowledge, position, and resources. This authority should not be used to dominate or control clients but only to provide help to them. This unequal relationship between practitioner and client imposes certain obligations on the practitioner. The practitioner has a specific role in responding to the clients' needs. The practitioner will learn much more about the client than the client learns about the practitioner. It is not the client's role to take care of the practitioner or to listen sympathetically to complaints about what a difficult day it has been, not getting a raise, or being in a minor accident. However, all of these are concerns the client might share with the practitioner.

Practitioners are more responsible for what happens, both within and outside of the professional relationship, than are clients. If the practitioner has some type of social or business contact with a client outside the professional setting (ranging from slight contact such as having children in the same soccer league, belonging to the same athletic club, or attending the same professional workshops; or considerable contact such as seeing each other socially or sharing business activities), these types of contacts are called *dual relationships*. Although professional codes state that dual relationships are inadvisable, inappropriate, or even forbidden, there may be occasions in a small community where slight outside contacts appear to be unavoidable. If a dual relationship cannot be avoided, the practitioner must stay aware of the complications involved. It can be quite difficult to be the practitioner in one situation and the consumer of a service, such as plumbing repair, in another situation. These two very different roles would have to be clearly differentiated. The practitioner is responsible for exploring the impact of any dual relationship with the client and being cognizant of how it might influence the professional relationship. Practitioners usually find that they have to work much harder to keep their professional role clear when they participate in dual relationships. Therefore, practitioners should not become involved in any major dual relationships and limit minor ones insofar as possible.

Practitioners must take responsibility for explaining the rules of a professional relationship. The relationship rules between practitioners and clients depend a great deal on the setting. Relationship rules often involve protecting confidentiality (a topic that is discussed later in this chapter), ensuring that the needs of the client take precedence over those of the practitioner, and clarifying assumptions that the client may have about any interactions outside of the professional one. Clients may hope to create a personal or friendship relationship with the practitioner after their professional relationship is over. A personal relationship with a client, even after the professional relationship has ended, is still a dual relationship according to most codes of ethics and therefore should be avoided.

A challenging area for practitioners is deciding if and when it is okay to accept gifts from clients. The codes of ethics in a number of disciplines forbid accepting gifts. However, practitioners from some disciplines believe that accepting small gifts can be a way of respecting cultural traditions or creating a relaxed atmosphere. When practitioners make home visits, accepting a cup of coffee or something to eat can be a way of showing respect. In group meetings members sometimes bring snacks for everyone. Having snacks is usually an accepted way of creating a comfortable environment. When clients cannot afford to pay for services, they may want to give practitioners small gifts as a way of expressing their gratitude. Since each discipline has different rules on accepting gifts, it is important to know and follow the ethical guidelines of your discipline.

Being a practitioner is a challenging job. It requires awareness of yourself and your actions both when you are working with clients and when you are not (Cottone & Tarvydas, 2003; Shepard & Morrow, 2003). No matter whether you are driving, at the movies, at the grocery store, or in other public places, you are still expected to act in a responsible manner. Becoming a practitioner means that people will observe your actions both on and off the job. Whether you like it or not, you will be judged wherever you are. Many practitioners are licensed by the state in which they reside, and this licensure can be affected if you are charged with crimes such as domestic violence or drunk driving, even though they are committed outside the times you are actually with clients (Bucky, Callan, & Stricker, 2005; Katsavdakis, Gabbard, & Athey, 2004; Remley & Herlihy, 2001; Sherman & Thelan, 1998).

HOMEWORK EXERCISE 3.1 | UNDERSTANDING PRACTITIONER/CLIENT RELATIONSHIPS

Think about relationships you have had with professionals (doctors, lawyers, teachers, etc.). List words that describe the role of the professional and the client or student. Clients who have never worked with a practitioner before may expect the practitioner's role to match the words in your list.

Now try an experiment with a classmate. In this exercise each of you will take turns performing two roles. The first role is to guide your blindfolded classmate around for 10 minutes. If possible, go outside. Your job is to keep your classmate as comfortable, secure, and safe as possible. You may want to ask your classmate if it would be okay to hold his or her elbow, hand, or shoulder as you guide him or her. You will need to give very clear

directions. After 10 minutes, trade roles so that the person who was blindfolded is now the guide. After each person has had a turn, in one list write down your thoughts and feelings when you served as the guide. In the next list, write down your thoughts and feelings when you were the person who was blindfolded. Using the insight you gained from your experience as a guide and as a person being guided, circle the qualities and characteristics of the guide that you believe were most important to helping the person being guided to feel safe, secure, and comfortable. Keep this list and refer to it as you read about qualities and characteristics that are important in a practitioner.

Who you are as a practitioner and the types of relationships you create with clients often are as important as what you actually do and say during your time with clients. To be effective, it is necessary to learn the information, structure, processes, and skills used in the helping relationship. Since you will be using yourself in the process of working with others, it is important to consider aspects of your personality that will help you to become an effective practitioner. Personal qualities or traits useful to practitioners include being accepting, adaptable, benevolent, caring, concerned, conscientious, creative, dedicated, empathic, flexible, friendly, a good listener, honest, intelligent, intuitive, kind, likable, magnanimous, open to new ideas, positive, respectful, sensitive, tolerant, and warm. These characteristics are listed alphabetically, not in order of importance. Each quality and trait is important. Since you are interested in this field, you probably have already developed many of these qualities.

HOMEWORK EXERCISE 3.2 | CURRENT ASSETS AND ASSETS TO DEVELOP

Take a moment to think about which of the listed personal qualities and traits you already possess. Which would you like to develop? Create two columns labeled "Current Assets" and "Assets to Develop." In the Current Assets column, list existing qualities and traits that will be useful in the role of practitioner. In creating the Current Assets column, it

may be helpful to think of what others have found positive about you as well as aspects that you like about yourself. Under "Assets to Develop," list qualities and traits you will need to develop to be an effective practitioner. You might want to include characteristics that previous teachers or supervisors have encouraged you to cultivate.

PROFESSIONAL ROLES AND RESPONSIBILITIES

The role of the helping professional is not as clearly defined as the roles of other professionals because situations vary so much, training is not standardized among the various helping professions, and the clientele is so diverse. Unlike the medical profession, for example, the role of the practitioner is often situation dependent. In other words, a social worker who is hospital-based will have expectations that are different from those of a school-based counselor. Medical personnel generally have the same expectations regardless of setting. Practitioners may be employed by a mental health agency, a family care agency, a social service agency, a school, or a health care facility. Each type of agency or setting has different expectations. In any setting there will be a great deal of diversity among clients with regard to factors such as age, gender, race, personal background, culture, socioeconomic status, sexual orientation, and level of ability or disability. Additionally, practitioners will be working with individuals, groups, families, and organizations. Training programs for helping professionals include associate, bachelor, masters, and doctoral-level training, and certification and licensure requirements that are state, federal, and profession specific. Okun (2002) differentiates between three levels of practitioners: those who have graduate or professional degrees; generalist workers who usually have undergraduate training and education and often work with graduate professional practitioners; and para-professional helpers who may not have formal education, including volunteers or informal helpers such as friends, family members, and colleagues. Non-degreed or associate-degree professionals are often employed as generalist workers. Specialized training may or may not dictate what the practitioner does, again depending on expectations and requirements of the setting. Egan (2002) noted, "Since helping is such a common human experience, training in both solving one's problems and helping others solve theirs should be as common as training in reading, writing, and math. Unfortunately, this is not true" (p. 3).

As you begin to develop your identity as a professional practitioner, you will be challenged to differentiate your professional role from your personal sense of self. Your personal beliefs about what is appropriate, valuable, or acceptable may be in conflict with professional values. As a professional you will have to set aside your personal values and opinions so that you can clearly see who your client is and what is appropriate, valuable, or acceptable for that particular situation or person. Recognizing and acknowledging your personal values, and not allowing them to inappropriately influence your professional behavior, will be an ongoing challenge throughout your career.

ETHICS, VALUES, AND LEGAL OBLIGATIONS

To make ethical decisions, practitioners need to be aware of their own personal values and socially based morals. Values are a part of all interactions with others. However, practitioners who lack awareness of their personal values and morals may impose them on others by giving advice, making decisions for clients, judging their actions, or helping in ways that have not been requested.

Cultural competence is an important aspect of the professional relationship because the practitioner's culture will influence his or her values. Being culturally competent means being aware of diversity issues and how they influence the professional relationship. It also involves becoming knowledgeable about how diversity influences your clients. Since each person, family, neighborhood, and community is unique, it makes sense to ask clients to explain their own situation. For example, Asian Americans do not all think or behave in only one way, and not all Christians share identical beliefs. Diversity includes differences in race, socioeconomic status, ethnicity, age, physical capabilities, spirituality, acculturation, gender, and educational experiences.

It is important for practitioners in any context to understand personal values, ethical responsibilities, and legal obligations. Whatever your professional role, you will need to spend considerable time learning about the nuances of the ethical code. Social workers, counselors, psychologists, marriage and family therapists, psychiatrists, nurses, and other helping professionals all have ethical codes of conduct that often include the general goals or objectives of the profession as well as enforceable ethical guidelines. However, the general guidelines are very similar for all practitioners. Although a complete review of every code of professional ethics for various disciplines is beyond the scope of this book, it is essential that your professional ethics guide your behavior as a practitioner and that you recognize times when you should consult with other professionals regarding possible ethical dilemmas.

When practitioners violate ethical standards, they usually transgress because they are (a) ignorant or misinformed; (b) practicing outside their area of competence; (c) insensitive to the needs of their clients; and/or (d) exploitative, irresponsible, or vengeful (Koocher & Keith-Spiegel, 1998; Mascari & Webber, 2006). Practitioners are responsible for recognizing issues, identifying relevant standards as determined by professional ethical guidelines and codes, and identifying relevant standards to help guide their actions. They must also know how to access appropriate resources for help. The website of each professional organization includes information about its code of ethics. Below are the web addresses of a number of organizations within the helping professions:

- American Association of Marriage and Family Therapy
  http://www.aamft.org/resources/LRMPlan/Ethics/ethicscode2001.asp
- American Counseling Association
  http://www.counseling.org/Resources/CodeOfEthics/TP/Home/CT2.aspx
- American Psychiatric Nurses Association
  http://www.apna.org/aboutapna/mission.html
- American Psychological Association
  http://www.apa.org/ethics/code2002.html
- Association of Addiction Professionals
  http://naadac.org/documents/index.php?CategoryID=23
- International Association of Marriage and Family Counselors
  http://www.iamfc.com/ethical_codes.html
- National Association of Social Workers
  http://www.socialworkers.org/pubs/code/code.asp
- National Organization for Human Services
  http://nationalhumanservices.org/ethics

As a practitioner you should study your profession's code of ethics and keep a copy of the code of ethics available to review. Each practitioner is responsible for following professional ethical guidelines in every situation. The agency where the practitioner is employed may have rules that differ from the stipulations of the practitioner's code of ethics. For example, the code of ethics of many disciplines does not allow practitioners to maintain relationships with clients after ending their professional relationship, but agencies that employ practitioners may or may not forbid such relationships. When there is a conflict or inconsistency between the agency rules and the professional ethical standards, practitioners are obligated to follow the ethical standards of their profession.

It is important to understand legal as well as ethical obligations. Legal responsibilities are not always clear and can vary somewhat from state to state. These legal mandates come from common law, legislation, regulations, and court decisions. They are subject to change based on new court rulings or new legislation. Any practitioner can be charged with breaking the law in either criminal or civil courts and/or charged with failing to abide by the ethical standards and be sanctioned by the professional organization as well as the state licensing body. Ignorance of the law and ethical standards is never an acceptable excuse for the breach of either. Legal obligations change with new laws and court decisions. It is the practitioner's obligation to stay current with these changes. The following is a summary of general legal obligations for the practitioner-client relationship (Cournoyer, 2004).

- *Duty to care:* Clients have the right to the provision of a reasonable standard of care. The practitioner is expected to carry out professional responsibilities in a competent manner. Professional competence includes availability to clients, ability to take action when there is danger to self or others, and appropriate record keeping.
- *Duty to respect privacy:* There are personal and symbolic areas that practitioners must not violate with clients. These include respecting the physical space that belongs to clients as well as not forcing them to reveal more information than they choose to disclose about themselves or their situation.
- *Duty to maintain confidentiality:* Sharing information about a client with a third party is a breach of confidentiality unless a waiver is signed by the client or other responsible party. Breaching *privileged communication* is generally considered unacceptable behavior for a practitioner, even if a judge demands such information as part of a legal proceeding.
- *Duty to inform:* The practitioner is required to inform prospective clients about the nature and extent of the services being offered as well as the legal obligations of practitioners concerning the reporting of abuse or neglect of children, elders, and dependent adults. There is also an obligation to explain the qualifications of the practitioner and the possible risks as well as benefits of treatment.
- *Duty to report:* All states have laws concerning the reporting of child abuse, child neglect, molestation, and incest. Vulnerable populations are covered by these laws: the elderly, children, and people who are physically or mentally disabled.

- *Duty to warn:* Most practitioners are legally obligated to reveal confidential information concerning a client's stated intent to harm another. The breadth and extent of how this law is to be carried out can vary by state or local jurisdiction.

HOMEWORK EXERCISE 3.3 | LEGAL CONFLICTS

Sometimes one set of legal duties of a practitioner conflicts with one another. Think of situations in which the duty to warn might conflict with the duty to maintain confidentiality. In what situations do you think it is essential to break confidentiality with a client? What do you think would be the most difficult aspect of sharing information without the client's consent?

EXPECTED COMPETENCIES

In this chapter, you have learned about professional relationships, roles, and responsibilities, including professional ethics, values, and legal obligations.
   You should now be able to:

- Explain the differences between professional and personal relationships.

- List four unique aspects of a client-practitioner relationship.
- Describe important legal and ethical obligations that practitioners should understand and keep in mind as they work with clients.

BUILDING RELATIONSHIPS

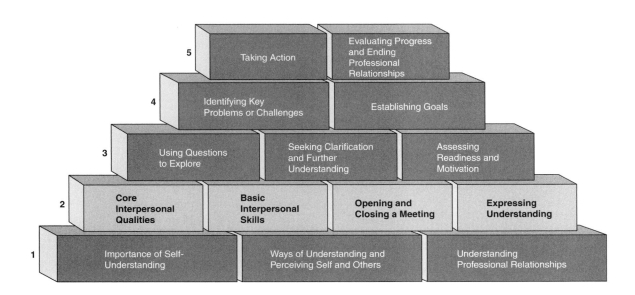

5   Taking Action | Evaluating Progress and Ending Professional Relationships

4   Identifying Key Problems or Challenges | Establishing Goals

3   Using Questions to Explore | Seeking Clarification and Further Understanding | Assessing Readiness and Motivation

2   **Core Interpersonal Qualities** | **Basic Interpersonal Skills** | **Opening and Closing a Meeting** | **Expressing Understanding**

1   Importance of Self-Understanding | Ways of Understanding and Perceiving Self and Others | Understanding Professional Relationships

Whether practitioners are working with a small system such as an individual or a family or a large system such as an organization, they need to understand how to structure and navigate the change process. This process includes the following phases: (a) preparing to meet with the client; (b) beginning the first meeting; (c) building a collaborative relationship with the client; (d) exploring strengths, capacity, resources, limitations, and challenges of the client; (e) defining the focus of the work or identifying problems and goals; (f) taking action, planning for goal achievement, and doing the work necessary to achieve goals; and (g) evaluating goal achievement, creating plans for maintaining progress, and ending the process. Each phase of the change process requires specific knowledge and skills. In Chapters 4 through 14 we will focus on the tasks and skills necessary to facilitate the change process. Each chapter builds on the previous chapters by exploring additional knowledge, tasks, skills, and qualities provided by the practitioner along with strengths brought by the client.

The chapters in Section II focus on the interpersonal qualities and skills involved in building effective relationships with clients. Chapter 4 outlines the core interpersonal qualities for working successfully with clients. Chapter 5 describes the basic skills of attending or fully focusing on clients, using good observational skills, and listening attentively. Chapter 6 introduces structuring skills, including preparing to meet with clients, beginning a meeting, explaining such things as confidentiality and legal obligations, and closing a meeting. Chapter 7 focuses on the crucial tasks and skills related to expressing understanding and demonstrating warmth and empathy.

CORE INTERPERSONAL QUALITIES

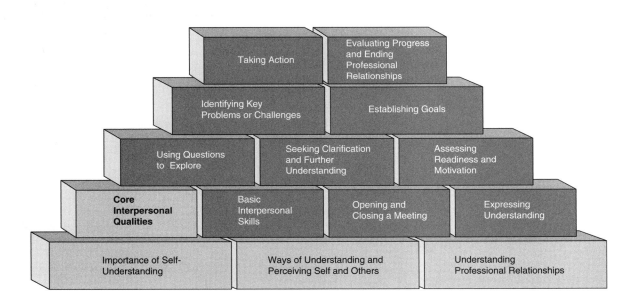

CHAPTER 4

In this chapter you will learn about the following topics:

Practitioner Tasks
- Understanding the impact and importance of the core interpersonal qualities of warmth, empathy, respect, and genuineness on relationships with clients.

Client Attributes
- Willingness to join in a working relationship

To begin the process of working together, clients must be willing to talk about what motivated them to see the practitioner. Even clients who are court-ordered to see a practitioner have a choice, although it is not an ideal one. Clients may have to choose between going to jail or seeing the practitioner, or between losing custody of their children or working with the practitioner. In such cases, the client may be mainly interested in discussing his or her distress and anger about having to see a practitioner. However, this client has demonstrated the ability to make a good decision—to choose going to the practitioner over going to jail.

Even when clients are willing to talk about their concerns, practitioners can only be successful if they are able to establish a working relationship with the client. In this chapter we will focus on the core interpersonal qualities that are necessary for building rapport and creating a solid working relationship that supports change. In future chapters you will learn appropriate ways to express and demonstrate each quality.

DEVELOPING WORKING RELATIONSHIPS

When working with individuals, couples, families, and groups to facilitate change, the quality of the relationship between the practitioner and the client is critically important. Carl Rogers (1951) identified the importance of this relationship several decades ago. Since that time, many studies have shown that the outcome of counseling is largely determined by relationship factors such as warmth, empathy, respect, and genuineness (Flaskas, 2004; Keijsers, Schaap, & Hoogduin, 2000; Lambert & Barley, 2002).

Clients identify the relationship with their practitioner as the essential factor in their success (Hopps, Pinderhughes, & Shankar, 1995; Smith, Thomas, & Jackson, 2004). This should come as no surprise. We all know from our own experience that it is easier to be open with someone whom we perceive as warm, understanding, respectful, genuine, and nonjudgmental.

HOMEWORK EXERCISE 4.1 | DEVELOPING WORKING RELATIONSHIPS

Think of recent times when you talked to a professional or someone in a position of authority. What qualities in the other person helped you to talk comfortably with that person? What qualities or behaviors in that person invited you to feel hurried, nervous, unimportant, or not heard?

Now think of a time when you were distressed and needed to talk with someone. Describe the relationship and the person with whom you would have felt comfortable expressing yourself. Think about what qualities in group relationships invite you to feel open, comfortable, and/or safe. Make a list of at least five qualities that are important to you in group relationships.

Warmth, respect, empathy, and genuineness are the core interpersonal qualities or attitudes essential for the development of good working relationships between clients and practitioners (Rogers, 1957; 1961a). Although beginning practitioners often think that methods, approaches, or skills are the critical factors in achieving good client outcomes, clients surveyed in many research studies reported that the relationship qualities of warmth, respect, genuineness, empathy, and acceptance were most important (Beutler, Machado, & Allstetter-Neufelt, 1994; Flaskas, 2004; Krupnick et al., 1996; Metcalf, Thomas, Duncan, Miller, & Hubble, 1996; Smith et al., 2004). Appropriately expressing these core qualities is necessary for developing trust and safety in relationships.

Warmth, respect, empathy, and genuineness are also vital for developing collaborative alliances or partnerships with clients. Such partnerships have been shown to be crucial for effective work with clients (Bedi, 2006; Dore & Alexander, 1996; Farber & Lane, 2002; Orlinsky, Grawe, & Parks, 1994; Krupnick et al., 1996; Thomas, Werner-Wilson, & Murphy, 2005). Knowing how to connect with each client in a meaningful way is an important condition for a successful outcome (Wiebe, 2002). This is also true for work involving larger systems. When practitioners work with a group of people, they need to build an empathic, respectful, genuine, collaborative alliance with each member of the group. We know a highly successful practitioner who works exclusively with large corporations. His success stems in large part from his warmth, humanness, and genuine concern about the people with whom he works, together with his ability to communicate these factors to individuals in the group as he works with the larger system.

CORE INTERPERSONAL QUALITIES FOR HELPING

WARMTH

Practitioners who are kind and accepting are perceived as *warm*, in contrast to people who appear detached, rejecting, or *cold*. In accepting, warm relationships, a climate of safety and trust develops, encouraging clients to think about their challenges in new ways and begin to explore a different way of acting (Farber & Lane, 2002; Lambert & Bergin, 1994). It is important to realize that what is experienced as an expression of warmth in one culture may be perceived differently in another. Awareness of your own culture's ways of expressing warmth as well as the ways of your client's culture is very important. It is also valuable to recognize how warmth was expressed in your family of origin, because your experiences can influence how you perceive the need for warmth in relationships.

Appropriate expressions of warmth, caring, compassion, or concern in a professional relationship are similar in some ways to expressions of warmth in friendships. Practitioners express warmth verbally by showing interest, acceptance, and concern for their clients. Warmth may be expressed nonverbally by smiling or using whatever facial expression fits with what the client is expressing, by being interested and attentive, and by giving your full attention to the client. Warmth can also be expressed by tone of voice. Even gestures can be perceived as open and inclusive or as closed and exclusive. In the next chapter, you will practice attending behaviors that express warmth nonverbally. In Chapter 7, you will practice ways to verbally express warmth.

HOMEWORK EXERCISE 4.2 | WARMTH

In the next few days pay attention to people you think of as warm and people you perceive as cold or aloof. Make a list of actions that express warmth and coldness. Now go back over your lists and circle the ways of expressing warmth that you believe would be appropriate in a professional relationship. For example, a person who runs up and hugs his or her friends would probably be considered warm, but that behavior would not be appropriate in a professional relationship. What about the person who calls others "honey" or "dear"? While you may consider that an expression of warmth, do you think that would be appropriate in a professional relationship?

EMPATHY

Most people who want to work with other people have already developed some level of empathy. As a helping professional you will need to enhance your ability to show empathy. Being empathic has been described as walking a mile in another person's shoes, but that is only part of empathy. True empathy is more like walking a mile in another person's shoes and experiencing the world as the other person would experience it. Being empathic involves having the willingness and flexibility to put yourself in the other person's reality (Gibson, 2006). Being empathic can be described as imagining yourself in the same situation as the other person, understanding that person's feelings, and seeing the situation from that person's point of view. Empathy also involves understanding the other person's assumptions, beliefs, and/or worldview. Remember what you learned in Chapter 2 about the constructivist perspective. Being empathic involves appreciating the way that others perceive or construct their world.

Empathy allows us to connect with people from very different backgrounds and experiences. Neuroscience has shown that almost everyone has some capacity to understand and share the feelings of others (Gibson, 2006). One of the challenges of being empathic is that it requires understanding another person's subjective experience while maintaining the capacity to differentiate yourself from that person. Taking on someone else's pain does not help the other person and is not empathy. If you as a practitioner *did* take on or experience your client's pain, the client would still be in pain, but you would be less effective, less objective, and less willing to fully connect because you would now need to attend to your own emotional distress.

Empathy is not the same as pity or sympathy. Pity involves sorrow or grief aroused by someone else's suffering. Often it implies a one-up position. When you offer pity, you may be seeing the other person as weak, vulnerable, helpless, and/or incompetent. When you feel pity, you tend to think: "you poor thing." Sympathy involves feeling affected by whatever affected the other person. In personal relationships sympathy and even pity may be appropriate. Your feelings may be affected by a friend or family member who is having a painful experience. In professional relationships it is important for you to be empathic without taking on or experiencing another person's pain because to do so would be emotionally draining for you and not helpful to your clients.

In Chapter 7 you will learn ways to express empathy. Briefly, being empathic involves listening attentively to what your clients are telling you, making every effort to comprehend what they are experiencing from their viewpoint, and expressing your understanding of your clients' experiences, including both painful and positive feelings. Validating the client's story is part of being empathic. Often clients have been told that their truth or understanding of a situation is wrong, stupid, silly, and/or ridiculous. This is particularly true when the client has been in an abusive relationship (Chang, 1996), or if the client is in a less powerful position such as a child, an elderly person, or a member of an oppressed group (Fivush, 2004). It is up to practitioners to recognize and accept the importance and validity of their clients' point of view and to understand their experiences and concerns.

HOMEWORK EXERCISE 4.3 | REFLECTING ON EMPATHY

In the next few days look for ways people express empathy. If you do not find any expressions of empathy, what are your thoughts about why that might be true? After three conversations, think about how you expressed empathy or might have expressed empathy. Write down these expressions of empathy and talk with someone in your class about your experiences being empathic.

DEVELOPING YOUR ABILITY TO BE EMPATHIC

A challenge for practitioners is learning to be empathic with people whose backgrounds—including challenges, age, experiences, race, or culture—are very different from their own. Developing the ability to be empathic is a lifetime task. Some good ways to develop knowledge, understanding, and empathy include the following:

- reading novels and professional literature about people from different backgrounds;
- joining in activities, talking to, and getting to know others who have different experiences;
- attending classes or workshops focused on specific groups of people;
- traveling to different countries and spending time with local residents;
- doing volunteer work in communities or neighborhoods very different from your own;
- watching popular movies about people who are different from you.

Anything that allows you to broaden or deepen your understanding of other people's experiences can enhance your ability to be empathic.

RESPECT

Respect involves acceptance, or as Rogers (1958) said, "unconditional positive regard." Unconditional positive regard involves expressing affirmation and appreciation of clients without condoning their harmful behaviors. It means looking for the good in others and seeing their strengths. Respectful practitioners communicate their

HOMEWORK EXERCISE 4.4 | DEVELOPING EMPATHY

Watch a movie and focus on one character whose experiences, life situation, and background differ from your own. (See Box 4.1 for a list of movies.) Your goal is to empathize with that character. As you watch the movie, think about how that character is experiencing what is happening. What are your hunches about that character's thoughts? What are your guesses about how the character is feeling (e.g., angry, sad, scared, glad, troubled, frantic, anxious, etc.)? What might have led the person to experience those feelings? Make every effort to see the situation from the character's point of view rather than how you would perceive the same situation. Write a

couple of paragraphs in the first person as the character in the movie. For example, instead of saying "I think the character felt sad," write as the character: "I feel angry when I think about my family putting me here" (*Girl, Interrupted*).

Write your thoughts about the aspects of the character that you would find difficult or easy to empathize with. Keep in mind that it is inappropriate to make generalizations about a group of people based on a character in one movie, but it is possible to get a sense of what it would be like to have experiences beyond your own.

regard for clients' thoughts, feelings, and abilities. They notice, acknowledge, and highlight their clients' strengths, capabilities, resilience, coping ability, potential, and resources. Practitioners who always need to be the expert in the client-practitioner relationship may not be experienced as respectful. It is better to realize and share with clients that they are the experts on their lives. Instead of telling a client, "Your family isn't good at problem solving" (as if you were the expert on his or her family), practitioners should be tentative in expressing their thoughts about the client. For example, a practitioner might suggest, "I wonder if your family hasn't learned to solve problems together." If the client finds this suggestion incorrect, practitioners who are respectful and genuine are willing to openly admit that their conclusion was a mistake and work with the client to correct misunderstandings.

Being respectful also involves being polite and following appropriate cultural norms. Practitioners must be able to work respectfully with clients from many diverse backgrounds. This involves learning about a client's background and knowing how people from that culture treat each other when showing respect. Ways to demonstrate respect will be covered in Chapter 8.

HOMEWORK EXERCISE 4.5 | RESPECT

Write a paragraph describing ways you demonstrate respect for yourself and other people. Now notice how others express respect. Also notice if certain groups of people receive more respect than other

groups of people. Almost all groups include some level of diversity, whether it involves different genders, races, backgrounds, educational levels, or ages.

GENUINENESS

Being genuine in a professional relationship involves being sincere, real, and authentic and allowing your humanness and uniqueness to be seen by clients. Practitioners who seem stiff, distant, or phony are experienced by clients as inauthentic. When the practitioner always has to be right and is unwilling to admit making mistakes, this can

BOX 4.1	WATCH A MOVIE TO PRACTICE EMPATHY

- *Real Women Have Curves* — a second-generation Mexican-American girl
- *Hoop Dreams* — an inner-city poor African-American boy
- *Mystic River* — an inner-city boy who is sexually abused
- *Girl, Interrupted* — a teenage girl who is mentally ill
- *American History X* — a boy in a neo-Nazi group
- *Bend It Like Beckham* — a second-generation Indian girl living in London
- *I Am Sam* or *Radio* — people with developmental disabilities
- *My Family* — a Mexican-American family living in L.A.
- *What's Eating Gilbert Grape* — a family dealing with issues related to autism, obesity, depression, and suicide
- *Soul Food* — an African-American family facing serious illness and death
- *Sleeping with the Enemy* or *What's Love Got to Do with It* — women struggling with partners who are physically abusive
- *The Notebook, On Golden Pond, Driving Miss Daisy,* or *Iris* — people facing challenges related to aging
- *28 Days, Losing Isaiah,* or *When a Man Loves a Woman* — women with drug and alcohol problems
- *Boys Don't Cry, Boys on the Side, Philadelphia,* or *The Crying Game* — people struggling with issues of sexual orientation
- *As Good As It Gets* — a man who is dealing with obsessive-compulsive disorder
- *A Beautiful Mind* — a man who has schizophrenia
- *Children of a Lesser God* — a woman who is deaf
- *The Green Mile, Dead Man Walking,* or *The Shawshank Redemption* — men in prison
- *The Saint of Fort Washington* — people who are homeless
- *Monster Ball* — the struggles of a single African-American mother
- *Joy Luck Club* — a second-generation Asian-American woman

also be experienced by the client as an inability to be authentic. In response, clients are likely to be reluctant to acknowledge their own errors. Ways to demonstrate genuineness will be covered in Chapter 13.

In addition to understanding the core interpersonal qualities for developing good working relationships, it is important to learn about common mistakes that can disrupt working relationships. Blaming, arguing, reacting defensively, and attempting to pressure clients indicate a lack of respect. Doing the thinking for clients may indicate a lack of respect for their abilities. Deciding what changes clients need to make, rather than working with them collaboratively, is disrespectful. Working harder than the client to solve the client's problems may indicate that the practitioner is not respecting the client's skills or the client's current circumstances that may be hindering change. When practitioners find themselves offering one suggestion after another despite the client's lack of receptivity, they are working too hard.

HOMEWORK EXERCISE 4.6 | GENUINENESS

You probably know some people whom you consider "fake." What do those people do and say that
makes you see them as fake? You also probably
know some people whom you consider honest,
forthright, open, or genuine. What do those people
do and say? You can ask other people what they
notice that leads them to think someone is fake or
genuine. Now make a list of the qualities and
behaviors that relate to being fake and those that
relate to being genuine.

COMMON MISTAKES

As you practice and develop the skills needed to be an effective practitioner, it is
important that you become aware of responses that are commonly used in conversations but are not appropriate for practitioners to use. Many of these responses may
appear to be helpful and are often used when someone is trying to solve a problem for
another person. As a practitioner, your role is to work with clients to help them define
their problems and goals and to help them find ways to solve problems and achieve
goals. Rather than taking over, parenting, preaching, or judging clients, your goal
should be to demonstrate your respect for their strength, capacity, and resources as
you help them find their own unique ways of responding to their challenges.

OFFERING ADVICE

It is common in everyday conversations to offer advice whether it is asked for or not.
Beginning practitioners often think they should be able to provide immediate help, so
they offer suggestions on how to solve the presenting problem. However, it is inappropriate for you as a practitioner to offer advice until you have fully explored the
person, challenges, and situation and have identified the client's goals. Offering advice
before you know what the clients have already tried can be experienced as not respecting
their strengths and capacities. Providing recommendations before you and the client
have identified goals is also not helpful. Even if you think your client is lonely and should
meet new people, suggesting that your client join a group in order to meet people would
not be appropriate unless you and your client had agreed on a goal of meeting people,
you had asked about ways your client had tried to meet people, and you had asked if
your client wanted a suggestion. Offering advice reinforces the practitioner as the
authority and "the knowledgeable one," instead of demonstrating the belief that the
client is able to solve problems and is the expert on his or her situation.

REASSURING

Reassuring is another response that is generally inappropriate even though it seems
supportive. Reassurance is generally not based in reality. Saying "it will be okay" sounds
nice but is inappropriate unless the practitioner knows for sure that it will be okay.

The purpose of offering reassurance to people is often to reduce their pain. As a
practitioner you need to remember that the pain clients feel about their problem can
motivate them to solve the problem. If the pain is about a loss, it is a natural response that
will usually decrease with time. Negating the importance of the clients' pain can lead

them to feel that they are not fully understood or respected. It is common for people to say things like "Don't worry about it." This statement indicates that people have or should have the capacity to stop worrying on command and/or that their worries are not significant. Think about a time when you were really worried and someone told you not to worry about it. Did that comment make you feel listened to? Did the comment reduce your concerns in any way? In your experience, has telling others not to worry helped them to quit worrying? Generally, this type of comment has the effect of minimizing the importance of their concerns. Although it is intended to be reassuring, telling someone who is worried not to worry sounds like telling him or her not to feel what s/he is feeling.

OFFERING EXCUSES

Offering excuses for the client's situation may appear to demonstrate understanding but may discourage the client from considering ways to improve or change the situation. For example, a practitioner might tell a client, "You have a learning disability that keeps you from being successful in school." The label of *learning disability* may be accurate, but it would be better to say, "I understand that you have a learning disability and want to find new methods of learning that will work for you." The statement, "How could you learn to be a good parent with such a poor example set by your own parents?" is making an excuse for the client's lack of parenting skills. Instead, the practitioner could say, "I understand that you do not want to parent your children the way your parents parented you. It sounds like one of your goals is to learn better ways to parent." Rather than making excuses, practitioners need to help clients set goals and find ways to achieve those goals.

ASKING LEADING QUESTIONS

Asking *leading questions* has the same effect as giving advice and should not be done, at least until the practitioner and client have established clear goals (Collins, 1990). An example of a leading question is, "Have you considered talking in a calm voice to your partner?" Imbedded in the question is advice. If clients want advice or suggestions, they will ask. Practitioners should help clients figure out the way to achieve their goals and create opportunities for them to try out new capacities or new ways of thinking and feeling. An overarching goal is often for clients to gain a sense of empowerment or knowledge that they can act in new and more effective ways. When practitioners give advice or try to quickly fix the problem, they may feel they have been helpful, but it will not lead to a greater sense of control, capacity, or empowerment for clients.

DOMINATING THROUGH TEACHING

While there are times when practitioners teach clients or provide them information, teaching in a way that is dominating or pushy is inappropriate. It can suggest that there is only one *right* way to do something. Think about how you would feel if you had not asked for a suggestion about how to study better and someone told you, "When you study, you must underline the key sentence in each paragraph and develop a written outline of everything you read." Communicating in a dominating way tends to invite people to feel shamed or rebellious and to withdraw or become defensive and argue.

Implying there is only one way to resolve an issue can lead to clients shutting down their own thinking and not searching for their own answers.

LABELING

Labeling is a sophisticated way to judge, criticize, or blame another person and is not helpful. Identifying a person as passive-aggressive, developmentally delayed, at risk, or resistant tends to limit the practitioner's view of the client's ability to change. While many practitioners consider labeling clients to be inappropriate at any time, others believe that labels can be useful. However, they insist on using person-first language—meaning you first speak about the person. For example, "He is a person who has acted in passive-aggressive ways" rather than "Working with that passive-aggressive person is difficult." You could say, "I have found working with Tom, who has been labeled passive-aggressive, to be difficult." Even though a label may accurately describe some aspect of a person, it doesn't portray the whole person.

INTERROGATING

Asking one question after another may result in clients feeling as though they are being interrogated. Remember, your job as a practitioner is to understand and work with your clients. Instead of listening to and expressing empathy concerning the client's situation, beginning practitioners often ask too many questions. "Why" questions are particularly problematic because they sometimes imply judgment and also invite defensiveness. Think about how you feel when someone asks you, "Why haven't you completed that task?"

HOMEWORK EXERCISE 4.7 | INAPPROPRIATE RESPONSES

Pretend that your client is a person who is obese and has begun to have health problems related to being seriously overweight. He has also had problems at work because he is not able to handle some of the physical aspects of his job. He reports that he has tried to lose weight, but each time he has gained it back. He believes that people are looking down on him for being overweight. He says, "I am feeling really discouraged because no one seems to understand how difficult dealing with weight problems can be."

Here are some examples of inappropriate responses:

- "Have you considered trying Weight Watchers? I understand that is a very good program."
- "You really must lose weight in order to help resolve your health problems."
- "I am sure if you put your mind to it you could lose weight and keep it off."

- "I bet your parents are overweight too and that is why you are having all these problems."
- "Why haven't you been able to stay on an appropriate eating plan?"

After each sentence above, refer to the following list and write down what type of inappropriate response is being used.

- Offering advice
- Reassuring
- Offering excuses
- Asking leading questions
- Dominating through teaching
- Labeling
- Interrogating

HOMEWORK EXERCISE 4.8 | Iɴᴀᴘᴘʀᴏᴘʀɪᴀᴛᴇ Rᴇsᴘᴏɴsᴇs Yᴏᴜ Hᴀᴠᴇ Exᴘᴇʀɪᴇɴᴄᴇᴅ

Think about a time when something was bothering you and you went to a friend to talk about it. Describe your reaction to the following hypothetical responses.

- "Let me tell you how to fix your problem."

- "Everything will be fine after a few days."

- "Don't worry about it."

- "You are never given more than you can handle."

- "Think of it as a growth opportunity."

Do these responses invite you to continue talking to the person, or do they make you want to end the conversation? What if the friend had simply listened to you or expressed understanding? Do you think you would have continued to share with that friend?

EXPECTED COMPETENCIES

In this chapter, you have learned about the essential interpersonal qualities needed for developing effective relationships with clients.

You should now be able to:

- Name and describe the four core interpersonal qualities that Rogers (1957) identified as essential to the development of a relationship with a client.

- Name, describe, and give an example of each of the seven common practitioner mistakes.

| # BASIC INTERPERSONAL SKILLS

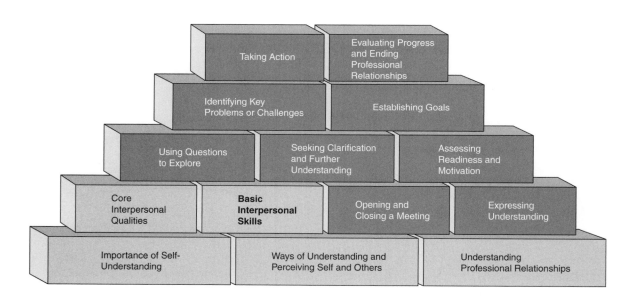

In this chapter you will learn about the following topics:

Practitioner Tasks
- Understanding the importance of careful observation, attending, and listening

Practitioner Skills
- Ability to observe, attend, and listen

Client Attributes
- Willingness to communicate as openly as possible

CORE INTERPERSONAL SKILLS FOR HELPING

Warmth, empathy, respect, and genuineness are core qualities that form the foundation for effective professional relationships. While these qualities are vital, practitioners must also master a number of interpersonal skills. Good professional relationships rest on accurately observing, effectively attending, and actively listening (Ackerman & Hilsenroth, 2001).

IMPORTANCE OF BEING A GOOD OBSERVER

Some people are naturally excellent observers, while others tend to focus on what is being said and forget to pay attention to other modes of communication. However, research has shown that much of the meaning in any communication is expressed nonverbally (Contarello, 2003; Van Buren, 2002).

Being a good observer helps practitioners better understand what clients are communicating. If the client communicates one message nonverbally and a different message verbally, the inconsistencies should be noted. Generally what is communicated nonverbally is closer to the truth. For example, if a client clenches his fist and hits the table while saying he is not angry, the discrepancy between what he is doing and what he is saying needs to be noticed and probably explored with the client. Careful observations supplement what the client tells you verbally; sometimes intensifying what is being said and sometimes contradicting it (Westra, 1996).

It is important to notice such things as facial expressions, eye movement and eye contact, body position and general movement, breathing patterns, muscle tone, gestures, and skin tone changes. For example, some people seem not to cry when sad, but a careful observer will notice a slight change in the amount of moisture in the person's eyes. When people are experiencing strong feelings their skin tone may change color, darkening or looking rosier than usual. This skin color change usually starts at the chest and moves up to the face. Sometimes only the neck darkens or a spot appears on each cheek. These observations will provide information about such things as the intensity of the client's feelings, the general energy of the client, and the emotion the client might be experiencing.

HOMEWORK EXERCISE 5.1 | BEING A GOOD OBSERVER

Sit in a public place and watch two people who are sitting and talking to each other for five minutes. Write down what you notice about facial expressions, eye movement and eye contact, body position and movement, breathing pattern, muscle tone, gestures, and skin tone changes. Use descriptive words rather than evaluative words. For example, you might say that his mouth was turned down; he looked at the floor mostly; sat slumped in his chair, leaning way back, rarely shifting position; sighed a few times; and seldom moved his hands. There were no indications of tension and no skin tone changes. You might guess that he is depressed but that is evaluative. Just describe what you saw. Here are some questions to stimulate your thinking about what you observed.

1. *Facial expression:* What did you see on the person's face? Did she have tears in her eyes? Was her mouth turned down? Was her brow wrinkled? Did she have circles under her eyes? Did she smile a lot?

2. *Eye movement and eye contact:* Did she look mostly at the floor, up at the ceiling, all around the room, or directly at the other person? Did she stare?

3. *Body position and movement:* How was she sitting? Was she leaning back against her chair, slumped over, slouched, upright and stiff, legs crossed, feet flat on the floor, legs curled under her, legs uncrossed, or ankles crossed? What about movement? Did she hardly move at all, move only slightly, or move around most of the time? Did she nod her head or swing her legs? Did her movement change, maybe sitting rigidly in the beginning and later becoming relaxed?

4. *Breathing pattern:* Did her breathing seem normal or did she often sigh, take deep breaths, or breathe in a shallow way?

5. *Muscle tone:* Did she seem tense? If so, what did you notice that caused you to believe that she was tense? Maybe her fists were clenched or her jaw seemed tightly closed. Or maybe you thought she was relaxed. What specifically did you notice that led you to believe she was relaxed? Maybe she was slumped or her face looked slack. Did she start out tense and then relax?

6. *Gestures:* What was she doing with her hands? Did her hands stay in her lap folded together? Were her hands moving around most of the time? Were her hands held together in tight fists? Did she make circles with her hands as she talked or rotate her arms so her palms faced up?

7. *Skin tone changes:* Did you notice any change in skin tone? If there was a skin tone change, describe it.

OBSERVING IN GROUPS

When working with groups of people, practitioners must be aware of what is happening at a verbal and nonverbal level with each of the members in the group. In a group or family meeting, that means watching everyone's body language or nonverbal communication as the meeting unfolds. Observing provides the practitioner with additional valuable information to use in understanding the clients and deciding how to respond. In groups, the practitioner should not only look at the person speaking but also scan the other group members (Jacobs, Masson, & Harvill, 1998; Rutan & Stone, 2001). Scanning encourages clients to speak to one another rather than to the practitioner exclusively. If a client is speaking to the practitioner and the practitioner begins to glance at others in the group, the client will generally follow his or her example and look to the group members for eye contact. If there are two group leaders, one leader can scan the group while the other leader is talking. Thoughtful observation is important to all types of groups (task groups, agency teams, or leadership teams). By observing group members' behaviors, the practitioner may notice such things as one member looking at the ceiling, another member whose eyes are closed, someone whose fists are clenched, and so on. Practitioners can make guesses about what these nonverbal behaviors are communicating and then may choose to ask if their hunches are accurate. For example, the practitioner might say, "I noticed that several folks in the group have their eyes closed. I wonder if you are getting tired of discussing this topic."

ATTENDING

Attending involves being completely focused on the client. The process of attending is not a new experience. We all have been in situations when we were fully present even though we were not aware of it, yet the skills related to attending are more difficult than it may seem on the surface. Often we believe we are paying full attention to other people, but in reality, we rarely pay attention to the messages our physical posture may be sending to another person, seldom closely observe the other person, infrequently focus fully on another person, and usually hear without really listening. The use of the attending skills is the foundation of any positive relationship (Anderson, Ogles, & Weiss, 1999).

In addition to closely observing the client, it is also important to think about ways to physically indicate readiness to work with the client. Although different cultures communicate involvement in different ways, there are some basic behaviors that generally convey this message. Readiness to be involved and to be fully present can be communicated in several ways. Leaning very slightly forward with a comfortable, relaxed, open, accessible body posture indicates attention and concern to most people. It is important to be relaxed and comfortable, but it is generally better not to lean way back as if you are resting rather than being attentive. It is also better to sit in a way that is more open and accepting rather than closed and defensive. Practitioners who fold their arms tightly across their chest may be experienced as being closed off. The client may respond to distancing behaviors on the part of the practitioner without being aware of doing so.

The practitioner's facial expression should be congruent with whatever is being discussed. If the client is talking about something sad or serious, the practitioner's face should express concern or somberness. For most people this comes naturally, but some people smile or even laugh when serious topics are being discussed. Maintaining regular eye contact, unless inappropriate because of cultural customs, is another way to express attentiveness. Practitioners should not stare at clients but should generally maintain eye contact with them as a way of showing interest.

Any type of distracting behavior draws attention to itself and away from the process. Nervous behaviors such as playing with a pencil, pen, or rubber band; rocking or turning in a chair; drinking from a water bottle and replacing the cap each time; or moving about a lot may distract clients and may cause them to lose focus on what they are saying. These behaviors may even be interpreted by clients as impatience or boredom on the part of the practitioner, leading the client to cut short what he or she was wanting to communicate.

Another way to communicate involvement is to use minimal encouragement. Nodding and saying "Uh-huh" lets clients know that the practitioner is paying attention to them. Repeating one or more of the last words in the client's sentence can be an effective method of offering minimal encouragement. For example, if the client said, "I am worried about what my manager will say," the practitioner might say, "Your manager?" thus letting the client know he was heard and inviting him to continue.

HOMEWORK EXERCISE 5.2 | ATTENDING

Pick a time when you are talking to someone and practice using as many attending behaviors as you can (sitting in an open, relaxed, and slightly forward position with a congruent facial expression; maintaining appropriate eye contact; minimizing distracting behaviors; and offering minimal encouragement).

After the conversation write down how you felt and what you were thinking. Which behaviors came naturally? Which behaviors did you find more challenging? Which did you forget to use? How did attending feel to you? What are your hunches about how the other person felt in response?

LISTENING

Listening is a step beyond attending and is one of the most important things practitioners do. In our busy society, we often do not listen carefully to one another. We hear the words but do not consider possible meanings. Listening involves not only hearing the words but also making every effort to understand the meaning the other person is trying to convey and to understand the implications of the material for the other person (Baum & Gray, 1992; Friedman, 2005). True listening involves focusing on what the other person is trying to communicate, not just the words s/he is using. Feeling truly listened to helps the client develop a sense of trust, be more inclined toward self-reflection, and experience respect and caring from the practitioner.

Listening as a practitioner is different from listening in conversations in social or work situations. To facilitate listening, practitioners must refrain from typical conversational behaviors such as talking about oneself, changing the subject, asking a lot of questions, and avoiding silence. Although listening may seem simple, it can be difficult because it requires that the practitioner pay complete attention to what the client is saying and doing, rather than to what the practitioner is thinking. Listening is usually a nonverbal activity. Practitioners may limit their responses to "uh-huh" or "mm" or one or two words of acknowledgment while listening. Other valuable ways to demonstrate listening will be addressed in Chapter 7.

Listening also involves noticing the client's communication style, including tone, volume, and speed of delivery. Listening to the way a client communicates includes noticing pauses, silence, and changes in his or her usual patterns of speech. It is important to give clients plenty of time to express their thoughts and feelings. Thus, part of listening is to slow the pace and allow some silence and to resist the temptation to talk in order to keep the conversation moving.

Even when practitioners are fully focused on listening, they may not understand the client because they misinterpret the client's words, lack knowledge about the client's culture, or are influenced by personal biases and prejudices. Some clients are clear communicators and are easy to understand. Others ramble and are hard to follow, while some use jargon or colloquialisms. Some have trouble expressing themselves in the practitioner's language. Others use a narrative style and communicate in a story form, and some speak in a confused or circular manner. Being a good observer and listener will help the practitioner overcome some of these obstacles to understanding what the client is trying to communicate.

HOMEWORK EXERCISE 5.3 | LISTENING

When you are having a conversation with someone, listen carefully to what the person says. Focus on listening more than talking. After the conversation, write down a summary of what the person said. Describe the person's tone or volume, speed of delivery, and style of speaking. Now do this again with another person. How were these conversations, when you were listening carefully, different from your usual conversations?

Think of a time that you felt someone was really listening to you. What was that like for you? Why do you think so few people are good listeners?

USING INTERPERSONAL QUALITIES AND SKILLS IN SIMULATED INTERVIEWS

Starting with this chapter, practice exercises will be included to provide you with opportunities to rehearse using the process and skills that make up professional practice. With enough practice, the skills and process of professional practice will come naturally to you. Beginning practitioners need to practice using professional skills and expressing core interpersonal qualities until they can use these skills and express these core qualities easily and comfortably (Weick, 1993) while fully focusing on their client and attempting to understand their client's reality (Mahoney, 1986a; Vodde & Gallant, 1995).

By completing the practice exercises, you will move from "knowing about" skills to "knowing how" to appropriately use the skills. Using skills in simulated situations has been shown to be the best way to develop expertise (Stone & Vance, 1976; Vinton & Harrington, 1994; Vodde & Gallant, 1995). As with learning any new behavior or skill, you may feel awkward, be afraid of making mistakes, or be hesitant about trying new behaviors. Initial feelings of awkwardness, discomfort, or tension as you use new skills are common with any learning process. Think about a group of skills that you learned some time ago, such as learning to drive. Take a minute to think about what it was like when you first drove a car, maybe with an instructor or parent. Now think about the time when you first drove alone. We often remember feeling tense and nervous and thinking that driving was a lot of work. It certainly didn't feel natural and comfortable. If we had to drive on a highway, we probably would have made mistakes and maybe even gotten in an accident. Think about what driving is like for you now. Probably by now the skills of driving are so automatic that you don't think about what you have to do. As with driving, repeated practice of the practitioner skills will develop your confidence and sense of competence until these skills will seem comfortable and natural.

Besides practicing skills, these practice exercises will give you the opportunity to learn more about the process of self-assessment and self-evaluation. Self-evaluation is a very important aspect of a professional career. Experienced and competent practitioners engage in a process of constant self-assessment and self-evaluation. They regularly define goals related to professional development and identify both their strengths and areas for growth related to skill development and knowledge acquisition (Bernotavicz, 1994; Orlinsky et al., 2005).

The practice exercises in this book provide opportunities to apply the skills you are learning and to get immediate feedback. In these practice exercises you will be working with a single person because working with one client is easier than working with several people or a group. Once you learn these skills, you will be able to use them with families, groups, and large systems.

In the practice exercises, you will form a group with two of your classmates, and the three of you will take turns playing the roles of client, practitioner, and peer supervisor. Each person will have an opportunity to experience being a client, to apply practitioner skills and receive feedback, and to give feedback.

Client role: In the role of client, you can discuss a problem in your life. Keep in mind, however, that the allotted time may not be enough to fully explain your situation. You can discuss a challenge that occurred in the past or role-play a client. If you do share a personal experience, choose something that you feel comfortable talking about with your classmates. If you have never been a client, being in this role will help you understand something about the vulnerabilities of being a client. After each practice meeting, the person in the role of the client will give feedback to the practitioner, focusing on whether s/he felt understood by the practitioner. It is helpful if s/he can describe what specific behaviors contributed to the experience of being heard.

Practitioner role: The practitioner will practice demonstrating the skills for the particular exercise. After each practice meeting, the practitioner will identify what s/he perceives as her or his strengths and weaknesses.

Peer supervisor role: After the practice meeting, the peer supervisor will give the practitioner feedback on use of skills related to the practice meeting. The peer supervisor will also complete the written evaluation form provided in the textbook.

In the role of peer supervisor, you will learn to evaluate the appropriate use of skills and interpersonal qualities. Although the many tasks of the peer supervisor are challenging to learn, you will benefit from closely observing fellow students and giving constructive feedback. As the peer supervisor, you will be the mirror reflecting back to the practitioner his or her strengths and areas for growth. The goal of the peer supervisor is to help the practitioner improve by identifying what the practitioner is doing well along with areas in which the practitioner needs to improve.

As a peer supervisor it is important to give specific, clear, direct, accurate feedback (Campbell, 2006; Rosenbaum & Ronen, 1998). It is not helpful to say, "You did a fine job." Instead, the peer supervisor should tell the person in the role of practitioner specifically what s/he did that was positive or negative, and when possible, tell the practitioner what impact s/he seemed to have on the client. For example, "You leaned toward your client and looked directly at her. After you did that for a while I noticed your client seemed to relax." Or, "You frequently fidgeted with your pencil. I noticed your client looking at the pencil. I think your behavior might have been distracting to your client."

When talking to the practitioner, focus on the behavior, not on the person. Do not make guesses, judgments, or interpretations about his or her actions. For example, you might say, "You leaned back in your chair" rather than "You didn't pay attention to your client."

The final task of the peer supervisor is to complete the evaluation form that is included with each practice exercise. This evaluation system has been used successfully by both graduate and undergraduate students (Baez, 2003; Chang & Scott, 1999; Menen, 2004; Pike, Bennett, & Chang, 2004).

Remember that mastering new behaviors requires practice. Some skills may seem easier to master and others more difficult. On some exercises, you may need to repeat practice exercises several times to adequately master the behaviors and skills. Since each practice exercise adds new behaviors and skills, it is important to become comfortable with one group of skills before moving on to the next practice exercise.

PRACTICE EXERCISE 1 | ATTENDING, OBSERVING, AND LISTENING

Exercise Objectives
- To practice communicating to a client your readiness to listen, willingness to focus on work with the client, and overall involvement with the process. These behaviors say to the client: "I am fully present and ready to be with you."
- To heighten your awareness of the nonverbal ways clients communicate.
- To practice listening to what the client is trying to communicate.

Step 1: Preparation
Form groups of three people. Each person will have the opportunity to play the roles of client, practitioner, and peer supervisor. Each meeting will last about 5 minutes.

Client Role
- Think about a problem that involves some reasonably strong feelings that you feel comfortable talking about for a few minutes.

Practitioner Role
- Review the behaviors involved in attending and important things to observe in the client in order to use them in the interview. (See evaluation form.)

Peer Supervisor Role
- Look over the evaluation form to review the behaviors involved in attending in order to evaluate the practitioner's use of these behaviors during the interview.
- Prepare to record verbal and nonverbal responses of the client and to keep track of the time.

Step 2: The Client Meeting

Client Role
- Tell your story for 5 minutes.

Practitioner Role
- Use the attending behaviors to communicate involvement and concentrate on observing all aspects of the client's communication.
- Listen, remaining silent except for expressing minimal encouragement.

Peer Supervisor Role
- On the evaluation form in the practitioner's book, put a check mark after each type of attending behavior used by the practitioner. *Each check mark is worth one point.*
- Keep track of the time and tell the practitioner and client when the 5 minutes are completed.

continued

PRACTICE EXERCISE 1 | Attending, Observing, and Listening *continued*

Step 3: Feedback

Client Role
- Share how you experienced the practitioner attending and listening to you.

Practitioner Role
- Evaluate your use of the behaviors that communicate attending.

Peer Supervisor Role
- Give feedback to the practitioner on the use of attending behaviors.
- Record the feedback in the practitioner's textbook for future reference.
- Ask the practitioner about observations of the client related to facial expression, eye movement and eye contact, body posture and movement, breathing patterns, muscle tone, gestures, and skin tone changes. Ask for description rather than evaluation.
- Give the practitioner a check mark for each area that s/he was able to describe.
- Ask the practitioner to summarize what s/he heard the client say. Examples of possible questions are given below:

  ○ Did you notice any shifts in the conversation?
  ○ Did you hear any changes in the volume and speed of the client's speech?
  ○ How would you describe the client's speaking style? For example, the practitioner might say, "The client had a clear, direct, logical way of speaking. His volume was rather quiet, but he tended to talk louder when discussing his son. He spoke rather slowly and deliberately."
  ○ Did you forget to listen at any time? If so, when? Any ideas about why you stopped listening?
  ○ Did anything happen that made it hard for you to listen?

- Using the evaluation form provided, evaluate the accuracy of the practitioner's summary of what the client said and description of the client's speaking style, volume of speaking, and speed of delivery.

Evaluation Form: Attending, Observing, and Listening

Name of Practitioner_____

Name of Peer Supervisor_____

Directions: Under each category (in italics) is a list of behaviors or skills. Give one check mark, worth one point, for each skill used by the practitioner.

Building Relationships

Attending

Give one point for each behavior used by the practitioner.

1. Open and accessible body posture
2. Congruent facial expression   _____
3. Slightly inclined toward the client _____
4. Regular eye contact unless inappropriate _____
5. No distracting behavior   _____
6. Minimal encouragement   _____
                                       _____

Observing

Give one point for each item accurately described by the practitioner.

1. Facial expression
2. Eye movement and eye contact   _____
                                       _____

PRACTICE EXERCISE 1 | ATTENDING, OBSERVING, AND LISTENING *continued*

3. Body position and movement   _____
4. Breathing patterns   _____
5. Muscle tone   _____
6. Gestures   _____
7. Skin tone changes   _____

Active Listening Skills Content and Process

Using the following listening scale, evaluate the accuracy and completeness of the practitioner's ability to summarize what the client said and to describe the client's way of speaking, including such things as speaking style, vocal tone and volume, and speed of delivery. On the following line write the score, from 1 to 5, for listening.   _____

Level 1: The practitioner did not summarize any of the major elements of content or describe anything about the client's way of speaking.

Level 3: The practitioner summarized four elements of content but did not describe anything about the client's way of speaking.

Level 5: The practitioner summarized all the major elements of content and accurately and fully described the client's way of speaking, including communication style, volume, and speed of delivery.

The peer supervisor will record the total score in the practitioner's book.

EXPECTED COMPETENCIES

In this chapter, you have learned skills for attending, observing, and listening, all of which invite clients to be actively involved in the process.

    You should now be able to:

- Describe three things to observe as you listen to clients.

- List three ways to attend or communicate involvement to clients.
- Compare typical conversational behavior with listening in the practice setting.
- Demonstrate the skills of attending, observing, and listening.

CHAPTER 6

OPENING AND CLOSING A MEETING

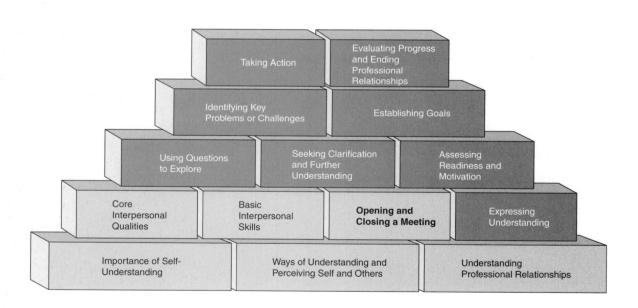

Taking Action	Evaluating Progress and Ending Professional Relationships
Identifying Key Problems or Challenges	Establishing Goals
Using Questions to Explore	Seeking Clarification and Further Understanding	Assessing Readiness and Motivation
Core Interpersonal Qualities	Basic Interpersonal Skills	**Opening and Closing a Meeting**	Expressing Understanding
Importance of Self-Understanding	Ways of Understanding and Perceiving Self and Others	Understanding Professional Relationships

In this chapter you will learn about the following topics:

Practitioner Tasks
- Preparing for work, giving clients the necessary information about the process, and closing the meeting

Practitioner Skills
- Ability to appropriately open and close a client meeting

Client Attributes
- Willingness to attend scheduled meetings and courage to begin the process of discussing challenges with a practitioner

Practitioners are responsible for structuring meetings with clients. In this chapter we will cover skills and techniques needed for preparing, beginning, and ending a meeting with clients. Developing effective skills in these areas is essential to the success of the entire process. For some clients, the first meeting with a practitioner is frightening. It takes considerable courage to schedule a meeting with a practitioner and then to follow through by coming to the meeting.

PREPARING FOR WORK

It is important to prepare before each client meeting. Preparing involves getting ready to meet with the client by doing such things as obtaining available client information; collecting supplies, forms, or possible referral information; and possibly talking to a supervisor or co-worker about the client. When preparing for the meeting, it is particularly important to think about the possible purposes of the meeting and what might be accomplished in the meeting. When preparing for a meeting with a task group, community group, or psycho-educational group, the practitioner may need to take considerable time to plan the agenda, decide what topics will be covered, think about how to help people get acquainted, and begin to think about plans for possible future meetings.

If the client belongs to a cultural group with which the practitioner is not already familiar, gaining at least a basic understanding of that cultural group is essential. As you learned in Chapter 1, culture influences language, behaviors, rules, and ways of understanding others and provides a framework of assumptions for understanding events and communicating that understanding to others. Gaining basic knowledge of each client's culture is vital to developing an effective relationship. Information about other cultures can be gained by reading literature written by authors from other cultures, learning about the relationship of one's own culture to other cultures, talking to key resource people from other cultures, and using other resources to get more information if needed. For example, books about diversity are listed on the websites of the American Psychological Association (http://www.apa.org), the National Association of Social Workers (http://www.socialworkers.org), and the American Counseling Association (http://www.counseling.org). Additional information can be found by searching the web for information on a specific culture. General information about a cultural group will, of course, not apply to all individuals, but it will give the practitioner a starting point for understanding the client's worldview.

After gathering as much information as possible, the practitioner should consider how the client might be feeling about the meeting. Clients are often anxious and uncomfortable about the first meeting. They may also feel embarrassed about asking for help. Practitioners should take some time for preparatory empathy or getting "in touch with the feelings and concerns that the client may bring to the helping encounter" (Shulman, 1992, p. 56). Even in task group meetings or organizational meetings, participants may be hesitant or uncomfortable about the first meeting.

It is also important for practitioners to prepare mentally by doing whatever is necessary to set aside possible distracting thoughts, relax, and get ready to fully focus on the client (Viederman, 1999; Williams et al., 2003). Each person has a different way of letting go of personal concerns and getting ready to center on clients. Some practitioners find that making "to do" lists of personal tasks helps them clear their minds. For some, walking around or eating helps them to be more alert. Taking a minute to meditate or take a few deep breaths is helpful to many. At times, practitioners need to take a moment to reflect on how their meeting with the previous client went, reassure themselves that they did the best they could, and move on to being fully engaged with the next client.

HOMEWORK EXERCISE 6.1　│　PREPARING TO BE FULLY PRESENT

Think about what you have done in the past to let go of thoughts about yourself in order to focus on someone else. Imagine that you received a troubling phone call just before a meeting with a client. What might you do to calm your mind about your own problems and to concentrate on your client?

HOMEWORK EXERCISE 6.2　│　PREPARING TO MEET WITH A NEW CLIENT

Pretend that you are a practitioner at a junior high school. One of the teachers has referred Paco, a 14-year-old Native American boy, to you. Although Paco is a good student, he has been quiet and withdrawn recently. His teacher thinks something might be bothering him. Write down your ideas about what Paco's first thoughts may be when he sees you. How do you think Paco might be feeling about meeting with you? What concerns do you have about meeting with Paco?

Now, pretend you are meeting with several people who live in the neighborhood where your agency is located. The residents are Mexican-Americans who have all lived in this country for at least five years and speak English reasonably well. They have expressed a desire to meet with someone at the agency about the possibility of starting a cooperative daycare center using space at the agency. Write down your ideas about how to prepare for this meeting. What hunches do you have about how these clients might be feeling about meeting with you? What do you think they might hope to accomplish in this first meeting?

BEGINNING A FIRST MEETING

SETTING THE TONE

Beginning meetings appropriately is essential, since first impressions are established quickly and often have lasting effects on relationships. Whether you are leading a group, meeting with colleagues to discuss a problem at your agency, meeting with a community leader, or meeting with a new or returning client, the first few minutes are vital in creating an atmosphere conducive to productive work together.

The practitioner is responsible for beginning the meeting. The beginning of a first meeting can be awkward, especially with a group or family. In the first meeting, people may feel uncomfortable and wonder what other group members and the practitioner are thinking about them. Often in first meetings, people are judging others and feeling judged. Clients may initially feel confused and uneasy, as well as hopeful about the possibility of getting help to resolve their challenges (Hanna, 2002). Structuring and organizing the initial meeting promotes trust and creates an atmosphere of safety.

In these critical first few minutes, the practitioner should invite the client to introduce himself or herself and state how s/he wants to be addressed. It is inappropriate to assume that clients are comfortable with having the practitioner use their first name. Proctor and Davis's (1994) research has shown that in cross-racial relationships it is particularly important for the practitioner to begin with last names and only use first names if the client requests the use of first names. It is appropriate for the practitioner to follow the lead of the client. If the client prefers first names, it may make sense for the practitioner to invite the client to use the practitioner's first name as well.

EXPLAINING THE PROCESS

People tend to feel more comfortable with professionals who fully explain the process, including what they are going to do and what will be expected of them. It is important to explain the purpose of the meeting, describe what will happen during the meeting, cover any ground rules for the meeting, and ask clients if they have any questions. Practitioners usually explain where the meeting will take place. For example, "We will be meeting in my office," "Let's talk together in your kitchen," or "I have reserved the conference room for our meeting." It is also important to identify how long the meeting will last. Since many clients have not met with a practitioner before and do not know what to expect, it is important to explain something about what typically happens in a first meeting. When meeting with an individual, the practitioner might explain that s/he will be mostly listening but also asking some questions to better understand the client. Starting with a task group, the practitioner might say, "In this first meeting, I see my role as helping everyone get acquainted, leading the discussion about the purpose of the meeting, and inviting everyone to discuss possible ground rules for our work together." Practitioners often include some discussion about the client's role in the work. For example, the practitioner might say to a family, "I hope each of you will share your thoughts and feelings about what is happening in your family."

In beginning a first meeting with a child or adolescent, it is important to cover the essential material in a way that the child or adolescent can clearly understand. Children and adolescents may not understand the purpose of the meeting with the practitioner and very likely will need some basic education about the practitioner and client roles. They certainly need to be told how long the meeting will last.

Beginning meetings with families and groups is similar in many ways to beginning with individuals. When working with families, it is important to provide the basic information using words that the children will understand. After going over the initial information, each person is often asked what s/he expects or hopes to change or accomplish. In initial family meetings it is particularly important to ask about expectations. Sometimes children have not been told the truth about the meeting. They may have been told that they were going to see a doctor who would examine them or give them an injection, or they may have been told they were going out for a treat like ice cream. Parents also may have unrealistic expectations, such as that the practitioner's role is to "make my child behave." After hearing these expectations, the practitioner can discuss realistic expectations with the family.

Some group practitioners open meetings with exercises that invite members to get acquainted or check in with the group. These exercises help group members feel more comfortable sharing their thoughts, feelings, and experiences with each other. An example of a beginning group exercise is to invite members to form pairs to discuss topics such as likes and dislikes related to music, movies, food, etc.; something unique about themselves; one fear about being in this group; one thing they hope to achieve by being in this group; and one thing they hope that the group will accomplish. When the pairs rejoin the group, each person introduces his or her partner and tells the group something about their conversation.

HOMEWORK EXERCISE 6.3 | BEGINNING A FIRST GROUP MEETING

Think about groups in which you have participated. Write down three ways the group leaders began their group meetings. Discuss whether you think these ways of beginning effectively set a comfortable tone for the group meeting. If you believe the group was started in a way that was not effective, discuss what you remember about what made it seem ineffective.

BEGINNING SUBSEQUENT MEETINGS

After the first meeting, there are many ways a practitioner may start a meeting. A common beginning phrase is "Where would you like to start?" This phrase puts the choice and responsibility on clients. Or the practitioner may identify where the meeting will start: "In our last task group meeting, we decided to begin this meeting by discussing how the new agency policies might affect low-income clients." Beginning with a summary of the previous meeting is also effective. For example, when working with a task group, the practitioner might begin by saying, "In our last meeting, we decided to move ahead with planning for the neighborhood park. Let's start by discussing ideas you have had since our last meeting about how to proceed with that project." Solution-focused practitioners recommend beginning any meeting by asking, "What progress have you noticed since our last meeting?" (DeJong & Berg, 1998). This beginning sets a positive tone and establishes expectations to look for improvements, to continue the work between meetings, and to believe in the possibility of ongoing positive change. Practitioners can take the opposite approach and ask clients about difficulties they experienced between meetings or when working on assigned tasks. However, this approach invites clients to look for problems and to believe that the practitioner expects them to have encountered problems since the last meeting. The practitioner may choose to begin with an observation or reflection about the previous meeting. For example, a group leader might say, "As I was thinking about our last meeting, I became aware that a few individuals didn't say much, and I'd like to begin by offering those people an opportunity to share their thoughts with us." After the initial meeting, some practitioners choose to begin meetings by waiting for the client to initiate the conversation, thereby giving the client the responsibility for setting the direction of the meeting.

CONFIDENTIALITY

Some of the most important elements to address at the beginning of the first meeting with individuals, families, or groups are the ethical issues related to your work together: expectations of keeping all communications confidential and situations when confidentiality will not be possible (Beahrs & Gutheil, 2001). It is vital that clients understand the rationale for the rules about confidentiality. As a practitioner, it is your responsibility to communicate that you care about the safety of your clients, especially the safety of those who are unable or limited in their ability to care for themselves; and to describe what types of information must be included in reports, what is optional but recommended, and what is not allowed.

Practitioners need to be sure that clients clearly understand the limits of confidentiality. Perhaps the most difficult area for clients to understand is the mandated reporting of possible harm to self or others, suspected child abuse (sexual or physical) and neglect, and elder abuse. The practitioner's responsibility to report these concerns to the proper authorities may cause clients to feel that they cannot trust the practitioner. In response to such a report, the client may end the relationship. They may think that the practitioner does not understand the reasons for their actions and statements, and thus feel betrayed by the practitioner. Clients do not think of the many forms of abuse when practitioners state that they must report if clients are a threat to themselves or others. Most parents do not see themselves as abusers but as disciplinarians. The same may be true of people who neglect or abuse elders or dependent adults. When explaining confidentiality, as when discussing any other topic, it is important to take the client's feelings into consideration. Sometimes using the word *refer* can lessen the sense that clients have been found guilty of an action and can help them to understand more about what the practitioner's responsibilities are versus the agency receiving the referral.

It is helpful to begin your discussion of confidentiality by covering the legal limits of your state, including the name of the state in your explanation. For example, you might say, "By California law I am required to provide you with information concerning the limits of confidentiality" (Pope & Vasquez, 1998). Sharing this information helps to put the boundaries of confidentiality in a context that clients can more easily understand. Most agencies will have a statement of confidentiality and informed consent that clients must sign before or during the first appointment. If the client is able to read and understand this material, it can reduce the amount of time spent explaining these issues. However, it is still the responsibility of the practitioner's to be sure that their clients understand written or spoken communication on this subject. Underage clients and clients with limited intelligence may need extra help in understanding the concept of confidentiality. Clients whose first language is not English may also have trouble fully understanding material written in English.

| BOX 6.1 | THE COMPLEXITIES OF CONFIDENTIALITY |

Duty to maintain confidentiality:
Client information must be kept secured and private from possible disclosure of information. This includes keeping files in locked cabinets, not discussing client information with others in such a way that the client can be identified, and not sharing client information without signed consent.

The exceptions and limitations that apply to the rules involving confidentiality are usually spelled out in state laws and mandated for those serving as practitioners.

Duty to protect and warn (controlled by law) encompasses the following areas:

A. Child abuse and neglect
B. Elder abuse and neglect
C. Intent to harm self or others
D. Subpoena—a court order requesting case material

There are non-mandated or optional times when client information may be shared (usually controlled by ethical limits and sometimes the law).

A. Third-party payers (usually insurance companies with client's consent)

B. Other medical professionals (with client's consent)
C. Family members (information provided to parents about their children)
D. Courts (subpoena and other requests for information)

There are situations in which it seems as if the clinician should be able to share information, but state laws may not consider this sharing mandated and thus any release of this information without the client's consent could constitute a breach of confidentiality. Examples of these situations are listed below:

A. Domestic violence
B. HIV/AIDS or other contagious diseases
C. Sexual abuse by a previous therapist

Different sites and different roles and responsibilities will affect the guidelines noted above. It is essential to know local and state laws concerning issues of confidentiality. Most states post these guidelines and laws on their websites. Clients can be encouraged to check out this information as well.

Another important piece of information to communicate involves who the actual client is and how records are kept (Fisher, 2003; Hedges, 2000). For example, if a client is mandated by the court to see a practitioner, it is important that the client knows from the beginning to whom the practitioner must report. All of this information must be communicated at the first meeting and may be addressed again as needed. Box 6.1 includes further information about the requirements of confidentiality, and Box 6.2 provides an example of opening remarks that a practitioner might offer at the beginning of a meeting.

MINORS AND CONFIDENTIALITY

When the person coming to the practitioner is considered a minor (the definition of a minor varies from state to state), the parents or guardians usually have the legal right to know what happens during meetings (Fisher, 2003; Haslam & Harris, 2004). The extent of the information revealed depends upon the practitioner and the situation. Many practitioners tell parents or guardians that they will only reveal specific information from the meeting if the child's behavior is a threat to self or others, such as being sexually promiscuous, using drugs excessively, threatening to run away, or

BOX 6.2	EXAMPLE OF WHAT A PRACTITIONER MIGHT SAY AT THE BEGINNING OF A MEETING

Hello, my name is Juanita Brown. I am a social worker here at the ABC agency. I understand your name is Mrs. Otsuka. Did I pronounce your name correctly? Would you prefer using first or last names? ——— Since you prefer first names, please call me Juanita.

Today, we will be meeting here in my office for 50 minutes to discuss the challenges you are facing. I will be listening to you and asking you some questions in order to get to know you and understand your situation. Sometimes I will summarize what I am hearing to be sure that I have understood you accurately.

Even though we have just met, I hope that you will decide to be open and honest as you tell me about the challenges you are facing. How does that sound to you? If you have any questions either now or at any time, I hope you will bring them up.

I want you to know that everything you say to me will remain confidential within the agency unless you give me written permission to share information with someone else. There are only a few exceptions. First, I am a mandated reporter, which means that if there is any suspicion of physical, emotional or sexual abuse of a child, elderly person or an incapacitated adult, I am required by law to report that information to the proper authorities. Also, if you tell me something that indicates that you are either a danger to yourself or someone else, I am required to take appropriate steps to ensure the safety of those involved. Would you like to talk more about the issue of confidentiality?

feeling suicidal or homicidal. It is particularly important for adolescents to understand the types of information that will be shared with their parents or guardians. This allows them to decide what they will share with the practitioner.

CONFIDENTIALITY IN GROUPS

Working with clients in groups raises additional issues of confidentiality. While practitioners understand confidentiality, clients may not. Nor do clients have professional ethical standards to uphold. If a client in a group reveals personal information to the group, are other group members free to share it with their family members or friends after the meeting has ended? Are group members free to discuss information from the group meeting in smaller groups if they meet for coffee after the group meeting has ended?

Just as with individual clients, it is best to discuss the limits of confidentiality at the first meeting. The purpose of the group and the setting in which it meets can make a difference. In a counseling or support group, the practitioner might recommend that the group members agree to not discuss the content of the meeting with anyone outside the group or with each other after the meeting has ended. However, in a community planning group, specific plans may be made regarding items that need to be shared with others. It is also important to let the group members know that despite such agreements, the practitioner cannot guarantee that group members will honor agreements. Clients must be warned that information revealed in the group might not be kept confidential.

HOMEWORK EXERCISE 6.4 | BEGINNING

In this exercise, you will compare how the beginnings of everyday conversations differ from the beginnings of professional meetings. First, sometime within the next week notice how you and your friends begin conversations. Write down three different ways that you notice people beginning a conversation.

After you have completed the first part of this exercise, think about a time when you had a meeting with a professional person who was new to you. Write down what the professional did and said that contributed to making the relationship comfortable or uncomfortable.

Finally, write a script for what you might say to begin a problem-solving meeting with an individual. How would you change that beginning if the person happened to be a 7-year-old child?

ADMINISTRATIVE CONTRACTS

In addition to providing verbal explanations to clients, many counseling organizations require that formal written administrative contracts be given to clients during the first meeting. These written guidelines, or administrative contracts, include relevant agency policies regarding topics such as changing appointment times, canceling appointments, payment for services, ethical factors that require clarification (e.g., a signed consent for treatment, limits of confidentiality, and client's rights), and information about the practitioner's qualifications and type of license. Practitioners should go over the administrative contract with clients and ask clients if they have questions about any of the information in the administrative contract. Contracts may include any or all of the following information:

- Detailed descriptions of the nature and the limits of confidentiality
- When disclosure is required by law
- What to do in case of emergencies
- Payment terms and reimbursement issues
- Confidentiality of records and e-mail communications
- Rights of the client to review records
- Telephone and emergency procedures
- Cancellation policies
- Information about the practitioner's qualifications

CLOSING A MEETING

The last few minutes of any meeting are almost as important as the first few minutes. In that period of time the practitioner will want to discuss the possibility of future meetings, to review what was covered in the meeting (including any tasks that were agreed upon), and to request feedback. It is up to the practitioner to assure that the meeting ends on time.

Practitioners may choose to discuss several topics near the end of a meeting. Discussing the client's feelings about seeking help is important. For many clients the decision to ask for help may be contrary to their personal or cultural beliefs. It may be useful to explore whether others know that the client is meeting with you and what the client believes the response of his or her friends or family might be. Supporting clients' courage in seeking help can give them more permission and determination to continue in the process with you.

Closing meetings on a positive note might include supporting the client's decision to seek help at this time; providing support, reassurance, and praise for the client's accomplishments; and expressing realistic hope about possibilities for the future. When these elements are included as part of the closing of a meeting, clients are more likely to return for the next scheduled meeting (Safran, Heimberg, & Juster, 1997). Since people seeking help often feel self-critical and insecure, focusing on client strengths can help enhance their sense of hope. Highlighting clients' strengths related to their accomplishments either during or between meetings invites them to see themselves in a more positive light. Knowing that you believe they are capable of change may engender the sense that they can improve their lives. The power of hope is an essential aspect of the work (Meyer et al., 2002). Most adults seeking the input of a practitioner have lost hope in some way and need to be supported in finding and seeing change possibilities. For children this hope may come in the form of finding someone who cares about them and believes they are valuable.

After the first meeting, the responsibility for ending a meeting may be given in part to the client. If this is the practitioner's preference, it is important to have a clock within visual range of the client and to explain that the meeting is their time and so you expect them to decide what is most important to cover in the available period of time. The client can then decide how to work within the time constraints.

When the meeting ends, it is not necessary or often even possible to have all issues resolved with clients, whether they happen to be individuals, group members, couples, or families. Unresolved issues can be addressed in the next meeting and may encourage growth between meetings. It can be helpful to state what you know to be unfinished business and to note that it can be addressed in the future. For example, the practitioner might say, "I am aware that you spoke about problems with your mother today. We can talk about that next week if you'd like."

Asking clients to reflect on their experiences is another way to close (Yalom, 1995). For example: "We have discussed appropriate ways to express anger today. What was your experience talking about that issue?" To allow ample time to close the meeting, the practitioner may find it necessary to interrupt the flow of the meeting to begin the closing process and complete the meeting on schedule.

HOMEWORK EXERCISE 6.5 | CLOSING

Just as there are differences between beginning everyday conversations compared to professional meetings, there are differences between how they end. Even in everyday conversations, it is important to close in some way. Notice how you end three different conversations. Write down what you said to close each of the conversations.

Next, imagine that you are ending a meeting with a family. In this meeting you have gotten acquainted with each family member and have heard each family member talk about the problems in the family. You have also begun to hear something about their hopes for the family. Write down two examples of what you might say as you end the meeting.

 DVD Example Check the *Developing Helping Skills* DVD for a demonstration of beginning a first appointment, attending, listening, minimal encouragement, and opening a meeting.

| **BOX 6.3** | **EXAMPLES OF CLOSING STATEMENTS** |

- "How would you like to end today?"
- "We have five minutes left."
- "This seems like a good place to stop for today."
- "We've talked about some important things today. Although we need to end for now, it seems like it might be helpful to continue our discussion about this next time."
- "We have five minutes left; do you have any closing thoughts about our meeting today?"
- "Let's talk about what we have accomplished today."

- "What did you find most helpful in our work today?"
- "I would recommend that we meet weekly for the next four weeks and then evaluate our progress. Does that plan sound okay to you?"
- "We are about out of time and have covered most of the points on our agenda. I think this is a good point to end."
- "Shall we meet again next week at the same time?"

INTRODUCTION TO PROBLEM-BASED LEARNING USING CASES

In order to further integrate what you are learning and to begin thinking about your new knowledge in relation to actual client situations, you will be working with a practice case using a modified problem-based learning method. Problem-based learning may be an unfamiliar technique that seems very different from more traditional learning methods such as reading your text and listening to in-class lectures. In problem-based learning, you will work in groups to explore real-life situations. Just as in the real world, you will receive one section of case information at a time. New sections of the case are introduced after you have read about the concepts needed to understand the next section of the case. Along with learning how to apply the new knowledge and practicing interpersonal skills, as you work with the cases you will identify relevant issues related to the case and explore additional information you will need to work effectively with the clients in the case. As in the real world, there are often no right answers to the problems and challenges in the cases. Two individuals or groups working on the same case might generate very different issues to explore. Discussing the case in a small group gives each group member the opportunity to share experiences, thoughts, and perspectives. Group members share in leading the discussion and recording the progress and decisions for the group. To increase effectiveness, it is important for groups to establish ground rules, such as the way members will report their information and what should happen when a member is absent or doesn't complete the assignment.

Just as practitioners discuss care-related dilemmas with their teams or colleagues, each member of your group will serve as a resource. Problem-based learning involves engaging in active learning, setting learning goals, discovering gaps in knowledge, and sharing responsibility for completing the assignments among group members. Using problem-based learning, your instructor serves as an advisor or guide, not the expert to look to for answers.

In order to help you better understand how to work with problem-based learning cases, the first section of an example case, *Jill Asks for Help*, is provided here. New sections will be included in the following chapters.

CASE | CASE, PART 1: JILL ASKS FOR HELP

Susan is the office manager for a community mental health center. She pre-screens all new clients. She receives a call from Jill who is requesting assistance with her "personal problems." Jill wants to be seen as soon as possible. Susan passes the information to Sylvia, who is scheduled to meet with the client the next day. Sylvia is a Licensed Clinical Practitioner. She is a slight, 40-year-old Mexican-American woman who is 5 feet tall and has short, dark hair.

Intake Form

Client Name:	Jill Evans
Age:	24
Ethnicity:	Caucasian
Marital Status:	Single, no dependents
Education:	M.Ed.
Employment:	Teacher of children with learning disorders and other special needs
Presenting Problem:	Trouble sleeping; feeling stressed; upset over a recent break-up; frustrated with new job
Referral Source:	Self-referred
Therapist:	Sylvia Perez, PsyD

Questions: Put yourself in the role of practitioner and answer the following questions.

1. What is the role of the practitioner in this type of agency or setting? (Consider visiting a similar agency and talking to a practitioner. You might also want to read the job description of practitioners in this type of agency.)
2. Are you prepared to work with this client? If not, what will you need to do to prepare?
3. What are your preliminary impressions related to the case?
4. What are the key facts in the case?
5. What additional information will you need prior to meeting this client? (Include this information in your report.)
6. What are some of the questions you might want to explore with the client?
7. What do you plan to say in the first few minutes?
8. What are your thoughts about the purpose of this first meeting?
9. How will you describe the purpose of this meeting?
10. Write out your opening statement to this client.
11. What issues of confidentiality might occur with this client situation?
12. What initial reactions might this client have when meeting with you for the first time? What are your hunches about how the client might react to you?
13. How will you build a relationship with this client?
14. How might your own spiritual, gender, culture, or ethical beliefs influence interactions with this client?
15. What concerns do you have about working with this client?
16. Do you have any biases, prejudices, or stereotypes related to this client?

Now that you have thought about opening and closing a meeting with Jill, you are ready to practice opening and closing a meeting in a role play with fellow students. Although these new skills may seem challenging at first, your preparation with the case example may help you to attend, observe, and listen to the person who is playing the role of the client.

PRACTICE EXERCISE 2 | Opening, Listening, and Closing

Exercise Objectives
- To practice appropriately opening a meeting.
- To practice appropriately closing a meeting.

Step 1: Preparation
Form groups of three people. Each person will have the opportunity to play the roles of practitioner, client, and peer supervisor. Each meeting will last about 10 minutes.

Client Role
- Think about a problem of your own that you feel comfortable sharing, or a client situation in which you can play the role of the client discussing a problem.

Practitioner Role
- Review the procedures for opening and closing a meeting. (This is the first meeting with this client. See the evaluation form.)
- Review the skills involved in attending, observing the client, and listening. (See the evaluation form.) You will not give any verbal responses to the client beyond minimal encouragement.

Peer Supervisor Role
- Look over the evaluation form to review the procedures for opening and closing a meeting. (This is the first meeting with this client.) Review the skills involved in attending, observing the client, and listening.
- Prepare to carefully observe and listen to the client and to keep track of the time.

Step 2: The Client Meeting

Client Role
- Tell your story or play the role of a client for 10 minutes.

Practitioner Role
- Open and close the meeting in an appropriate way for a first client meeting.
- Use the skills involved in attending, observing the client, and listening.

Peer Supervisor Role
- On the evaluation form, put a check mark next to each behavior used by the practitioner for

attending and opening and closing a first meeting with a client.
- Pay close attention to what the client says.
- Write brief notes about what you observe in the client.
- Keep track of the time and let the client and practitioner know when 8 minutes are over so the practitioner can close the meeting.

Step 3: Feedback

Client Role
- Share how you experienced the practitioner attending and listening to you.

Practitioner Role
- Evaluate your use of the behaviors for opening and closing a first meeting and behaviors that demonstrate attending, observing, and listening.

Peer Supervisor Role
- Give feedback to the practitioner on opening and closing a first meeting and the use of attending behaviors.
- Ask the practitioner about observations of the client related to facial expression, eye movement and eye contact, body posture and movement, breathing patterns, muscle tone, gestures, and skin tone changes. The peer supervisor will ask for description rather than evaluations.
- Give the practitioner a check mark for each area that s/he was able to describe.
- Ask the practitioner to summarize what s/he heard the client say. Examples of probing questions include the following:
  - Did you notice any shifts in the conversation?
  - Did you hear any changes in the volume and speed of the client's speech?
  - How would you describe the client's speaking style? For example, the practitioner might say, "The client had a clear, direct, logical way of speaking. His volume was rather quiet, but he tended to talk louder when discussing his son. He spoke rather slowly and deliberately."
  - Did you forget to listen at any time? If so, when? Any ideas about why you stopped listening?

PRACTICE EXERCISE 2 | Opening, Listening, and Closing *continued*

- ○ Did anything happen that made it hard for you to listen?

- • Using the listening scale, evaluate the accuracy of the practitioner's summary of what the client said and description of the client's speaking style, volume of speaking, and speed of delivery.

- • Record the feedback in the practitioner's text-book for future reference.

Evaluation Form: Attending, Observing, Listening, Opening, and Closing

Name of Practitioner_____

Name of Peer Supervisor_____

Directions: Under each category (in italics) is a list of behaviors or skills. Give one check mark, worth one point, for each skill used by the practitioner.

Building Relationships

Attending

Give one point for each behavior used by the practitioner.

1. Open and accessible body posture _____
2. Congruent facial expression _____
3. Slightly inclined toward the client _____
4. Regular eye contact unless inappropriate _____
5. No distracting behavior _____
6. Minimal encouragement _____

Observing

Give one point for each item accurately described by the practitioner.

1. Facial expression _____
2. Eye movement and eye contact _____
3. Body position and movement _____
4. Breathing patterns _____
5. Muscle tone _____
6. Gestures _____
7. Skin tone changes _____

Active Listening Skills Content and Process

Using the listening scale in Appendix A, evaluate the accuracy and completeness of the practitioner's ability to summarize what the client said and to describe the client's way of speaking, including aspects such as speaking style, vocal tone and volume, and speed of delivery. On the following line write the score, from 1 to 5, for listening. _____

Beginning Skills

Give one point for each topic covered by the practitioner.

1. Introduce yourself and describe your role. _____
2. Seek introductions. _____
3. Identify where meeting will be held. _____
4. Identify how long meeting will last. _____
5. Describe the initial purpose of the meeting. _____

continued

PRACTICE EXERCISE 2 | OPENING, LISTENING, AND CLOSING *continued*

6. Explain some of the things you will do.   _____
7. Outline the client's role.   _____
8. Discuss ethical and agency policies.   _____
9. Seek feedback from the client.   _____

Closing Skills (for a meeting)

Give one point for each skill used by the practitioner.

1. Practitioner identified that the meeting was about to end.   _____
2. Practitioner provided a summary of the meeting.   _____
3. Practitioner reviewed any tasks that the client agreed to complete. _____
4. Practitioner discussed plans for future meetings.   _____
5. Practitioner invited client feedback about the work.   _____
6. Practitioner asked client about any final questions.   _____

EXPECTED COMPETENCIES

In this chapter you have learned about preparing, opening, and closing a meeting with individual clients, groups, and families.

You should now be able to:

- Summarize the important elements of confidentiality in working with clients.
- Summarize key activities you need to do to prepare for a meeting.

- Give an example of how you might open an initial meeting with an individual and with a group.
- List the important elements to include when you open a meeting with a new group or client.
- Give an example of how you might open a second meeting with a family.
- Give two examples of how you might close a meeting.
- Demonstrate opening and closing a meeting.

EXPRESSING UNDERSTANDING

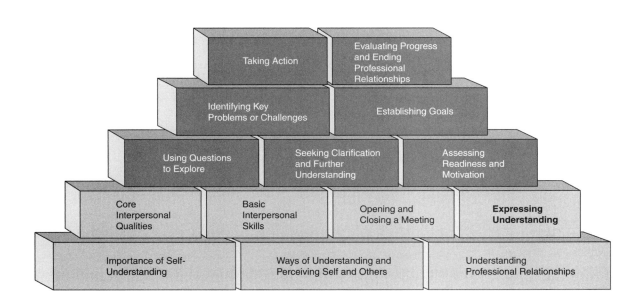

In this chapter you will learn about the following topics:

Practitioner Tasks
- Focusing on empathically understanding each client's unique situation

Practitioner Skills
- Ability to reflect feelings, to reflect content and feelings, to summarize, and to explore meanings

Client Attributes
- Willingness to discuss thoughts and feelings about challenges

At this point you can begin to see how each building block rests on the previous blocks: how each new skill group builds upon your previous knowledge and skills. In order to let clients know you understand their problems or challenges and their context, you will use many skills. In this chapter you will learn about five ways to express empathic understanding:

1. reflecting feelings
2. reflecting content
3. reflecting feelings and content
4. summarizing
5. exploring meanings

In order for this process to continue, clients must be willing to discuss their thoughts and feelings about their challenges and concerns. It is important to remember that openly discussing concerns with a stranger requires considerable strength on the part of the client.

THE IMPORTANCE OF EMPATHIC UNDERSTANDING

A particularly valuable way to invite clients to further explore their situation is to express empathic understanding. As discussed in Chapter 4, empathy involves making every effort to understand others from their point of view. Expressing empathy means communicating an understanding of another person's experience, behavior, viewpoint, meanings, and/or feelings. Empathy is *seeing* the world as that person sees it, not as you would see it if you were in his or her place; *feeling* the way that person feels about a situation, not as you would feel if you were in that situation; *understanding* the meaning that person is giving to events, and grasping the assumptions that influence his or her particular worldview. Whether clients have backgrounds, experiences, and problems similar to your own or whether the opposite is true, accurate understanding requires a great deal of exploration and thought. When meeting with clients who are similar to you, you can easily make the mistake of thinking that these clients are just like you rather than taking the time to understand their own uniqueness. With clients whose experiences and background are very different from your own, understanding from their point of view may require considerable time and effort.

Empathy is not characterized by saying, "If I were you," or "I know just how you feel;" rather, it is characterized by saying, "I understand that you see it in this particular way." Expressing empathy encourages openness and trust and is essential in establishing relationships with clients (Gibson, 2006).

Expressing empathy is only possible if you truly listen to other people and attempt to understand them. Unfortunately, we rarely fully listen to each other and even more rarely express our understanding of what someone else has said. Students often say they feel awkward or uncomfortable expressing empathic understanding. This discomfort is reasonable considering our societal norms about interpersonal communication. Generally, it is considered more acceptable to simply nod or say something like "mm-hmm" when listening to someone instead of sharing what you heard them say. As a practitioner, you may assume that your client feels understood, but the best way to ensure that your clients know you *do* understand is to share what you have heard, beyond saying, "I understand." When practitioners summarize a client's story, they create an opportunity for the client to correct any misunderstandings and to elaborate or explain the content further. If practitioners want to invite active participation in meetings with any type of group, it is important that they respond with some indication of hearing and understanding each person who speaks. It is often useful to have other group members do the same to be sure that they have correctly grasped what others are saying.

HOMEWORK EXERCISE 7.1 | LISTENING FOR EMPATHIC RESPONSES AND BEING EMPATHIC

During a conversation with at least two other people, pay attention to the process of the conversation. Does one person let the other person know that she was heard? Is there any expression of understanding? Do you have a sense that they are truly listening to each other or even paying attention to each other? How can you tell whether they are listening or not? Is it a serial conversation in which one person talks and then the next person starts talking without really connecting to what the first person said?

In another conversation, see what happens when you listen to the other person and make an effort to understand from the other person's point of view. Find a way to let the other person know that you understand what s/he is saying beyond an "okay," a nod, or "hmm."

In a meeting, notice who gets responded to and who does not. If a person is not responded to, does s/he continue to try to get heard, withdraw, get angry, or react in another way? Is there some pattern about who gets responded to and who does not? For example, are men more likely than women to get responses, or are members of the dominant group more likely to get responses than others?

EXPRESSING EMPATHIC UNDERSTANDING

Skills to express empathic understanding include reflecting feelings, reflecting content, reflecting feelings and content, summarizing, and exploring meanings. Using these skills allows the practitioner to express understanding of the client's feelings, thoughts, opinions, points of view, values and expectations, worldview, situation, and challenges.

REFLECTING CONTENT

When reflecting content, practitioners restate their understanding of what the client has said. As practitioners reflect back their perception of the clients' reality, clients will experience the practitioners' attempt to understand and can correct any misunderstandings. In these exchanges between practitioners and clients, practitioners gain a deeper understanding of their clients. Clients experience being listened to and may clarify their thinking as they explain their situation to their practitioners. Practitioners sometimes begin reflecting comments with "Are you saying...", "What I hear you saying is...", "As I understand it...", or "It sounds like..."

Examples of Reflecting Content

- To a group member: "I hear that you think we should do more exploration before committing to this course of action."
- To a family: "It sounds like you have experienced a number of challenges recently."
- To an adult individual: "As I understand it, you are thinking seriously about asking for a divorce."
- To a child: "So your mom has been sick a lot recently and you are not sure what is going to happen."
- To an individual: "It sounds like the traveling that your job requires has been very difficult for you since your baby was born."

HOMEWORK EXERCISE 7.2 | REFLECTING CONTENT

In the next few days listen for comments that reflect content. Since this skill is rarely used in regular conversation, you may not find any examples. Write down five reflecting content comments that you could make to let someone know that you understand what s/he is saying.

REFLECTING FEELINGS

Reflecting feelings requires that the practitioner use empathy to join with the client, to understand how it feels to be the client with all the client's unique qualities and perspectives, and to communicate this understanding. It is not enough to think about how the client may be feeling. As a practitioner you must also express your hunches to let your client know that you understand his or her feelings. Reflecting feelings often allows the client to experience being understood at a core level (Egan, 2002). Reflecting feelings is a very different experience from the way a friend might respond. A friend might say, "I know exactly how you feel," whereas a practitioner responds, "You seem to be feeling sad" or "I wonder if you're sad about that."

Reflecting feelings requires that the practitioner understand the client's feelings even though the practitioner may not have had the same feelings or similar experiences. After reflecting feelings or content, the practitioner can ask, "Am I understanding you correctly?" or "Did I get that right?" These questions give the client an opportunity to correct any misunderstandings. Reflecting feelings may be accompanied by (a) a softer voice or leaning forward to imply deeper connection when the client is expressing fear, shame, or sadness, or (b) more firmness if the client is expressing anger, disgust, or dismay. Expressing understanding or acceptance of a client's feelings may be shared nonverbally by using congruent facial expressions.

Examples of Reflecting Feeling
- *Client:* "You know, I haven't heard from any of them. If they are too busy, they could at least e-mail me."
  Practitioner: "It sounds like you feel sad about that."
- *Client* (sounding angry and speaking with a tight jaw): "I feel like we just aren't getting anywhere."
  Practitioner: "You look like you are feeling impatient with me and our progress."
- *Client on a team:* "Some of the people on this team just aren't carrying their weight."
  Practitioner: "I'm guessing that you are feeling kind of frustrated."
- *Child family member (looking scared):* "When they start fighting and yelling, I just run up to my room."
  Practitioner: "I wonder if you feel kind of scared."

REFLECTING FEELINGS IN FAMILIES AND GROUPS

In groups, practitioners may encourage members of the group to reflect feelings. This is also a good approach when working with families. In either case, the practitioner can prompt people by asking, "How do you think (name of the person) might be feeling?" It is helpful for group members or family members to be encouraged to reflect feelings because this is a valuable skill for them to learn and it also helps the individual who is talking realize that s/he is understood. To create this atmosphere in a family or group, it is important for the practitioner to model expressing empathy by reflecting feelings.

Examples of Reflecting Feeling in Families and Groups
- "The group seems hesitant to talk about the fact that we didn't get the grant we applied for. I wonder if you folks are feeling discouraged."
- "I sense low energy in the room, almost sadness. Is anyone else experiencing this feeling?"
- "Several members of the family seem angry with each other."
- "You folks look a bit tired tonight."

HOMEWORK EXERCISE 7.3 | REFLECTING FEELINGS

Reflecting feelings may seem awkward because it is something people in our society rarely do. Remember that any new behavior feels uncomfortable at first. Reflecting feelings requires that you have a good vocabulary of "feeling words." Make a list of six words that are additional ways to express each of the following feelings: sad, mad, scared, glad. Put each list in order from the most intense expression of the feeling to the least intense expression of the feeling.

In three different conversations or situations, think about what you might say to reflect feelings. Write down your thoughts. At least once in a conversation express your understanding by reflecting what you believe the person to be feeling. Notice how the person responds.

REFLECTING FEELINGS AND CONTENT

Frequently practitioners reflect both feelings and content in the same sentence. Using this skill allows the practitioner to include more information in the reflective comment. Reflecting content or reflecting feelings in the beginning of a relationship with a client is especially helpful as the practitioner is learning about the client's situation. As the practitioner has more understanding of the client, s/he may use the technique of reflecting feelings and content. For example, with a client who has expressed considerable distress about her sister's angry behavior toward her and who looks like she is about to cry, the practitioner said, "You seem quite sad as you talk about what is going on between you and your sister."

Examples of Reflecting Feelings and Content

- "It sounds like you were shocked when your wife told you that she wanted you to leave."
- "So in a way you are grieving about losing your job."
- "It seems like everyone in the group is feeling hurt and a little angry that Mary Ann didn't show up for the picnic."
- "So before your dad left, the two of you used to watch ball games together and now you feel sad and really miss him whenever the ball games are on."

HOMEWORK EXERCISE 7.4 | REFLECTING FEELINGS AND CONTENT

Think back to the movie you watched for the assignment in Chapter 4. Write down five comments reflecting feelings and content that you could make to the movie character you focused on.

Each practitioner develops a different style related to using reflecting skills. Some practitioners use mostly reflecting feelings and content and others tend to use reflecting feeling or content. Many practitioners attempt to express what is not being expressed by the client. If the client is just talking about the facts, the practitioner may make a reflecting comment that involves a hunch about the client's feelings. If the client seems almost overwhelmed with feelings, the practitioner may find it useful to talk about the facts of the situation. Reflecting comments help clients understand the connection between their thoughts and their feelings. The most important reason for offering a reflecting comment is to let the client know that s/he is understood.

SUMMARIZING

Summarizing is another way to express empathic understanding. Summarizing is the same as reflecting but generally covers more information. Sometimes clients have so much information to share that practitioners listen for some time before making a reflecting comment. When the practitioner does make a statement, it might be a summary of the many things the client has been talking about. Summarizing is often a good way to close a meeting. Using a closing summary, the practitioner will outline the key points of a whole meeting.

Since there are often many points of view in a group or family, reflecting comments are particularly important when meetings include more than one client (Jacobs, Masson, & Harvill, 1998; Seligman, 2004). To assure that all members have a complete understanding of key points, a summary at the end of the meeting is essential.

Examples of Reflecting Comments and Summarizing

1. *Client:* "I am really trying hard in school, but I just can't seem to get the grades I want."

   Practitioner: "You sound discouraged because even though you are working hard in school, you are disappointed with your grades." (reflecting feelings and content)

2. *Client:* "When I'm angry with my friend, I tell her how I feel and then she does the same kind of thing again."

   Practitioner: "It sounds like you are unhappy about the way your friend treats you." (reflecting feelings and content)

3. *Practitioner:* "As I remember our last meeting, we focused on how distressed you felt about your wife's rollercoaster behavior toward you. When she is being friendly, you feel good and get more work done, and when she is distant, you worry and have trouble sleeping and focusing at work. Is that how you remember it?" (summarizing)

4. *Practitioner:* "We have discussed both sides of the issue and noted the pros and cons of each direction we could go. I appreciate how difficult this discussion has been for some of you. It appears that some members of the group seem to be troubled when people disagree with each other." (summarizing)

5. *Practitioner:* "Everyone in the group seems relieved that we have agreed to keep all the information confidential." (reflecting feelings and content)

6. *Practitioner:* "Jaime and Mary, you seem to be ready to take charge of some of the family problems. It has been hard to disagree with your children on what should happen next. I can imagine that you children are upset because you think that your opinions don't count." (summarizing)

HOMEWORK EXERCISE 7.5 | SUMMARIZING

Using your movie character again, write down three summarizing comments that you could make. Make a summarizing comment about what happened in the first part of the movie, near the middle of the movie, and at the end of the movie.

EXPLORING MEANING

Understanding the meaning of an event is not as straightforward as understanding its content or the feelings related to it. To understand meaning, practitioners need to be good observers of the behavior and tone that accompanies the content. They also must listen for the possible meaning a client is giving to a situation, action, thought, or feeling. For example, earlier in this chapter we mentioned a client who was upset that her sister was angry with her. The practitioner listened to understand the meaning the client was giving to this event. As the practitioner expressed understanding, it became clear that although the client had not been close to her sister since the death of their mother, she longed for a better relationship with her sister. In an attempt to express the meaning, the practitioner said, "It sounds like when your sister acts in uncaring ways, you feel sad about not having the kind of close relationship you would like. Is that right?"

When working with clients that come from a background, culture, ethnicity, language, or experience that is different from your own, it is particularly important to continually express understanding and give clients a chance to further explain what they have said. For example, if a college student from the dominant United States culture doesn't work up to his potential in college, it may be interpreted as a lack of maturity rather than disrespect for his parents. If a college student from a Chinese-American cultural background doesn't get excellent grades in college, his performance may be seen as a disgrace to his family.

Think back to what you learned in Chapter 2 about the constructivist perspective. We are constantly involved in constructing or giving meaning to our reality. The meaning we attach to an event will depend on many factors, including our cultural background, education, mental stability, family, age, experiences, etc. It is up to the practitioner to explore with clients what meaning or meanings they are giving to situations. For example, a well-educated, white male client felt he was a failure because his boss seemed unfriendly toward him and only focused on the areas in which he needed to improve. There were many other possible interpretations of his boss's behavior, but this was the meaning that made sense to this client. An African-American male client with almost straight As in a graduate program focused on the fact that another student was getting higher grades than he was. He interpreted this to mean that he wasn't working hard enough.

Sensitivity to diversity issues and the meaning that the client gives to situations will provide a framework for a positive working relationship. When developing relationships, it is important to deal directly with diversity variables. For many clients, having a worldview similar to that of the practitioner is more important than differences such as age, ethnicity, race, gender, sexual orientation, education, and physical differences. However, for some clients, obvious differences between the practitioner and client may be a barrier to developing an empathic relationship. Language differences present significant challenges even if the client speaks the same language as the practitioner. If the client is using a second language rather than her native language, she may not be fluent enough to express how she feels. This is further compounded when English is the second language of both practitioner and client. Language differences will obviously influence the nature of communication and perhaps the ability to understand each other either literally or in terms of the way words are used. When language differences exist, it is particularly important to frequently reflect or summarize. After hearing the summary, the client can be encouraged to correct any misunderstandings. This process may need to go both ways so that the practitioner also asks the client what she has heard the practitioner say.

Example of Exploring Meaning

Your client says, "I've never talked this much with a white woman, but I guess it will be okay." While saying this, you notice that your client looks concerned or scared and is wringing her hands. Your observations might lead you to say, "I can understand that it might be hard to talk with someone who seems so different from yourself. Let's begin by talking about what it is like for you to be talking to me, a white woman."

HOMEWORK EXERCISE 7.6 | EXPLORING MEANINGS

When talking to someone who is different from you in cultural background, age, gender, and/or experience, express your understanding of what you think the person means or intends to communicate. For example, you might say, "It seems like you are doing a lot of thinking about whether to continue in your current job. Is that right?" In another situation you might express, "I understand that it is really a challenge to juggle all the things you are doing." Write down what you said and how the other person responded.

EXPRESSING WARMTH

In Chapter 4 you learned about the importance of expressing the core interpersonal qualities, including warmth. In this chapter we are reintroducing warmth as a quality that is usually paired with empathy. Often warmth is shown in the way the practitioner looks at the client, pays attention to the client, and/or has a facial expression of concern or acceptance. The practitioner's tone of voice or even the way of sitting may express warmth and caring.

In the next practice exercise, you will evaluate your ability to appropriately express warmth and empathy. For each quality, an evaluation scale is included to help you specifically identify how well you demonstrate each quality. When doing the practice exercises, you may find that you are so focused on using skills correctly that you do not express as much warmth as you would naturally express. As using professional skills becomes more natural for you, expressing warmth will become easier and begin to feel more authentic.

HOMEWORK EXERCISE 7.7 | EXPRESSING WARMTH

For the next few days, pay attention to ways that you and other people express warmth. What about other people's behavior communicates that they are cold, detached, or lack warmth? Also notice situations where the expression of warmth might be misleading.

When clients feel understood, they are likely to continue talking about their situation and further exploring their challenges. The next practice exercise focuses on expressing understanding by reflecting feeling, reflecting content, reflecting feelings and content, summarizing, and exploring meanings. Using these skills encourages clients to explore further.

PRACTICE EXERCISE 3 | EXPRESSING UNDERSTANDING, WARMTH, AND EMPATHY

Exercise Objectives
- To practice expressing your understanding of what your client is communicating by reflecting feelings, reflecting content, reflecting feelings and content, summarizing, and exploring meanings.
- To practice expressing warmth and empathy in appropriate and effective ways.

Step 1: Preparation
Form groups of three people. Each person will have the opportunity to play the roles of client, practitioner, and peer supervisor. Each meeting will last about 10 minutes.

Client Role
- Think about a problem that you encountered in the past. These exercises will be much more authentic if you talk from your own experience.

Practitioner Role
- Think about important things to observe in the client and to use in the interview.
- Review the behaviors introduced in this chapter: using responses that reflect the client's feelings, content, feelings and content; summarize; and explore meanings.

Peer Supervisor Role
- Review the behaviors introduced in this chapter. (See evaluation form.)
- Prepare to record verbal and nonverbal responses of the practitioner and to keep track of the time.

Step 2: The Client Meeting

Client Role
- If the experience you plan to discuss happened more than a year ago, give the practitioner the necessary basic information, e.g., "This happened when I was a junior in high school."
- Talk for a brief period, pausing to give the practitioner a chance to respond during the telling of your story.

Practitioner Role
- Use the skills of reflecting the client's feelings, content, feelings and content, meaning, or summarizing several things the client has said.
- Observe the client's nonverbal communication.

Peer Supervisor Role
- Watch the practitioner's behavior and check each attending behavior consistently used by the practitioner, and notice the client's behavior.
- Keep track of the time and alert the practitioner and client when 9 minutes have passed so the practitioner has time to close the meeting.
- Check off the items for opening and closing the meeting.
- Write down each of the practitioner's statements. Writing out each practitioner statement is very difficult but critical in order to accurately identify statements, to give solid feedback, and to effectively evaluate the practitioner's work. You may abbreviate, use a form of shorthand, or just write the first group of words in the statement, or you can tape record the interview and transcribe or listen to the tape.

Step 3: Feedback

Client Role
- Share how you experienced the practitioner reflecting, summarizing, and exploring meanings.

Practitioner Role
- Evaluate your use of reflecting, summarizing, and exploring meanings.

Peer Supervisor Role
- Ask the practitioner to describe what s/he observed in the client and summarize what s/he heard the client say.
- Give the practitioner a check mark for each area that s/he was able to describe.
- Based on your notes, give feedback to the practitioner on the use of reflecting the client's feelings, content, feelings and content, exploring meanings, and summarizing several things the client has said. Give the practitioner a check mark for each skill used.
- Discuss with the practitioner the appropriate score for warmth and empathy.
- Record the feedback in the practitioner's textbook for future reference.
- Identify any inappropriate response made by the practitioner. See the list on the next page.

PRACTICE EXERCISE 3 | EXPRESSING UNDERSTANDING, WARMTH, AND EMPATHY *continued*

Empathy Evaluation Scale

Level 1: *Once during the meeting* the practitioner communicated an understanding of the client's experience and feelings with enough clarity that the client indicated agreement.

Level 3: *Three times during the meeting* the practitioner communicated an understanding of the client's experience with enough clarity that the client indicated agreement.

Level 5: *Five times during the meeting* the practitioner communicated an understanding of the client's experience with enough clarity that the client indicated agreement.

Warmth Evaluation Scale

Level l: The practitioner communicated *little or no concern* for the client and appeared cold, detached, and/or mechanical.

Level 3: At least half the time, the practitioner communicated verbal and nonverbal expressions of concern and compassion that were appropriately suited to the unique needs of the client.

Level 5: The practitioner consistently communicated verbal and nonverbal expressions of concern and compassion that were appropriately suited to the unique needs of the client.

EVALUATION FORM: EXPRESSING UNDERSTANDING

Name of Practitioner_____

Name of Peer Supervisor_____

Directions: Under each category (in italics) is a list of behaviors or skills. Give one check mark, worth one point, for each skill used by the practitioner.

Building Relationships

Attending

Give one point for each behavior used by the practitioner.

1. Open and accessible body posture   _____
2. Congruent facial expression   _____
3. Slightly inclined toward the client   _____
4. Regular eye contact unless inappropriate   _____
5. No distracting behavior   _____
6. Minimal encouragement   _____

Observing

Give one point for each item accurately described by the practitioner.

1. Facial expression   _____
2. Eye movement and eye contact   _____
3. Body position and movement   _____
4. Breathing patterns   _____
5. Muscle tone   _____
6. Gestures   _____
7. Skin tone changes   _____

Active Listening Skills Content and Process

Using the listening scale in Appendix A, evaluate the accuracy and completeness of the practitioner's ability to summarize what the client said and describe the client's way of speaking, including such things as speaking style, vocal tone and volume, and speed of delivery. On the following line write the score, from 1 to 5, for listening.   _____

continued

PRACTICE EXERCISE 3 | EXPRESSING UNDERSTANDING, WARMTH, AND EMPATHY *continued*

Beginning Skills

Give one point for each topic covered by the practitioner.

1. Introduce yourself and your role.   _____
2. Seek introductions.   _____
3. Identify where meeting will be held.   _____
4. Identify how long meeting will last.   _____
5. Describe the initial purpose of the meeting.   _____
6. Explain some of the things you will do.   _____
7. Outline the client's role.   _____
8. Discuss ethical and agency policies.   _____
9. Seek feedback from the client.   _____

Closing Skills (for a meeting)

Give one point for each skill used by the practitioner.

1. Practitioner identified that the meeting was about to end.   _____
2. Practitioner provided a summary of the meeting.   _____
3. Practitioner reviewed any tasks that the client agreed to complete.   _____
4. Practitioner discussed plans for future meetings.   _____
5. Practitioner invited client feedback about the work.   _____
6. Practitioner asked client about any final questions.   _____

Skills that Express Understanding

Give one point for each skill used by the practitioner.

1. Reflecting feelings   _____
2. Reflecting content   _____
3. Reflecting feelings and content   _____
4. Summarizing   _____
5. Exploring meanings   _____

Common Mistakes or Inappropriate Responses (subtract 1 point for each)

(offering advice, reassuring, offering excuses, asking leading questions, dominating   _____
through teaching, labeling, interrogating)

Core Interpersonal Qualities

Using the scales, evaluate the appropriateness and effectiveness of the practitioner's expressions of empathy, warmth, and respect. On the following lines write the scores, from 1 to 5, for warmth and empathy.

Score for warmth
Score for empathy   _____

Empathy Evaluation Scale

Level 1: *Once during the meeting* the practitioner communicated an understanding of the client's experience and feelings with enough clarity that the client indicated agreement.

Level 3: *Three times during the meeting* the practitioner communicated an understanding of the client's experience with enough clarity that the client indicated agreement.

Level 5: *Five times during the meeting* the practitioner communicated an understanding of the client's experience with enough clarity that the client indicated agreement.

PRACTICE EXERCISE 3 | EXPRESSING UNDERSTANDING, WARMTH, AND EMPATHY *continued*

Warmth Evaluation Scale

Level 1: The practitioner communicated *little or no concern* for the client and appeared cold, detached, and/or mechanical.

Level 3: At least half the time, the practitioner communicated verbal and nonverbal expressions of concern and compassion that were appropriately suited to the unique needs of the client.

Level 5: The practitioner consistently communicated verbal and nonverbal expressions of concern and compassion that were appropriately suited to the unique needs of the client.

EXPECTED COMPETENCIES

In this chapter you have learned about showing empathy using skills such as reflecting client feelings; reflecting content; reflecting feelings and content; summarizing; and exploring meanings of what the client has said.

You should now be able to:

- Give an example of reflecting feeling that could be used with an individual, family, or group.
- Give an example of reflecting content with an individual, family, or group.

- Give an example of a response reflecting feelings and content that could be used with an individual, family, or group.
- Give an example of a summary statement that could be used with an individual, family, or group.
- Give an example of exploring meanings that could be used with an individual, family, or group.
- Demonstrate four ways to express understanding.

Exploring and Assessing with Clients

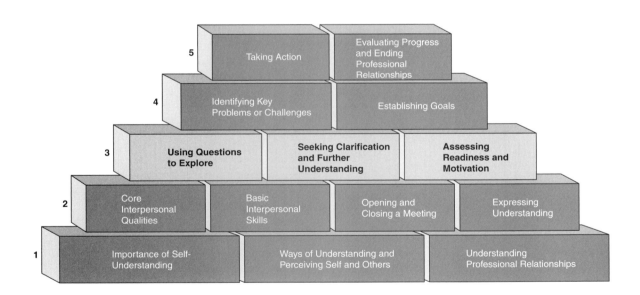

5	Taking Action	Evaluating Progress and Ending Professional Relationships
4	Identifying Key Problems or Challenges	Establishing Goals
3	**Using Questions to Explore**	**Seeking Clarification and Further Understanding**	**Assessing Readiness and Motivation**
2	Core Interpersonal Qualities	Basic Interpersonal Skills	Opening and Closing a Meeting	Expressing Understanding
1	Importance of Self-Understanding	Ways of Understanding and Perceiving Self and Others	Understanding Professional Relationships

Building on the basic relationship skills covered in Section II, you will learn skills and tasks in Section III related to exploring, assessing, elaborating, and gaining a deeper understanding of clients. Chapter 8 presents information about using questions to further explore. Ways to demonstrate respect are also covered. Chapter 9 introduces ways of seeking more in-depth information and covers important areas to assess. The focus of Chapter 10 is on assessing client readiness for change. Part of that assessment considers the client's level of motivation for change and hindrances that may prevent the client from moving forward.

As in the previous section, the process of exploration can happen only if clients bring their strengths to the process. Clients need to be willing to explore their thoughts, feelings, resources, and situations involved in the challenges they are facing.

USING QUESTIONS TO EXPLORE

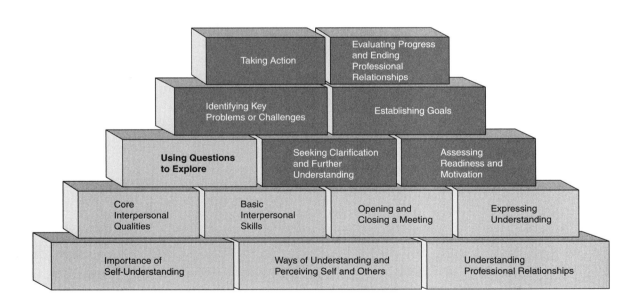

In this chapter you will learn about the following topics:

Practitioner Tasks
- Using questions appropriately to explore

Practitioner Skills
- Appropriate use of open-ended and closed-ended questions

Client Attributes
- Willingness to explore problems and strengths

Reflecting and summarizing are excellent ways to let clients know that they have been heard and understood. After expressing your empathic understanding of your client, you may decide to ask a question to direct the client to focus on a particular area or to say more about some topic. As a practitioner, you need to fully understand your client's concerns. If the practitioner has done a good job of building the relationship by expressing understanding, as discussed in the previous chapter, the client is more likely to be willing to continue exploring. In this chapter you will learn to use several types of questions appropriately, and you will also learn the various purposes of asking questions. Exploring your client's strengths is as important as understanding his or her problems. Focusing on strengths is one way to demonstrate respect. Of course, exploring will be successful only if the client is willing to share further information.

Exploration involves asking questions to gain more information about a particular area or to gain greater depth of information. In everyday conversation, we usually stay at a surface level of understanding and rarely ask for more information. Practitioners can be helpful only if they have a full picture of the situation. In order to fully comprehend a client's situation, practitioners often need to explore beyond what the client has initially shared.

TYPES OF QUESTIONS

In this chapter you will build on your previous skills and learn to appropriately ask open-ended and closed-ended questions. Asking questions to get information is a skill that most people use, so it comes naturally when you are in the role of practitioner. Although gathering information is important in all forms of helping, it is important to check with your client by expressing understanding, by reflecting feelings, content, content and feelings, or summarizing before asking questions. Asking questions without expressing understanding first may be experienced as "grilling" or interrogating. Although you may be more comfortable asking questions than expressing empathy, it is important to express empathy first and to avoid asking too many questions.

OPEN-ENDED QUESTIONS

Open-ended questions invite clients to broadly explore a particular topic. Open-ended questions generally begin with *who, what, when, how,* or *tell me more*. When these words are used, the questions are usually open-ended. An example of an open-ended question is "How do you feel about that?" *Why* questions are also open-ended but require clients to rationalize and justify and can put them on the defensive. It is better to avoid the use of *why* questions whenever possible.

Some questions are open-ended but go beyond what the client has expressed. If practitioners ask questions using language that the client has not used, this may limit rather than expand the area of exploration. For example, if the client has not mentioned anger and the practitioner asks, "What is it about that situation that makes you angry?" the practitioner has assumed that the client is feeling anger related to something in the situation. It would be more effective to ask, "When you think others are not taking you seriously, how do you feel?"

Open-ended questions often begin with these phrases:

- Will you tell me more about...
- What are your feelings about...
- Who could help...
- What seems to help...
- How did you feel about...
- How frequently do you...
- How important is...
- Will you explain more about...

Examples of Open-Ended Questions
- What other parts of your life is the problem affecting?
- What other people are affected by this problem?
- Who has helped you with this problem?
- How have other people helped you with this problem?
- What made you decide to seek help at this time?
- What has improved since the last time I saw you?
- What led you to come discuss this problem with me now?
- How long has this problem been going on?
- What would your life be like if this problem wasn't going on?
- Do you know anyone else who has had a similar problem?
- Do you know how they solved it?
- Have you ever talked to a practitioner before about this problem? If so, how was working with a practitioner helpful to you?
- How have you solved other problems in your life?
- What do you understand about the kind of help I might offer you?
- How has it felt to talk about the problem today?

HOMEWORK EXERCISE 8.1 | OPEN-ENDED QUESTIONS

Write down five open-ended questions that you might use with an adult, five that might be appropriate with a child, and five that you think would be helpful with a frail older person living in a nursing home. Write down five open-ended questions you might use working with a family, five open-ended questions you might use working with a group, and five open-ended questions you might use with a larger system such as a community group, an agency, or a neighborhood.

CLOSED-ENDED QUESTIONS

Closed-ended questions can be answered with one word such as *yes* or *no*. Using closed-ended questions is appropriate when the practitioner needs to obtain specific information. Examples of such questions are "How old are you?", "What is your address?", and "How many other people live in your house?" When practitioners need to obtain specific information related to eligibility requirements, discharge needs, and immediate needs, the use of closed-ended questions is appropriate. However, if the practitioner wants to invite the client to explore a topic more fully, an open-ended question is more appropriate.

Skilled practitioners choose the type of question to ask based on their goals. Beginners often overuse closed-ended questions. Since closed-ended questions ask for limited and very specific information, they do not invite clients to fully explore a topic and may indicate that the practitioner is not interested in obtaining more information. If clients treat open-ended questions as closed-ended questions by giving one-word responses, you may need to encourage them by saying, "Tell me more." Adolescents are often masters at turning open-ended questions into closed-ended questions. For example, if you ask, "What did you learn in school last week?" they might reply "Nothing." In Chapter 11 you will learn more about working with clients who may not want to talk with you.

HOMEWORK EXERCISE 8.2 | CLOSED-ENDED QUESTIONS

In the next week pay attention to the kinds of questions people ask. Write down ten questions that you hear in everyday conversations. Identify each question as closed-ended or open-ended and briefly describe how the question was answered.

MULTIPLE QUESTIONS

Some ways of using questions are less effective than others. For example, practitioners should not ask more than one question at a time. Asking several questions at once invites confusion, and generally clients will just reply to one of the questions. This prevents the practitioner from obtaining potentially important information from the question the client did not answer. For example, a practitioner might ask the client: "Is it hard for you to both work and study? How does your family feel about this?" Sometimes the second question is similar to the first question, but in this example there are two different questions. The first question focuses on the client's thoughts and the second question on his or her family's feelings. Questions that have multiple-choice answers also can inhibit the client's exploration. An example might be, "How do you feel about that: sad, confused, angry?" However, when clients are not used to expressing their feelings or reporting on them, asking a multiple-choice question initially may give them a larger vocabulary for describing what they are experiencing.

HOMEWORK EXERCISE 8.3 | MULTIPLE QUESTIONS

In the next few days pay attention to the types of questions people ask you and the questions you ask others. You will probably hear some open-ended questions, some closed-ended questions, and some multiple questions. Identify which type of questions you use most frequently. Notice how people respond to multiple questions.

PURPOSES OF QUESTIONS

QUESTIONS TO EXPLORE PATTERNS

Questions can be used to identify connections or patterns. The practitioner may want to help clients see possible connections between their problems and their behavior, thoughts, feelings, ways of coping, and/or relationships. For example, the practitioner might say, "I hear that you believe that people don't take you seriously. What have you noticed about the way you talk that might relate to people not taking you seriously?"

QUESTIONS TO INVITE A NEW APPROACH

Questions can also be used to ask clients to consider new or different approaches. For example, "What are other ways that you might talk or act so people would take you seriously?" Working with a task group, the practitioner might say, "I understand that you believe that the administration is unwilling to consider your proposal. What else might you do that would be helpful when presenting the proposal to the administration?"

QUESTIONS TO EXPLORE STRENGTHS

In Chapter 2 we discussed the strengths perspective and the importance of focusing on strengths. As practitioners explore problems and challenges with clients, they need to also look for their strengths. Whether the client is an individual, a family, a group, or neighborhood, looking for strengths is essential. Often it will be the clients' strengths that will help them resolve the problems. There are many ways to invite clients to turn their focus from problems to strengths and resources. Here are a few examples of possible questions and statements that can be used to invite clients to identify strengths.

Examples of Questions to Explore Strengths
- What do you do well?
- What are you good at?
- What do you like about yourself?
- What do other people say they like about you?
- How have you made it through the challenges you faced in the past?
- What is something you did as a child that you were proud of?
- What about when you were a teenager, what did you do that you felt good about?
- What is something you have done that was hard?

- What does your family do that is fun?
- What does your family do that you all have to help with?
- Tell me about the people in your life who have helped you out.
- Tell me about the relatives that you like.
- Who has your family turned to for help in the past?
- What are some good things that this organization or neighborhood has been able to do?
- Tell me about a time that you helped someone else.
- What are some of the ways that people in your family help each other?
- If someone else had a problem similar to yours, what would you suggest that person do?
- Think of someone that you know who has solved a problem similar to yours. What did that person do that might work for you?
- Of the things you have already done to resolve this problem, what has worked the best?
- What have you learned from dealing with these challenges?
- What skills helped you solve previous challenges?
- How have you resolved previous challenges?
- What are the positive qualities that led you to ask for help at this time?

HOMEWORK EXERCISE 8.4 | ASKING QUESTIONS ABOUT STRENGTHS

Write down five additional questions you might use to find out about strengths. (*Hint:* You can ask about strengths and achievements in the past including qualities needed to accomplish certain tasks or goals; for example, "Tell me about the strengths and skills that you used when you learned to drive.")

IDENTIFYING STRENGTHS

Although practitioners are often working with people who feel troubled and need to deal with what is most challenging in their life, it is very important to go beyond empathizing and to listen for, ask about, and express your understanding of their strengths. Practitioners need to look for and focus on clients' abilities, resources, and resilience in facing challenges; clients' capacity to cope in difficult situations; and clients' willingness to keep trying. Highlighting what clients have already achieved expresses to them that the practitioner understands and supports the efforts they have made (Saleebey, 2002c).

Examples of Comments that Help Clients Acknowledge Strengths
- *To a group:* "It seems like each of you contributed a great deal of time to make this project such a success."
- *To children in a family:* "As I listen to you talking about how you have managed during the time your mom has been sick, I am aware of how capable each of you is in pitching in to help with the laundry, house cleaning, and cooking."
- *To an individual:* "I know that standing up for yourself is new for you, but it sounds like you were clear and assertive with your boss."

- *To a couple:* "I think that figuring out that you need help and getting it shows you each have a lot of commitment to your relationship."

HOMEWORK EXERCISE 8.5 | IDENTIFYING STRENGTHS

Think of someone in your life who saw and identified one of your strengths. What was that experience like for you? Now think about when things you didn't do well were noticed and highlighted, while things you did do well seemed to be ignored. An example might be when you were a child and got nine out of ten spelling words right on a test. Were you told, "Good job! You got nine right." Or instead, were you asked, "Why did you miss one?" As a practitioner, do you want to be the person who focuses on the one word that was missed or on the nine words that were correct?

Now think about three friends or family members. Identify one or more of their strengths.

DEMONSTRATING RESPECT

Asking about strengths and identifying them specifically are ways of demonstrating respect. In Chapter 4 we discussed the importance of demonstrating respect in relationships with clients. Respect can be expressed by believing and validating the client's story; by showing interest in the client's thoughts and feelings; by asking about strengths, resources, potential, and capacities; and by identifying his or her strengths. Using language that expresses a belief that clients can change and are able to solve their problems also shows respect for clients.

Examples of Demonstrating Respect
- "I can see how many different ways you've tried to solve this problem. Will you tell me about other things you have considered, but haven't been able to use yet?" (showing interest in the client's thoughts and asking about strengths and potential)
- "You seem quite angry about how your boss has been behaving. It must be a tough place to work. How do you think I might help you?" (validating the client's story and showing interest in his or her wants and needs)
- "When you resolve this problem, what are some things that will be different in your family?" (expressing belief in the client's ability to change)
- "Who else in the agency might be willing to work with us to resolve this problem?" (asking about resources)
- "As I understand it, you have done a lot of thinking about the problems this organization is facing. You have talked to a number of people about their understanding of the problem and have decided to commit time and energy to resolve this problem. You have taken some important steps in problem solving." (identifying strengths)

HOMEWORK EXERCISE 8.6 | DEMONSTRATING RESPECT

Over the next few days, notice what people do or say that you believe demonstrates respect. Also notice what people do or say that you believe demonstrates a lack of respect.

CASE | CASE, PART 2: FIRST MEETING WITH JILL

Jill enters the office and sits tentatively on the couch. Sylvia notes that Jill is taller than average, with an athletic build. She is dressed professionally and has medium-length hair that appears to be the result of a short cut that has grown out without any subsequent shaping. She is pale and doesn't appear to be wearing any makeup. She crosses her legs and tucks her hands under them. After covering the beginning information, including confidentiality issues (mandated reporting, etc.) and informed consent, Sylvia begins her interview with Jill.

SYLVIA: Tell me what brings you in today...

JILL: Well... (*pause*) I've never been in counseling before so I don't really know what to say. In fact, I don't think I've ever felt this way before. (*pause*) Usually, I am the one my friends call when they have a bad day and now I'm the one having all the bad days, it seems. I mean, generally I can just step back and figure out what needs to be done and just do it, but this is different. Anyway, I've been talking with some of my friends and one of them suggested that counseling might be helpful, so that's part of it... (*pause*) umm... but I guess I've been having some trouble with life lately, and it seems like I just can't snap out of it so I'm hoping that coming here might help.

SYLVIA: So this is a very new experience for you. You're generally the type that others turn to for help and you're used to figuring out your challenges, but this is different. You mentioned that you've been having some "trouble." Would you tell me more about that?

JILL: Well, I feel like I'm not sleeping very well and I just don't feel like doing much these days. And yesterday, I couldn't find my car keys... I always put them on the key rack next to the door... but instead of being able to just look for them, I started to cry. I never do that. Oh... and last week, I found myself staring into space while giving my students some free time to work on homework. The problem is that I've been working hard on getting them to stay focused on whatever task we are doing, and I feel like I should be able to concentrate if I am going to ask them to do that. I don't know... I guess I just feel like I'm falling apart and I don't like it.

SYLVIA: It sounds like it has been hard for you lately. How long has this been going on?

JILL: Hmm... I guess a couple of months now. It's frustrating. I'm sick of feeling like this. And I don't know what to do about it. I've never had this happen before...

SYLVIA: It sounds like you have been quite troubled. Tell me what was happening in your life a couple of months ago.

JILL: Well, my boyfriend and I broke up, but he's over it already and I feel like I should be, too. I mean, it's been two months already! And he's got a new girlfriend and I'm sitting here bummed out. (*short pause*) Why can't I get past this?

Jill continues by telling Sylvia that she and her boyfriend dated for 5 years and planned to get married next summer. She describes the evening of the breakup in detail, stating that they talked for a couple of hours after he said he felt like he never had a chance to date other people and wanted to do some experimenting while still planning to marry Jill. She said she would not be willing to continue dating with those new rules, and he said his mind was made up. He told her to put his personal items in a box on her porch and he would pick them up or she could tell him when he could stop by (at a time when she wouldn't be home) to retrieve them himself. Jill's friends told her he was seeing someone about 3 days after they broke up. At this point in the interview, Jill's eyes begin to tear up a little...

SYLVIA: You seem sad right now...
(*pause*)... Jill is crying at this point.

JILL: Sometimes I just feel like I don't know what to do with myself anymore. We did everything together, practically, and everything I do reminds me of him. Most days, I just don't want to get up anymore...

Questions
1. How has your initial perception of the client changed?
2. What new facts have you learned?
3. What are your current impressions or hunches about the case?

4. What additional information do you need to gain? (Include this information in your paper.)
5. Write out three additional things that the practitioner might have said to express understanding.
6. Identify the statements the practitioner made that express understanding.
7. What types of exploring questions might you use in working with this client?
8. Write a summarizing statement that the practitioner might use with Jill.
9. What do you already know about the client's strengths and resources (including cultural resources)?

PRACTICE EXERCISE 4 | USING QUESTIONS TO EXPLORE, AND EXPRESSING WARMTH, EMPATHY, AND RESPECT

Exercise Objectives
• To practice using questions to explore and demonstrating warmth, empathy, and respect

Step 1: Preparation
Form groups of three people. Each person will have the opportunity to play the roles of client, practitioner, and peer supervisor. Each meeting will last about 10 minutes.

Client Role
• Think about a problem you encountered in the past that you feel comfortable sharing. It may be one that is now resolved. These exercises will be much more authentic if you talk from your own experience.

Practitioner Role
• Review the use of questions. (See evaluation form.)

Peer Supervisor Role
• Review the use of questions. (See evaluation form.)
• Prepare to write down everything the practitioner says.

Step 2: The Client Meeting

Client Role
• Tell your story, but stop talking after every few sentences to give the practitioner a chance to practice using his or her skills.

Practitioner Role
• Use all of the skills and behaviors you have learned so far, as appropriate.
• After reflecting or expressing understanding, use an open- or closed-ended question to explore further, and identify and ask about strengths.

Peer Supervisor Role
• Keep track of the time and tell the practitioner and client when 9 minutes are completed so the practitioner has time to summarize what has been covered and close the meeting.
• Since attending, observing, and listening have been evaluated several times, these items will not be included in this evaluation.
• Check off the items for opening and closing the meeting.
• Write down each of the practitioner's statements and questions. You may abbreviate, use a form of shorthand, or just write the first group of words in the statement, or you can tape record the interview and transcribe or listen to the tape.
• Keep track of any inappropriate responses.

Step 3: Feedback

Client Role
• Describe how you experienced the practitioner.

Practitioner Role
• Evaluate your use of expressing understanding, identifying strengths, and questioning.

Peer Supervisor Role
• Give feedback to the practitioner from your notes on the use of reflecting the client's feelings, content, feeling and content, exploring meanings, and summarizing.
• Read and discuss the practitioner's statements and questions.

continued

PRACTICE EXERCISE 4 | USING QUESTIONS TO EXPLORE, AND EXPRESSING WARMTH, EMPATHY, AND RESPECT *continued*

- Check off the practitioner's use of skills for expressing understanding and gaining more information.
- Evaluate the practitioner's use of the core interpersonal qualities of warmth, empathy, and respect. (All of the scales are in Appendix A.)
- Record the feedback in the practitioner's book for future reference.
- Identify any inappropriate responses.

Respect Evaluation Scale

Level 1: The practitioner did not invite discussion of and/or recognize the client's strengths, resources, and/or capacities, and/or showed a lack of respect for the client's abilities such as helping or providing answers that the client did not ask for.

Level 3: *Once during the meeting,* the practitioner invited discussion of and/or recognized the client's strengths, resources, and/or capacities, and the practitioner did nothing that showed a lack of respect for the client's abilities such as helping or providing answers that the client did not ask for.

Level 5: *Three times during the meeting,* the practitioner invited discussion of and/or recognized the client's strengths, resources, and/or capacities and the practitioner did nothing that showed a lack of respect for the client's abilities such as helping or providing answers that the client did not ask for.

EVALUATION FORM: USING QUESTIONS TO EXPLORE

Name of Practitioner_____

Name of Peer Supervisor_____

Directions: Under each category (in italics) is a list of behaviors or skills. Give one check mark, worth one point, for each skill used by the practitioner.

Building Relationships

Beginning Skills

Give one point for each topic covered by the practitioner.

1. Introduce yourself and describe your role.   _____
2. Seek introductions.   _____
3. Identify where meeting will be held.   _____
4. Identify how long meeting will last.   _____
5. Describe the initial purpose of the meeting.   _____
6. Explain some of the things you will do.   _____
7. Outline the client's role.   _____
8. Discuss ethical and agency policies.   _____
9. Seek feedback from the client.   _____

Closing Skills (for a meeting)

Give one point for each skill used by the practitioner.

1. Practitioner identified that the meeting was about to end.   _____
2. Practitioner provided a summary of the meeting.   _____
3. Practitioner reviewed any tasks that the client agreed to complete. _____
4. Practitioner discussed plans for future meetings.   _____
5. Practitioner invited client feedback about the work.   _____
6. Practitioner asked client about any final questions.   _____

PRACTICE EXERCISE 4 | USING QUESTIONS TO EXPLORE, AND EXPRESSING WARMTH, EMPATHY, AND RESPECT *continued*

Skills that Express Understanding

Give one point for each skill used by the practitioner.

1. Reflecting feelings _____
2. Reflecting content _____
3. Reflecting feelings and content _____
4. Summarizing _____
5. Exploring meanings _____
6. Identifying strengths _____

Exploring

Questioning Skills

Give one point for each skill used by the practitioner.

1. Expressed understanding before asking questions. _____
2. Used open-ended questions when appropriate. _____
3. Asked one question at a time. _____
4. Used closed-ended questions when appropriate. _____
5. Asked questions about strengths. _____

Common Mistakes or Inappropriate Responses (subtract 1 point for each) _____
(offering advice, reassuring, offering excuses, asking leading questions, dominating through teaching, labeling, interrogating)

Core Interpersonal Qualities

Using the scales in Appendix A, evaluate the appropriateness and effectiveness of the practitioner's expression of empathy, warmth, and respect. On the following lines write the scores, from 1 to 5, for warmth, empathy, and respect.

Score for warmth _____
Score for empathy _____
Score for respect _____

Respect Evaluation Scale

Level 1: The practitioner did not invite discussion of and/or recognize the client's strengths, resources, and/or capacities, and/or showed a lack of respect for the client's abilities such as helping or providing answers that the client did not ask for.

Level 3: *Once during the meeting*, the practitioner invited discussion of and/or recognized the client's strengths, resources, and/or capacities, and the practitioner did nothing that showed a lack of respect for the client's abilities such as helping or providing answers that the client did not ask for.

Level 5: *Three times during the meeting*, the practitioner invited discussion of and/or recognized the client's strengths, resources, and/or capacities, showed positive regard to client, and did nothing that showed a lack of respect for the client's abilities such as helping or providing answers that the client did not ask for.

EXPECTED COMPETENCIES

In this chapter, you learned to use questions to explore the client's situation and identify strengths. You should now be able to:

- Explain practitioner tasks related to exploring.
- Explain the difference between closed-ended and open-ended questions and give examples of each.

- Discuss ways that questions can be used to explore patterns, to invite a new approach, and to explore strengths.
- Give examples of how questions can elicit information about a client's strengths.
- Identify three ways to demonstrate respect.
- Demonstrate appropriate use of questions.

SEEKING CLARIFICATION AND FURTHER UNDERSTANDING

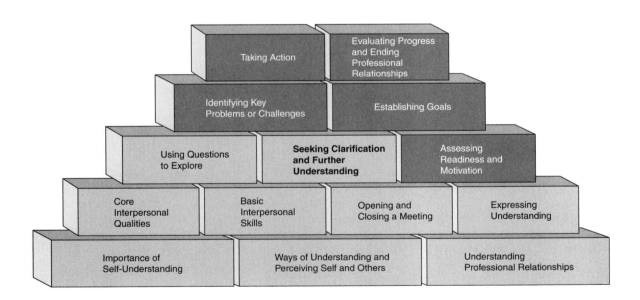

In this chapter you will learn about the following topics:

Practitioner Tasks
- Identify gaps in information and seek further clarifying information and understanding about important aspects of the problem(s) or challenge(s), person(s), and situation

Practitioner Skills
- Ability to use questions to clarify information and obtain further understanding

Client Attributes
- Willingness to explore thoughts, feelings, and conclusions and to consider such areas as the history of the problems and effects of the problems.

In this chapter, you will continue to develop your ability to use your professional skills and understanding of the unique aspects of a practitioner-client relationship. Effective practitioners are able to recognize when and how to gain further clarification of a topic in order to more fully understand the client's situation. It is up to the practitioner to notice when topics are not being fully explored or are only superficially discussed. In these situations the practitioner should seek more information. In this chapter you will learn the skills related to seeking clarification and gaining further information. You will also learn about the importance of allowing silence so clients can reflect on the process.

THE NEED TO GAIN FURTHER INFORMATION

In ordinary conversation, people often communicate in verbal shorthand, only discussing topics in a superficial way. Most people assume that other people use words in the same way they do, that others can somehow fill in the information that is left out, and that others understand how conclusions are reached. Communicating in this way involves many assumptions and often leads to misunderstanding. As a practitioner, it is important to listen for gaps in information and notice the points that are not clear. Since practitioners need to fully understand their clients, it is important for them to seek clarification by asking clients for more specific information.

SEEKING CLARIFICATION

Seeking clarification encourages clients to explain their experience in depth or with more specific details. If clients thoroughly explain their behaviors, feelings, and experiences, then the nature of the problem, challenge, or situation will be clearer to the practitioner. If the practitioner is unclear about what clients are saying or meaning, the clients also may be unclear about their troubling situations. For example, if a client says, "I'm depressed," the practitioner should not assume that depression means the same thing to the client as it does to the practitioner. The practitioner might ask for more information by saying, "I understand that you are feeling depressed. What is depression like for you?" In a group meeting, several people may agree that the clients of the agency are not treated with respect. It is up to the practitioner to explore further by making a remark such as, "I hear that you are concerned about how your clients are being treated. Will you give me examples of ways that clients are treated with respect?"

When asking questions for clarification, practitioners can explore the meaning of words and body language. For example, the practitioner could say, "I noticed that several people in the group began looking at the floor when we started discussing who was willing to go and talk to the mayor. Will one of you tell me more about what you are expressing by looking at the floor?" (exploring meaning of body language). The practitioner might explore the meaning of a word and say, "You mentioned that people in this family are often angry at each other. Will you give me an example of what happens when people are angry in your family?" (exploring the behaviors related to anger).

Exploring the basis of conclusions drawn by the clients is another area that often needs further exploration by the practitioner. For example, if a member of a task group says, "Okay, I guess that I will have to do all the work of putting together the PowerPoint® presentation," the task group leader might say, "It sounds like you think you will have to prepare the presentation by yourself. Will you tell us what happened to make you decide that you would have to do all the work of putting the PowerPoint presentation together?"

Examples of Questions to Seek Clarification

Client statement: "He is always getting mad at me over nothing."

Possible questions:

- o "Tell me about what he did the last time he got mad at you." (asking for further information)
- o "How often was he mad at you yesterday?" (asking for further information)
- o "Would you give me an example of a time when he got mad at you over nothing?" (asking for further information)
- o "What does he do when he is mad at you?" (exploring behaviors described as "mad")

Client statement: "I just know she doesn't love me anymore."

Possible questions:

- o "Would you tell me how you know she doesn't love you anymore?" (asking for basis of conclusion)
- o "What has she done or said that makes you believe that she doesn't love you anymore?" (asking for basis of conclusion)
- o "If she did love you, what would she do?" (exploring meaning of "love" to the client)

Client statement: "I think the other people in this group just don't care about whether this project gets completed on time or not."

Possible questions:

- o "Will you tell me what you have noticed that makes you think others don't care about whether this project gets completed on time or not?" (asking for basis of conclusion)

- o   "Will the rest of you tell us your thoughts about people's commitment to completing this project on time?" (asking for further information)
- o   "What are some things you think the people in this group could do to show that they were invested in completing the project on time?" (asking for further information)

Using questioning to expand and clarify is particularly important with families and groups because it encourages interaction among members as they expand on their thoughts and feelings. Using clarifying questions can lead to everyone having a clearer picture of what is being communicated. Clarification can also increase awareness of similarities and differences among members.

Examples of Clarifying Questions in Groups

- •   "Several people mentioned thinking this neighborhood is going to the dogs. Will you give me some examples of what you mean?"
- •   "I understand that you would like the agency to be more efficient. Will you tell me what you believe will be different when you are more efficient?"
- •   "I heard several folks say that you thought that doing group assignments would not work. What do you think doesn't work about group assignments?"
- •   "It sounds like you believe that people in this family don't feel close to each other. Will you tell me what happens when people don't feel close to each other in this family?"

HOMEWORK EXERCISE 9.1 | SEEKING CLARIFICATION

Read each of the following sentences and write down two questions you might ask to get more information.

1.   No one in this neighborhood cares about the drug problems.
2.   I just know that my teacher doesn't like me and is going to give me a low grade.
3.   I know the other kids in this group will be mean to me.
4.   The people in this agency don't really care about the clients.
5.   My mother had a nervous breakdown, so she can't help how she acts.
6.   My parents just don't understand kids. They won't let me do anything.
7.   In this family we just don't communicate very well.

   The next time you are in a conversation with several other people, pay attention to whether people take time to ask about what the other person means or whether they just wait until one person has stopped talking so they can start talking.

CLIENT'S ROLE IN CLARIFICATION

The practitioner may be highly skilled at noticing missing information and asking clarifying questions, but to go further with exploration, the client must also be willing and able to explore more deeply. This willingness to explore more deeply is generally based on feeling comfortable or safe with the practitioner. As you know from your life experiences, some people develop a sense of trust very quickly while others are more hesitant. Experiences of abuse, oppression, and mistreatment often lead people to be cautious about trusting. If clients are not willing to explore more deeply, practitioners should not push them but rather accept what they are ready to do. Asking clients to talk about their hesitancy to share information may be helpful. The practitioner should also consider his or her role in the client's caution. When clients resist exploring further, it may be an indication that the practitioner is trying to move too quickly. Perhaps the practitioner has tried to gain further information before adequately establishing a trusting relationship with the client. Some people have not had the opportunity to explore their thoughts and feelings or be introspective. It may take them some time to develop this ability. If the client seems uncomfortable exploring further, the practitioner should go back to expressing understanding in order to build a trusting relationship.

ALLOWING SILENCE

Sometimes allowing silence is the best way to invite clients to elaborate further. It is important to allow clients time to think and process what has been said. The practitioner may have said something or asked something that the client needs time to consider. Although allowing silence may seem awkward to beginning practitioners, it is an appropriate and respectful response, particularly at times when the client is expressing strong feelings and needs time to reflect.

Silence allows time for emotions to be experienced or thoughts to become clarified. Allowing silence is a nonverbal response that has been described as one of the most useful interventions available to practitioners (Belkin, 1984; Moursund, 1993). When it appears that clients need time to deal with what has been said, practitioners should allow some silence. It is important to remember that some topics, particularly those that involve intense or strong feelings, require more time to process. In addition, although you may process information quickly and be ready to respond almost immediately, this is not true of all people. Some people need quiet in order to think about what they are hearing and feeling. Practitioners need to be sensitive and allow clients the time they need to think.

As with other responses, silence must be used purposefully. Some clients consider silence an indication of lack of interest or even rejection. Practitioners should observe nonverbal clues that could indicate that the client is uncomfortable with the silence. Clients who are mandated to be in the session may not want to talk. Some practitioners choose to remain silent because they believe that the client will decide to talk when s/he is ready. Each situation and each client needs to be thoughtfully considered.

Sometimes it is important to ask about the silence. For example, the practitioner might say, "What were you thinking about during the silence?" During a silent period, the practitioner may look at the client or decide not to keep eye contact as a way to give the client more space.

Examples of Allowing Silence
1. *Individual client:* "I don't know why I get sick so often . . . maybe it is the stress in my life, the fast pace . . ."

     Practitioner: (*silence, giving the client time to think about her comment*)

2. *Group member:* "I'm not sure where we should go from here, but it seems like we need to make a decision."
    Practitioner: (*silence, giving group members time to reply*)
3. *Family member:* "I really wish that we could do something together without fighting."
    Practitioner: (*silence, giving other family members time to respond on their own*)

HOMEWORK EXERCISE 9.2 | ALLOWING SILENCE

Think about your own experience with silence when you are with other people. Are you comfortable with silence, or do you feel anxious or uncomfortable if a conversation stops? In one conversation in the next few days, try allowing 10 seconds of silence rather than immediately starting to talk if there is a pause in the conversation. How did you feel in the silence? If silence is uncomfortable for you, you might try counting slowly to ten and encouraging yourself to be quiet for the whole 10 seconds.

IMPORTANT AREAS FOR EXPLORATION

Three broad areas that are generally important to explore further in counseling situations are problems or challenges, person or persons, and situation or environment. When telling their story, clients usually discuss several of these broad topics. It is up to the practitioner to notice what is not being discussed and to explore those areas that are not covered by the client.

EXPLORING THE PROBLEMS OR CHALLENGES

To better understand the client's challenges, it is important to learn about the history of the problem by exploring or asking questions. You might ask a client, "When did this problem begin?" Asking the client about previous attempts to solve the problem is one of the most critical questions, because this question gives clients an opportunity to talk about what they have tried: "What have you already done to resolve this problem?" Finally, to better understand the problem, the practitioner should determine the severity and frequency of the problem: "How often does this problem occur?" or "On a scale of 1 to 10, how problematic is this situation for you?"

EXPLORING THE PERSONS INVOLVED

Learning about how the problem or situation affects the people who are involved is also essential. Usually the client talks about how s/he feels about having the problem. If not, the practitioner might ask, "How are you feeling about having this problem?" As the practitioner explores the severity of the problem, s/he will also need to explore how the problem is affecting the person's functioning. The practitioner might say, "I heard that you are very worried about your son. I wonder if your concern is affecting other areas of your life, like your ability to sleep or do your job." The pain of many problems may cause appetite loss, insomnia, inability to concentrate at school or at work, irritability, withdrawal, crying easily, etc. To gain a full understanding of the impact of the problems on the client, it is often important to ask how frequently the problem occurs. For example, the practitioner might say, "I hear that you are quite concerned about your son. Tell me more about how often this concern is your overriding experience."

EXPLORING THE SITUATION OR ENVIRONMENT

A client's overall life situation or environment affects his or her ability to work on problems, so practitioners should explore the resources and supports available to the client's. A client who recently moved to a new area and has few friendships is in a different situation from a client who lives near friends and/or family. The practitioner could ask, "Will you tell me about the people who have helped you with this problem?"

Since problems usually affect people other than the client, part of exploring the situation involves asking about others who may be affected by the problem. Asking about the effect of the problem on others helps the practitioner gain a better understanding of the client's situation. For example, the practitioner might say, "I understand that you are very troubled by the problems on your job. I am guessing that your challenges at work are affecting other people in your life. Will you tell me about others who may be affected?"

A final part of gaining a basic understanding of the client's situation is learning about the other important demands and stresses in the client's life. Returning to the example of the client who is worried about her son, the practitioner would want to find out whether the client has a good job, adequate financial resources, and many friends. If she does, then her ability to work on the problem will be much greater than it would be if she were unemployed, worried about money, and had few friends.

DVD Example Check out the *Developing Helping Skills* DVD for a demonstration of expressing understanding, exploring, seeking clarification, and gaining further information.

PRACTICE EXERCISE 5 | SEEKING CLARIFICATION AND FURTHER UNDERSTANDING

Exercise Objectives
- To practice asking questions to seek clarification, to practice allowing silence, and to practice gaining specific information about person, problem, and situation.

Step 1: Preparation
Form groups of three people. Each person will have the opportunity to play the roles of client, practitioner, and peer supervisor. Each meeting will last about 10 minutes.

Client Role
- Think about a problem you can discuss with the practitioner.

Practitioner Role
- Review expressing understanding and using questions to gain more understanding of the problems or challenges, person, and situation.
- Review using questions to seek clarification:
  - Clarifying the meaning of words and phrases (e.g., "In what way is he mean to you?").
  - Exploring the basis of conclusions drawn by the client (e.g., "What leads you to think that he is planning to leave you?")
  - Eliciting further clarifying information (e.g., "Do you mean . . . ?"; "Are you saying . . . ?").

continued

PRACTICE EXERCISE 5 | SEEKING CLARIFICATION AND FURTHER UNDERSTANDING *continued*

Peer Supervisor Role
- Review expressing understanding, using questions to seek clarification, and using questions to gain an understanding of the problems or challenges, person, and situation.
- Listen to whether topics related to person, challenges, and situation are adequately covered.
- Prepare to record verbal and nonverbal responses of the client and to keep track of the time.

Step 2: The Client Meeting

Client Role
- Tell your story, stopping after every few sentences to give the practitioner a chance to practice using his or her skills.

Practitioner Role
- Use all of the skills and behaviors you have learned so far.
- If the client does not discuss an important topic related to person, problem, and situation, then ask questions to more clearly understand these areas.
- Use questions to seek clarification, and allow silence when appropriate.

Peer Supervisor Role
- Keep track of the time and tell the practitioner and client when 9 minutes are completed so the practitioner has time to summarize what has been covered and close the meeting.
- Check off the beginning and ending skills used by the practitioner. In order to evaluate the practitioner's use of skills, the peer supervisor will write down each practitioner statement and question.
- Give the practitioner one point for each response that expressed understanding, for each

questioning response, and for each area covered within the categories of person, problem, and situation.
- Write down each of the practitioner's statements and questions. You may abbreviate, use a form of shorthand, or just write the first group of words in the statement, or you can tape record the interview and transcribe or listen to the tape.

Step 3: Feedback

Client Role
- Describe how you experienced the practitioner.
- Identify any inappropriate responses.

Practitioner Role
- Evaluate your use of skills that seek clarification and how well you covered person, problem, and situation.
- Identify any inappropriate responses.

Peer Supervisor Role
- Give feedback to the practitioner from your notes on skills that seek clarification.
- Evaluate how well the practitioner covered the key points related to person, problem, and situation.
- Using the evaluation form, check off each response used.
- Give feedback on inappropriate responses. One point is deducted for each inappropriate response.
- Evaluate the practitioner's use of the core interpersonal qualities of warmth, empathy, and respect. (All of the scales are in Appendix A.)
- Record the feedback in the practitioner's book for future reference.

EVALUATION FORM: SEEKING CLARIFICATION AND FURTHER UNDERSTANDING

Name of Practitioner_____

Name of Peer Supervisor_____

Directions: Under each category (in italics) is a list of behaviors or skills. Give one check mark, worth one point, for each skill used by the practitioner.

Building Relationships

PRACTICE EXERCISE 5 | SEEKING CLARIFICATION AND FURTHER UNDERSTANDING *continued*

Beginning Skills

Give one point for each topic covered by the practitioner.

1. Introduce yourself and describe your role. _____
2. Seek introductions. _____
3. Identify where meeting will be held. _____
4. Identify how long meeting will last. _____
5. Describe the initial purpose of the meeting. _____
6. Explain some of the things you will do. _____
7. Outline the client's role. _____
8. Discuss ethical and agency policies. _____
9. Seek feedback from the client _____

Closing Skills (for a meeting)

Give one point for each skill used by the practitioner.

1. Practitioner identified that the meeting was about to end. _____
2. Practitioner provided a summary of the meeting. _____
3. Practitioner reviewed any tasks that the client agreed to complete. _____
4. Practitioner discussed plans for future meetings. _____
5. Practitioner invited client feedback about the work. _____
6. Practitioner asked client about any final questions. _____

Skills that Express Understanding

Give one point for each skill used by the practitioner.

1. Reflecting feelings _____
2. Reflecting content _____
3. Reflecting feelings and content _____
4. Summarizing _____
5. Exploring meanings _____
6. Identifying strengths _____

Exploring

Questioning Skills

Give one point for each skill used by the practitioner.

1. Expressed understanding before asking questions. _____
2. Asked open-ended questions when appropriate. _____
3. Asked one question at a time. _____
4. Asked closed-ended questions when appropriate. _____
5. Asked questions about strengths. _____

Problem/Challenge, Person, and Situation

Give one point for each topic discussed.

Problems or Challenges

Previous attempts to solve problem _____
History of the problem(s) _____
Severity or intensity of the problem(s) _____

continued

PRACTICE EXERCISE 5 | SEEKING CLARIFICATION AND FURTHER UNDERSTANDING *continued*

Person

Feelings about having the problem(s)   _____
Effects of the problem(s) on other areas   _____
(such as health, sleeping, ability to function at school or work)

Personal strengths   _____

Situation

Effects of the problem on other persons   _____
Available social support and/or strengths in environment   _____
Other demands and stresses in the situation/environment   _____

Seeking Clarification

Give one point for each skill used by the practitioner.

1. Exploring the meaning of words and body language   _____
2. Exploring the basis of conclusions drawn by client   _____
3. Eliciting further clarifying information   _____
4. Allowing silence   _____

Common Mistakes or Inappropriate Responses (subtract 1 point for each)   _____

(offering advice, reassuring, offering excuses, asking leading questions, dominating
through teaching, labeling, interrogating)

Core Interpersonal Qualities

Using the scales in Appendix A, evaluate the appropriateness and effectiveness of
the practitioner's expression of empathy, warmth, and respect. On the following
lines write the scores, from 1 to 5, for warmth, empathy, and respect.

Score for warmth   _____
Score for empathy   _____
Score for respect   _____

EXPECTED COMPETENCIES

In this chapter, you learned to use questions to clarify what the client is saying.

You should now be able to:

- Identify the practitioner's tasks related to going further.
- Give examples of questions (with individuals, groups, and families) that invite a deeper understanding of what the client is saying by seeking clarification.
- Identify when allowing silence is important.

- Give an example of a question that explores previous attempts to solve the problem, the history of the problem, and severity or intensity of the problem.
- Give an example of a question that explores feelings about the problem and effects of the problem on functioning.
- Demonstrate appropriately seeking clarification.
- Demonstrate gaining further understanding related to person, problem, and situation.

Assessing Readiness and Motivation

CHAPTER 10

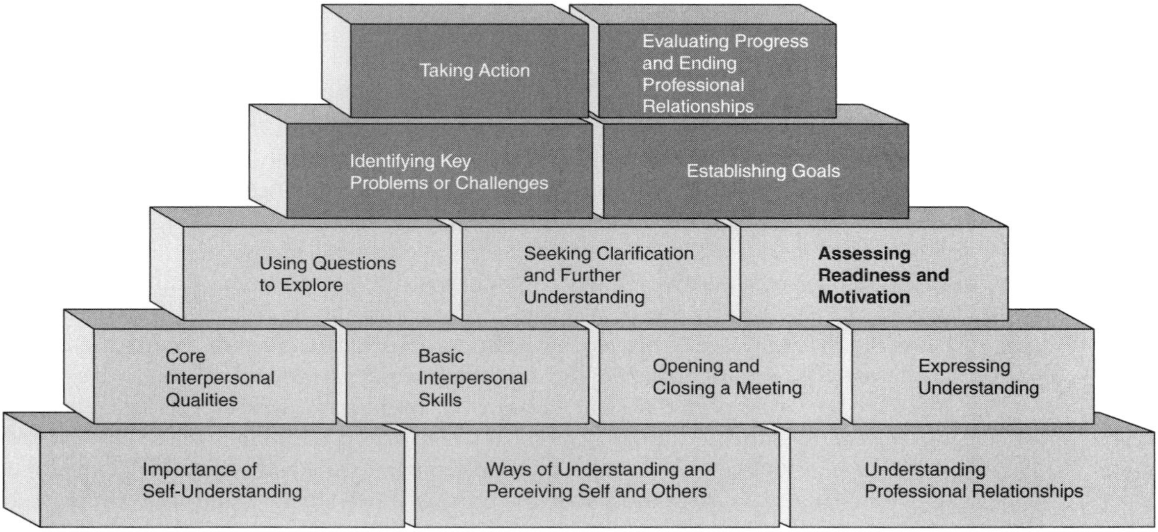
Taking Action
Evaluating Progress and Ending Professional Relationships
Identifying Key Problems or Challenges
Establishing Goals
Using Questions to Explore
Seeking Clarification and Further Understanding
Assessing Readiness and Motivation
Core Interpersonal Qualities
Basic Interpersonal Skills
Opening and Closing a Meeting
Expressing Understanding
Importance of Self-Understanding
Ways of Understanding and Perceiving Self and Others
Understanding Professional Relationships

In this chapter you will learn about the following topics:

Practitioner Tasks
- Assessing level of readiness
- Assessing level of motivation

Practitioner Skills
- Willingness to thoughtfully consider and accept what the client is ready and able to do at this time

Client Attributes
- Willingness to discuss readiness to do the work

After fully exploring the problems, persons, and situation, the practitioner needs to assess clients' readiness to make changes and their motivation to change. Some clients are required or forced to go to counseling and have little interest in making changes. As you explore with clients their problems and situations, you will find that some clients feel they had to go to a practitioner but have no interest in making changes, some are just beginning to think about making changes, and others are ready to focus on changes. Still others have begun to solve problems and need help in taking the necessary steps to achieve their goals. Skillful practitioners explore clients' levels of readiness and motivation before beginning to identify problems and goals.

STAGES OF READINESS TO CHANGE

Prochaska (1999) identified five stages of change discovered through research on the processes of change as people modify their health habits (smoking cessation, weight reduction, and sobriety). The stages-of-change theory has since been applied to other areas, including couples and marital counseling, and the counseling of violent criminals, child sexual offenders, and batterers (Baucom, Shoham, Mueser, Daiuto, & Stickle, 1998; Belcher et al., 1998; Dowden & Andrews, 2000; Fishman, Taplin, Meyer, & Barlow, 2000; Kear-Colwell & Pollock, 1997; Trevos, Quick, & Yanduli, 2000; Walker Daniels & Murphy, 1997). To establish effective working relationships with clients, it is important for practitioners to understand the readiness of the client to change and to work appropriately with the client at his or her level. This can be especially challenging when working with a group or family that has members at different stages of readiness for change. Although we know that people move through these stages as they face making changes, we also know that the process is not always sequential. People may move to the next stage for a while and then move back to a previous stage, possibly because of fear of what lasting changes may cost them or maybe because other demands in their lives are taking precedence.

PRE-CONTEMPLATION

The initial stage of readiness for change is *pre-contemplation*. At this stage clients do not see the need for change in their actions or feelings. They often do not see their behavior or situation as a problem that should be addressed, may not connect their problems with anything that can be changed, or may blame problems on others.

These clients sometimes see practitioners because someone else encouraged or required them to do so.

Examples of People in the Pre-contemplation Stage

- A person who abuses substances but, despite many arrests for driving under the influence, does not consider himself or herself to have a problem that needs to be addressed.
- A gang that lives in a community with high levels of violence but who believe they can continue perpetrating violence and not be personally affected.
- A husband who comes along to counseling because his wife thinks they have problems but who doesn't see any problems himself.
- A person who has had a serious health crisis and has been told to change his or her eating habits but states, "I have always eaten this way, and I am not going to change now."

Practitioners working with clients in the pre-contemplation stage should focus on raising their clients' awareness of the urgency of the issues and the pain and fear that these issues might cause. Practitioners may also attempt to engender hope that things can be different. It is not possible to set goals for behavioral change with people who are in this stage. The change that is desirable is to help clients move toward contemplating that a change could improve their lives. Specific ways of working with people in each stage of change will be discussed in Chapter 11.

CONTEMPLATION

The second stage of readiness for change is *contemplation*. At this stage the individual or group is aware that there is a problem, but they are not yet ready to pay the price of change. In this stage people are thinking about the possible costs and benefits of changing. It may be helpful for the practitioner to discuss the client's perception of both the advantages and disadvantages of changing. The client may view change as a future possibility but not something to commit to now. A client may state that "sometime" in the next six months or a year s/he may be interested in making some changes.

Examples of Statements Made by Clients in the Contemplation Stage

- "I am just not ready to make any changes right now."
- "I have wondered if some of the problems on this team are because I am kind of dominating, but on the other hand, I think we get more accomplished because I am pushy."
- "My boss thinks I should get over my fear of making speeches, but I am just not sure if that is something I can do."
- "I keep getting sent to the principal's office for fighting and then I can't play in the next football game. I don't like getting in trouble, but I have to stand up for myself."
- "We have talked about forming a committee to address some of the problems in this organization, but I wonder if we could really accomplish anything."

In working with clients who are at this stage, practitioners need to carefully propose small steps that may lead to a greater willingness to change in the near future.

In the case of a married couple who do not spend enough time together to develop a healthy relationship, the practitioner may decide to focus on the pleasure derived from the few times they were together or the joy they experienced in their relationship before they were married. Exploring these feelings may encourage the partners to think about changes they could make to spend more time together.

PREPARATION

The third stage of readiness for change is *preparation*. Usually at this stage clients are preparing to set goals and are thinking about the steps necessary to achieve their goals. Often they have already made some progress and are planning to make more progress. Goals can now be delineated more clearly, and the timing of beginning steps can be proposed. Generally people need to be at this stage before a major change will be possible.

Examples of People in the Preparation Stage
- A person who has been told to prepare to move into a supervisory role and seeks counseling with the goal of gaining confidence in his or her ability to supervise other people.
- A task group that has decided to work on a particular problem and asks a practitioner to help them set realistic goals and develop an action plan.
- A couple who are committed to working out their problems and ask for help in learning to solve particular issues.

Working with people's readiness to change can be very challenging in the case of families and community groups. Sometimes a loud naysayer will stop or slow down the whole process. It is then necessary to explore that person's hesitation or ambivalence about making a change. S/he is likely in either the pre-contemplation or contemplation stage. Sometimes people who are not ready to make a change will be willing to give up their resistance and allow the other group members to carry the project forward. In other situations, a person who isn't necessarily opposed to a goal but isn't willing to work to achieve the goal will choose to work on another committee or on a part of the project they can support.

ACTION

The fourth stage is the *action* stage. In the action stage, clients are ready to take specific steps and may even take steps with little or no support from the practitioner. Many people who are ready to make changes do so without seeking help. Those in the action stage may only need the practitioner's reinforcement, some new information to help them be more creative in seeking change, or help in seeing which of their previous efforts have worked or not worked. Clients in this stage make practitioners look good because they quickly set goals and take action.

Examples of People in the Action Stage
- An obese client, when faced with life-threatening eating issues, joins Weight Watchers, learns to follow the program, and loses a significant amount of weight.

- A parent, whose children have been removed from the home because the parent used harsh, abusive means of discipline, says that s/he wants to learn other ways to discipline, willingly goes to a parenting class, and talks with the practitioner about ways to use what s/he is learning.
- A child realizes that s/he will not be able to play on a team without earning passing grades and starts attending an after-school tutoring class in order to bring up his or her grades.
- A task group establishes a clear goal, identifies steps to achieve their goal, and talks with a practitioner about ways to work together most effectively.

If the practitioner assumes that clients are ready for action before they are really ready, the practitioner may become frustrated when there is no movement on proposed goals or when goals are hard to clarify. Clients may feel ashamed that they don't seem to be able to make the changes the practitioner has suggested. Because many clients are not ready to take action when they first seek the help of practitioners, it is important for practitioners to carefully assess each client's level of readiness rather than to assume that every client who comes for help is at the preparation or action stage and to proceed based on this assumption.

MAINTENANCE

One of the most challenging stages is *maintenance*. This stage requires as much careful planning as the previous stages. Change upsets the balance of our lives. We want to celebrate changes without looking at how the changes will be maintained. Practitioners need to help clients develop ways to hold onto their successes and explore how past successes have been maintained.

Examples of Clients in the Maintenance Stage
- An organization develops more effective ways of problem-solving and plans regular meetings so potential problems can be addressed before they become bigger issues.
- An individual learns to stop procrastinating on projects and makes plans to check in with someone who will provide honest feedback about whether the problem seems to be reappearing.
- An alcoholic continues to be involved with AA.
- A person has lost weight with the help of Weight Watchers and continues to attend meetings at least once a month.

TERMINATION

In Prochaska's (1999) stages-of-change model, *termination* is not the end of the process but rather the point in time when there is no temptation to return to the problematic behavior. As you know from your own experience, it may take a very long time before you have complete confidence that you will never go back to the problematic behavior. For many people it will always be important to stay focused on maintaining the change. For example, an ex-smoker may report occasionally wanting a cigarette years after quitting.

Relapse is not uncommon with any major change. Clients need to be made aware of the possibility of relapse and helped to view relapse not as a failure but as a learning experience. Relapses can provide clients with the opportunity to learn ways to be increasingly successful in achieving their goals. When clients relapse they may go back to any one of the previous stages. Practitioners will have to assess which stage the clients are in as a result of their relapse and plan interventions accordingly. In Chapter 11 we will discuss further guidelines for choosing interventions appropriate to the level of the client's readiness to change.

HOMEWORK EXERCISE 10.1 | STAGES OF CHANGE

Generally, when we deal with problems we move through each stage of change. Identify the stage of change revealed in each of the following situations:

- If you have a sore tooth, your first thought is "It's probably nothing serious."
- As time goes by, you begin to think, "Maybe I should do something about it, but going to the dentist is painful and expensive, so maybe I can wait."
- You might then decide, "I am definitely going to call the dentist and make an appointment."

- You actually go in for the appointment.
- The dentist might recommend more regular check-ups in the future.

Now think about a change that you have made and identify each of the stages that you went through. Next, think about a problem or issue you have identified on which you have not taken action. What support would you need in order to move on to the next stage?

ASSESSING STAGE OF CHANGE

The following questions suggested by Norcross and colleagues (1989) are helpful to ask when determining a client's stage of readiness for change.

- "Do you currently have a problem with _____?"

  ○ If the answer is "yes," the client is in the contemplation, preparation, or action stage of change.
  ○ If the answer is "no," the client is in the pre-contemplation or maintenance stage of change.

- If the answer to the previous question is "yes," ask, "When do you intend to deal with the problem?"

  ○ If the answer is someday, the client is in the contemplation stage of change.
  ○ If the answer is in the next few weeks or some specific date in the near future, the client is in the preparation stage.
  ○ If the answer is "right now" or the client has already begun to deal with the problem, the client is in the action stage.

- If the answer to the previous question indicates that the client has no plans to deal with the problem, ask, "What leads you to say that?"
    - If the client responds, "Because it is not a problem," the client is in the pre-contemplation stage of change.
    - If the client responds, "Because I have already dealt with that problem," the client is in the maintenance stage of change (Prochaska, Norcross, & DiClemente, 1994).

The stages of readiness for change are summarized in Table 10-1.

TABLE 10.1 | STAGES OF CHANGE

Stage of Change	Brief Description
Pre-contemplation	Does not consider the issue to be a problem.
Contemplation	Is thinking about the problem but ambivalent about whether to address it or not. No intention to change within the next 6 months.
Preparation	Intends to take action within the next 30 days and has taken some behavioral steps in that direction.
Action	Is ready to take action or has changed overt behavior for less than 6 months.
Maintenance	Has changed overt behavior for more than 6 months.
Termination	No temptation or desire to engage in unhealthy behavior in any situation, and 100% self-efficacy or confidence that s/he can engage in healthy behavior in all situations. Even under stress, when depressed, bored, lonely or angry, still doesn't return to the previous habit.

HOMEWORK EXERCISE 10.2 | MATCHING THE PROBLEM STATEMENT TO THE CLIENT'S STAGE OF CHANGE

After each statement of the problem, identify the stage of change that the practitioner is describing to the client.

- "You have been unable to decide whether to continue in school or drop out."
- "It seems that this task group has reached your initial goals. You are now thinking about how to stabilize the changes you have made."
- "Your family has done a lot of talking about the level of fighting that has been happening recently. It seems like you have thought about the problem a lot and have decided on the steps to take to resolve it."
- "So your wife thinks you have a drinking problem, but you don't see this as a problem."
- "It sounds like you have decided to work together on a plan to enhance services for Mexican-American clients."

ASSESSING MOTIVATION TO CHANGE

In addition to assessing the client's level of readiness to change, practitioners must also consider the client's level of motivation related to the problem. The level of motivation depends on all the factors that influence clients to be compelled and/or have a need to act in order to resolve an issue or problem. Individual factors include resources, capacity, personal interest, amount of discomfort, involvement, and the belief that one is capable of taking the needed action. Motivation is also influenced by factors outside the individual, including pressure from family members or friends, from court orders (steps needed to regain custody of children), and societal pressure for public health (smoke-free workplaces and television advertisements about healthy behaviors, such as the importance of diet and exercise).

HOMEWORK EXERCISE 10.3 | MOTIVATION FOR CHANGE

Think of a time when you thought you ought to make a change in one of your habits. What factors encouraged you to make the change or motivated you, and what factors reduced your energy, enthusiasm, or motivation to make the change?

Motivation for change is affected by many things. If clients experience practitioners as being genuine, providing regular feedback, having positive regard, and being focused on their issues, motivation tends to increase. If practitioners are aware that there is tension or a breakdown in their collaboration with clients, then addressing this problem non-defensively and making the necessary adjustments in their own behavior enhances the motivation for change. In order to maintain motivation, it is important not only to notice possible problems in the relationship between the client and practitioner, but also to regularly ask for feedback from clients. Here are a few questions that practitioners might use (Norcross, 2007):

- "Would you tell me your thoughts about the progress you are making?"
- "Are you satisfied with the progress you are making?"
- "Are you satisfied with the way we are working together?"
- "How are you experiencing your relationship with me?"

Of course, if the client is dissatisfied in some way, it is important to explore the problem and work with the client to resolve it.

DISCOUNTING

An important step in determining a client's motivation to change is to assess whether the client identifies the problem as important, painful, or troubling enough to be worth the effort to fix, or if the client is discounting the problem. Discounting is a cognitive distortion that allows people to avoid dealing with a problem. Discounting is a thinking pattern that leads to denying the existence of problems or minimizing their significance (Melor & Sigmund, 1975). Motivation can be seriously limited by discounting. Individuals, couples, families, groups, and organizations all use this thinking pattern.

There are four levels of discounting. The most destructive type of discounting is thinking that there is no problem or denying that a problem exists. Examples of this type of discounting include an individual who thinks being 50 pounds overweight is not a problem, a family that believes disciplining children by hitting them with a belt isn't a problem, a task group that thinks the fact that they haven't started working on an assignment that is due in a few days is not a problem, and a business that thinks the fact that their product isn't completely safe will never cause them any problems.

The next level of discounting involves thinking the problem is not significant, but at least realizing it exists. This level is less serious but still prevents action toward solving the problem. Using the same examples, the overweight person could accept being 50 pounds overweight as a problem but not a serious one. The family might say that some people see hitting children with a belt as a problem, but it is not something for them to be concerned about because it doesn't happen very often. The task group could say that getting started late is a problem but not a serious one, because students work on things at the last minute all the time and they still get them done. The business could say that their product isn't completely safe but most people are not negatively affected so it's not important to change it.

There is no motivation to change a situation unless we identify it as a problem causing painful consequences and believe that something can be changed to alleviate these consequences. Discounting the solvability of a problem is not as serious as discounting the existence or the seriousness of the problem, but it still blocks motivation to make changes. At this level of discounting, the individual might say being 50 pounds overweight is a serious problem, but everyone in the family is overweight and there is nothing that can be done about it. The family recognizes that disciplining the children by hitting them with a belt is considered a serious problem by many people in their community, but they also believe that it is the only effective way that they can make their children behave. The task group could say, "We wanted to get a good grade on this project and knew that starting on it so late may mean that won't be possible, but everyone was too busy. We just couldn't do it any other way." The business could say that selling a product that is unsafe is taking a risk, but it is a profitable product and they don't know any way to improve its safety.

At the next level of discounting, the individual or group realize that others have changed this behavior or situation but do not think they can change. The individual might state, "I don't think I can lose weight, but I know that my friend has been able to." The family could say, "We haven't been able to discipline our children except by hitting them, but our neighbors took a parenting course and learned several new ways to discipline their children." The task group might state, "For this assignment we weren't able to start working until two days before the project was due, but some of the other groups in class somehow found enough time to work together." The business might say, "We haven't found any way to be profitable except by continuing to sell an unsafe product, but there are other similar companies who have found alternative safe and profitable products." In each case, change is only seen as possible for others. Clients who are discounting their ability to solve the problem may be at the contemplation level of readiness to change. They are beginning to think that the problem is solvable and to wonder if they could solve the problem.

If a practitioner determines that clients are discounting at any level, the first step is to help them understand that the problem exists, is serious, and is solvable by the client. This process of working through the levels of discounting might take considerable time. Since most of us are uncomfortable with change, discounting to avoid facing problems is quite common. Sometimes clients avoid the pain of one set of problems with addictions or other avoidance patterns. Discounting can be subtle, and if practitioners are not careful, they can find themselves convinced that the clients are correct in their perceptions. This is especially true if the practitioner has discounted a similar problem in his or her own life.

Some areas to consider when assessing discounting include the following:

- Does the client acknowledge that a problem exists?
- Does the client identify the problem as important or significant?
- Does the client believe that this type of problem can be solved?
- Does the client believe that s/he could possibly solve this problem?

Example of Discounting

Pretend that you just received a low grade on a paper. You might handle this painful situation by denying the problem: "It's nothing. Grades don't matter." Or you might minimize the significance: "One low grade isn't important." You could decide that nothing could be done about the problem: "That instructor is just a tough grader." Or maybe the problem could be solved, but not by you: "I know some people have gotten better grades after talking to the instructor about his expectations, but I can't go and talk to him. I am just too scared."

HOMEWORK EXERCISE 10.4 | DISCOUNTING

Think of a problem in your life that you have been discounting. Discuss this situation with a partner. Talk about ways you have avoided dealing with the problem. Note how you may have minimized the significance of the problem, underestimated your personal ability to solve the problem, or denied that the problem could be solved. Was there a time when you denied the existence of the problem and found ways to avoid feeling the pain that it was causing you?

OTHER FACTORS THAT INFLUENCE MOTIVATION TO CHANGE
STRENGTHS, CAPACITY, AND RESOURCES

In addition to recognizing a problem and believing that change is possible, the client's capacity, resources, and strengths also have significant effects on the level of motivation to change. You learned previously about identifying strengths in the client and the client's environment. Clients who have many personal strengths, good social support, and adequate resources tend to be more motivated than those with more limited strengths, social support, and resources. Remember what you learned about resilience in Chapter 2. Resilience is an important strength. Clients who are more resilient are likely to be more motivated because they know from previous experience that they are able to cope with challenges. For example, think about the possible differences in motivation in the following two female clients. Both clients came to the agency with concerns about their adolescent sons who had begun to perform poorly in school. Both clients have full-time jobs. Client A is married, is active in her church, lives near her family, and earns an adequate income. She has a positive outlook on life and believes that other people are helpful. Client B is a single mother who recently moved to town and has a poverty-level income. Because of the many challenges she has faced, she is discouraged about her life and does not have much confidence in the goodwill of other people. It is fairly easy to guess that client A, with good support, resources, and resilience, may have more energy or motivation available to focus on how to best help her son than does client B.

Below are some areas to assess when thinking about a client's strengths, capacities, and resources:

- Past ability to solve or manage problems
- Level of resilience (this includes such things as positive outlook, trust in others, confidence in ability to cope, positive self-esteem, and strong cultural identity)
- Common sense or ability to use past experience and knowledge to figure out what to do
- Support from friends, neighbors, church, family, community
- Financial support
- Eligibility for social service support
- Adequate housing
- Safe area to live
- Adequate schooling to obtain or maintain employment

HOMEWORK EXERCISE 10.5 | STRENGTHS, CAPACITY, AND RESOURCES

Talk to someone in your class about the strengths, resources, and capacities each of you have available to help with solving problems. Write out a list of strengths, capacities, and resources you each have. Create a list of at least 15 strengths, resources, and capacities that could help you deal with problems.

LEVEL OF STRESS AND DEMANDS

The level of stress and demands in a person's life also affects motivation. In Chapter 1 you learned that anything that upsets your normal routine is stressful. Stress becomes a problem when a person experiences more stressful events than s/he can cope with adequately. At that point the person becomes more vulnerable to accidents, illness, and inappropriate behavior. Similarly, we all have demands in our lives, but we only experience these demands as problems when the level of demands is higher than we can comfortably handle. For example, if students face numerous assignments that are due at the same time they are taking final exams, they might experience the demands as too high. After getting past exam week and turning in their papers, the same students would probably feel much less stress. Clients who have faced extensive stress in the last year and have high demands in their current lives often have more trouble staying energized or motivated to work on any problems that go beyond dealing with the stress and demands they face on a daily basis.

Let's go back to Clients A and B who were discussed previously. We know that Client B recently moved to this area and that moving is very stressful. What if we found out that she had gotten divorced in the last year and, because of the divorce, her financial situation changed and now she has to work full-time for the first time in many years? Client A has not experienced significant stress in the last year. Empathizing with Client B, you might guess that the additional problem of her son not doing well in school could make her feel overwhelmed and unable to cope. She might need to focus on her feelings about the changes in her life before she would have much motivation to work with her son.

Below are some areas to consider when assessing levels of stress and demands:

- Number of children and other people in the household
- Demands of job
- Caretaking responsibilities for family members
- Deaths, illnesses, major health challenges
- Changes such as moving, job changes, marriage or divorce, new relationships, relationship break-ups
- Additional demands related to attending school, church involvement, volunteer activities, etc.

HOMEWORK EXERCISE 10.6 | IMPACT OF STRESS AND DEMANDS ON MOTIVATION

Think of a time in your life when you faced high levels of stress and demands. Now pretend that another problem has been added, such as finding out that one of your parents is ill and will soon be hospitalized. At this point, the stress and demands may seem beyond your coping skills. What would you do? Would your motivation to get high grades decrease? Would you act in ways that are atypical for you, such as withdrawing or being irritable?

HOPE

While high levels of stress or limited resources may weaken motivation, hope can serve to increase motivation and is critical to all practitioner-client relationships. Without hope, neither clients nor practitioners can effect change. By acknowledging clients' pain and helping them to feel hopeful that they can make the changes necessary to alleviate their problems, practitioners can enhance their motivation to move through the process of change.

Hope is created by many experiences. Think back to what you learned about worldview constructs in Chapter 2. People who believe that they have the power and capacity to change, that other people will help them, and/or that they can succeed in the world are likely to be hopeful. Belief in one's ability to make a change—a sense of capability to bring about a desired effect—is an important element of hope (Bandura, 1989; Bodenheimer, Lorig, Holman, & Grumbach, 2002). Another element of hope is having an internal locus of control. A person with an internal locus of control believes that his or her behavior will produce desired changes. A person with an external locus of control, by contrast, believes that there is no connection between his or her behavior and the desired outcome (Beyeback, Morejon, Palenzuela, & Rodriguez-Arias, 1996).

Various life experiences influence an individual's sense of hope. Martin Luther King, in his well-known speech "I Have a Dream," engendered hope in a community of people who had lost hope as a result of oppression. Others may have lost hope due to illness, poverty, cultural or religious beliefs, or continued experiences of rejection or failure. Considerable support from others may be needed to renew hope. Many clients come to practitioners because they cannot see any way to solve their problems. They feel hopeless and stuck. When hope is renewed, it provides the energy that will drive the changes that they want to make in their lives.

Practitioners can help clients feel more hopeful. They bring their previous experience, education, and beliefs about change to any meeting with clients. When change is not as quick or easy as clients want, practitioners provide support and encouragement that change is possible. Mahoney (2003) calls those working in the helping professions "socially sanctioned protectors of hope" (p. 196). A worldview that protects the practitioner's sense of hope is essential. Otherwise, burnout and cynicism will result from the type of work that brings healers into difficult and painful situations. However, developing positive future visions (Murphy & Dillon, 2003) does not mean that practitioners gloss over pain or offer false reassurance of quick and easy solutions to problems. Maintaining hope in the face of what can seem like insurmountable problems to clients is what practitioners must learn to do (Hanna, 2002). Once practitioners have listened to the client's pain and expressed empathy, they can focus on the potential within the person or the situation.

Another element of hope is the *placebo effect*. Research on counseling and medicine consistently shows that when people believe that something will help them, it often does. In medical research a high percent of improvement has been shown to be due to the placebo effect (Cho, 2005; Wylie, 1996). Practitioners' belief in the efficacy of their methods has a powerful effect on clients (Wampold, 2001). In counseling situations, studies demonstrated that clients who expect therapy to be successful experience more gains (Frank & Frank, 1991; Kim, Ng, & Ahn, 2005). In situations when the client does not have positive expectations and is feeling discouraged about the possibilities for change, the practitioner can enhance hope by focusing on each small improvement made by the client. Another way to enhance hope is by focusing on what the future will be like after the problems have been solved. "The simple act of imagining a different future can free clients from a hopeless perspective" (Butler & Powers, 1996, p. 231). In studies of what clients identify as helpful, 58% reported that *acquiring hope* was important (Murphy, Cramer, & Lillie, 1984; Steinglass, Bennet, & Wolin, 1987).

Let's go back to Clients A and B and add hope into the equation. We know that Client B has limited social support and resources and a heavy burden of stress and demands in her life. What if she also is feeling hopeless and says, "You know, my son has always had trouble in school. I never believed he'd be able to go all the way through high school." This low level of hope will further decrease her motivation. If the same client said, "My son is very intelligent. He has always been a good student. These problems started after we moved and he enrolled in this new school. I think there have just been too many changes in the last year for all of us." What level of hope does that statement indicate?

Below are some areas to consider when assessing levels of hope:

- the client's belief that s/he may be able to make needed changes
- problems the client has solved in the past

- successes the client has had in resolving past challenges
- the client's belief in the practitioner's ability to help
- the client's belief in his or her ability to be effective, to reach goals, and/or to take action

HOMEWORK EXERCISE 10.7 | HOPE

Think of a time when you had a problem and felt confident and hopeful that you could resolve it. What was that experience like for you? What role do you believe that your hope for success played in your ability to solve the problem?

Now think of a time when you had a problem and felt hopeless about getting it solved. What was that experience like for you? What role do you believe that your sense of hopelessness played in your ability to solve or not solve the problem? What if you had talked to someone who told you they had helped someone with a similar problem before and felt confident that they could help you? How would that have affected your level of hope?

CASE | CASE, PART 3: SECOND MEETING WITH JILL

SYLVIA: So how did this week go for you?

JILL: Well, it was about the same, I guess. I was hoping that I would feel better by now and it was a little better, but not much has changed.

SYLVIA: It sounds like you are a little disappointed that things have not improved as much as you hoped they would. Is there anything in particular that you were hoping would change?

JILL: I just thought that talking about all of this would make me feel better. I really want to get back to my old self and I guess I was hoping that talking to you would have made that happen.

SYLVIA: What is your "old self" like?

Jill proceeds to tell Sylvia about her love for the outdoors, including hiking, fishing, running, going to the beach, and socializing with friends in her spare time. She also noted that she enjoyed preparing for class and doing a good job with her students.

SYLVIA: You have generally enjoyed staying active, and it sounds like this break-up and new job have really put a damper on your ability to continue doing the things you love.

JILL: Absolutely! I am tired of sitting around my house all the time, but I don't know what to do because everything I do reminds me of Seth, my ex-boyfriend. I never did any of those things alone...he was always with me...and we did these things together in college, too...so now I just go to work, come home, correct papers, cry a little and go to bed unless one of my friends calls and forces me to do something. (*She begins to cry.*) I guess I'll just have to get used to being alone.

SYLVIA: Tell me more about what it feels like to be alone.

JILL: (*long pause*) I guess I'm so used to being with Seth, I've forgotten how to be on my own. I've never really been on my own because we've been together since college. Now I just go to work and come home to my empty apartment. (*Her voice gets louder.*) This was not what I expected my life to be right now. I should have been planning a wedding!

SYLVIA: It sounds like you are really sad and disappointed.

JILL: I guess I am also angry at Seth for doing this to me. I miss the fun times I used to have with Seth and with my friends. I just wish I could stop thinking about him so much. It makes me sad and then I get discouraged and don't feel like doing anything. I want to get back to the old me, but I don't know how. Can you help me?

| CASE | CASE, PART 3 SECOND MEETING WITH JILL *continued* |

SYLVIA: Yes, I can. We are about out of time for today. In our next meeting, let's spend some time talking about the problems you really want to focus on and figure out what your goals are. Will you think about your goals between now and our next meeting?

JILL: Yes, I will do that.

Questions

1. What new facts have you learned?
2. What are your current impressions or hunches about the case?
3. What additional information do you need prior to your next meeting with this client? (Include this information in your report.)
4. What are the three most important issues or problems to address with the client?
5. What did the practitioner do well in this session?
6. What, if any, mistakes did the practitioner make?
7. Identify the ways that the practitioner used skills for seeking clarification. Are there any other points that you think should have been clarified? If so, name those points.

8. What strengths do you identify in the client? What might the practitioner have said to further highlight the client's strengths? What questions might the practitioner ask to further explore strengths?
9. What else do you think should be explored related to the people, the problems, and the situation?
10. Review what you learned in this chapter about assessing the client's stage of change. What do you think this client's stage of change is? What further exploration would you do to confirm that the client is in this stage of change?
11. Discuss the client's level of motivation. What else would you want to explore to further determine level of motivation?
12. Look back to the point in the meeting when Sylvia chose to explore Jill's feelings about being alone. Sylvia might have also asked Jill to talk more about her friends and their support of her. Write a script showing how Sylvia might have explored this topic further with Jill.

EXPECTED COMPETENCIES

In this chapter you have learned about assessing readiness to work on problems, the effect of discounting on motivation, and the importance of hope. You should now be able to:

- Describe the five stages of readiness for change identified by Prochaska (1999) and give an example of each stage.

- Give an example of a discounting statement.
- Identify factors that influence motivation.
- Name two ways practitioners can invite hope in clients.

DEFINING THE FOCUS OF WORK

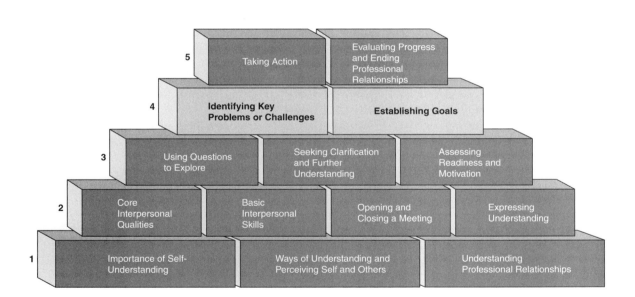

In this section we address ways to clarify client issues. This is one of the most challenging stages for most new practitioners. Without a clear understanding of problems and goals, clients will rarely take life-changing action. In Chapter 11 you will learn skills to help clients identify the problems they are ready and motivated to work on. In Chapter 12 we discuss practitioner tasks that encourage clients to create general goals as well as goals that are *M*easurable, *A*ttainable, *P*ositive, and *S*pecific (MAPS). If goals meet the MAPS criteria, successes are quickly evident and can be celebrated. By the end of this section, you will be ready to move on to learning about ways to help clients take action to reach their goals.

IDENTIFYING KEY PROBLEMS OR CHALLENGES

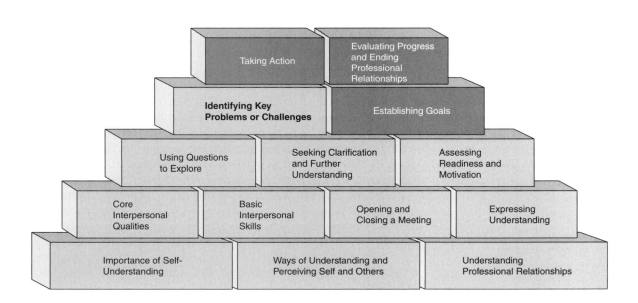

In this chapter you will learn about the following topics:

Practitioner Tasks
- Assisting clients to identify the challenges they are willing to work on
- Breaking those problems into manageable parts

Practitioner Skills
- Ability to appropriately use advanced reflecting, noticing patterns and themes, partializing problems, rolling with resistance, and identifying discrepancies

Client Attributes
- Willingness to move beyond blaming and to identify specific challenges to work on

After fully exploring the problems, persons, and situation and assessing the client's level of readiness and motivation, practitioners help clients identify their primary problems or the problems they want to focus on at this time. The process of helping a client move from statements such as "My life is just falling apart," or "This team will never be able to accomplish anything" to clearly stated problems can be challenging. Problem identification requires all the skills you have learned so far plus six new skills introduced in this chapter. Even the most experienced practitioner cannot identify problems for work if clients are not ready and willing to think about the part they play in the problems or to identify what they are willing to change. As we all know, looking honestly at our role in problems takes considerable strength and courage.

UNDERSTANDING THE CLIENT'S PROBLEMS

Some clients come to a practitioner with a clear idea of the problem(s) they are ready to focus on. For example, the client may be an individual or a family working with a hospital social worker to find appropriate placement for an elderly parent who needs ongoing medical care. A child may request to work with a school counselor due to his frustration with getting several low grades in math. An agency team must work together to figure out how to cut $10,000 from the budget, or a community has only one park that is rundown and unsafe for the children and wants to create options for safer places to play. Even in situations where the problem seems obvious and clear, a skilled practitioner will fully explore the issues, knowing that there may be many other problems that also need attention in order to solve the problem identified by the client. To follow up on the example of the child who got low grades in math, exploration might reveal that his dad, who always encouraged him in math and is very good at math, separated from the family and moved out of town. Now the child rarely sees his father. If the practitioner accepted the low grades in arithmetic as the only problem to address, s/he might refer the child to a female math tutor. This intervention might not be helpful because the child's problem of missing the support and encouragement of his father would not be addressed.

Learning to think like a professional is a complicated process. To make it easier to conceptualize how to move from hearing clients discuss their problems to clearly identifying the problems and goals, it might be helpful for you to think through a process that may be more familiar, such as dealing with a leaky roof.

Imagine you are working for a home repair company. A couple comes to you complaining that their roof is leaking and asks you to fix the problem. There are a number of steps to take to determine exactly what you can and will do to help the couple with their problem. As you are exploring the problem, you should also be developing a relationship with the couple. Without some sense of trust and connection, the potential customers might go to another repair company. The problem exploration will probably include determining the answers to the following questions:

- What is the extent of the problem?
- How is the problem affecting the structure of the house and those who live in it?
- How long has the problem been in existence?
- How frequently does the roof leak, and how much water comes in?
- What has caused the problem?

  - Is it due to neighbors throwing rocks and breaking the roofing material so that even if it is fixed the neighbors may destroy the repairs?
  - Is it due to a lack of maintenance or the number of years since the roof was last repaired?
  - Is it a superficial problem or one that indicates that the entire roof needs to be replaced?

- How urgent is it that the problem be solved?
- Is there an emergency?
- Could the leak be an indication that the foundation is unsound and the entire house is sinking and shifting so that even if the roof is repaired, it will likely leak again?

As an experienced home repair consultant or roofer, you must also consider such things as the homeowners' financial and time constraints. You should consider the homeowners' ability to deal with the disruption of repairs as well as costs. Some homeowners do not have the money to do any repairs and must learn to live with the leak. It may be that no amount of money will fix the roof for long, and the homeowners will have to decide how they want to respond to this news. It may be that the homeowners have the money to do the repairs but not the desire to do a thorough repair job, or they may not be ready to do the whole repair at this time. Rather than moving forward, the people with the leak may decide to do nothing or may just postpone any changes due to a lack of motivation to fix the problem now since the rainy season is almost over. As discussed in the last chapter, the practitioner, like the roofer, needs to fully explore the clients' readiness to make changes and work with what the client is ready to do. If the people with the leaky roof told you that all they were ready to do was put a piece of plastic over the hole in the roof, you might say that in your professional opinion that would only be a temporary fix; however, you could not make the homeowners replace the roof.

To continue this leaky roof scenario, you would also need to think about possible goals and/or other solutions to the problem. You might think that the most appropriate goal would be to rework the foundation of the house so that it provides more support for the walls and subsequently, the roof. You might recommend a new roof if the foundation is strong. You would know that, if necessary, the homeowners could do as little as putting a piece of plastic over the hole in the roof. You could talk with the homeowners about the possible goals, but it is up to the people with the leaky roof to decide which goal is appropriate. The practitioner, like the roofer, must fully explore the problem and the clients' readiness to make changes before talking with the clients about possible goals. Once the decision has been made about which goal is appropriate at this time, the roofer or practitioner will discuss the process the homeowners or clients will use to achieve the goal and complete the work. An agreement is reached and a contract is signed.

The process of coming to an agreement about problems and goals involves doing a thoughtful and complete assessment. When clients do not take steps to solve the problem and reach their goals, beginning practitioners may forget that a possible explanation is that the practitioner may be focusing on a problem that is not important to the client or one the client is not yet ready to solve. Think back to what you learned in Chapter 10 about readiness to solve problems and levels of motivation. Using our roofing example, the homeowners may be in the contemplation stage and thinking about the pros and cons of solving the problem, but not yet in the action phase and ready to solve the roof problem. The first problem the homeowners might need to address is the fact that they spend more money than they make and therefore have no extra money to deal with emergencies like the roof leaking. Maybe the problem is that the home-owners are stuck in low-paying jobs and just cannot get ahead financially until they work on the problem of having low-paying jobs. Many clients (or people who need roof repairs) do not seek professional help until the problems in their life have persisted for some time and seem overwhelming to them. Therefore practitioners need to carefully explore all aspects of the problems that are troubling their clients.

DEALING WITH CRISIS

In most client situations, there is plenty of time to fully explore the problems. However, in a crisis situation, the practitioner may have to take action quickly without fully exploring the problems. A crisis situation exists anytime the immediate problems are so serious that the individuals involved are in shock and/or are unable to cope with the situation. Crisis situations include such things as interpersonal violence (murder, rape, or bombings), major natural disasters (flood, tornados, fires, and hurricanes) or some form of personal loss (being fired, unexpected death of a family member, and sudden abandonment by a significant other). At a time of crisis, practitioners need to focus on dealing with the immediate needs of those involved. After assessing the level of the crisis, the practitioner needs to determine the most effective immediate response. When clients are in shock or are unable to cope, the practitioner may need to be much more directive than would usually be appropriate. If the practitioner has no training in dealing with crisis or the client needs the services of another professional such as a police officer, physician, or a clergy person, the practitioner needs to refer the client to the appropriate professional. When the crisis situation is defused, clients will then be able to cope with the remaining challenges. In the future, you will want to learn more about crisis intervention and the numerous ways crises can be handled. For now, here are a few guidelines:

1. Do your best to stay calm. Your ability to acknowledge the crisis and offer hope and help are essential. Slow breathing will help to keep you calm. You should also remind yourself that you can seek the help of your supervisor.

2. The safety of everyone involved is your first priority. How to create that safety is your first task. You may need to seek the help of others such as your supervisor, other practitioners, or other professionals. This is okay.
   You do not have to solve the issue on your own in order to appear competent and confident. Established professionals rely on each other in times of crisis.
3. At times of crisis it is particularly important to use all the skills you have learned so far: listen carefully, ask questions for clarification, and be empathic and warm.

HOMEWORK EXERCISE 11.1 | DEALING WITH CRISIS SITUATIONS

Describe a time when you or someone you know experienced a crisis. What helped most in resolving the situation? Did you get help from others? What happened once the crisis was over? Do you have residual feelings about the outcome of the crisis?

Sometimes unresolved feelings from our own personal crises can hinder our ability to handle the crises faced by our clients. What unresolved crisis from your life might hinder your ability to effectively help a client facing a similar crisis?

In every situation except crisis, practitioners and clients need to fully explore person, problem, and situation and assess stage of change and motivation before defining the problems clients are ready to focus on. Several new skills will be useful in this phase of work with clients. We will introduce these new skills by looking at the stages of change in which these skills are most helpful; however, you will find many other times when these skills are useful.

WORKING WITH CLIENTS IN THE PRE-CONTEMPLATION STAGE

Clients in the pre-contemplation stage do not see any need to make a change. They may not perceive their behaviors or feelings as problems or may not believe they are able to change. Practitioners working with clients in the pre-contemplation stage should focus on raising their awareness of the issues and the pain and fear that these issues might be causing. Practitioners may also attempt to engender the hope that things can be different. For clients in the pre-contemplation stage, practitioners work to help clients move toward contemplating that a change would improve their lives.

BLAMING OTHERS FOR THE PROBLEM

Sometimes people in the pre-contemplation stage begin the process of working with a practitioner by seeing the problems as belonging to someone else. When clients blame others for their problems, it is difficult to identify problems that they want to address. They tend to stay focused on wishing they could change the behavior of others. When clients believe their problems are the fault of others, they may believe that making changes is not possible.

If they are blaming others, individual clients may identify problems by making statements like these:

"My boss doesn't support me."

"My husband doesn't communicate with me, and he drinks too much."

"The Child Protective Service worker is unfair to me."

"The judge threw the book at me."

If the client is a family, they may identify the problem as failing to get along with their in-laws, the high crime rate in the neighborhood, or prejudiced teachers at their children's school. If the client is a group of teenage boys referred to counseling by the probation department, they might identify the problem as laws that are too harsh, a "mean" probation officer, or someone "out to get them." If the client is a neighborhood group, they might see the problem as the city failing to spend any money on their neighborhood, limited jobs because of businesses moving out, or neighbors leaving junk in their yards.

The challenge for the practitioner is to listen empathically to the clients' narrative, explore and express understanding of the client's challenges, and encourage clients to realize that they only have control over themselves. Moving the focus from something clients cannot change to something the client can change gives clients the opportunity to effectively make changes. As we all have experienced, complaining about someone else's behavior can continue indefinitely without resulting in any changes in the other person's behavior. When practitioners focus on what their clients can do, they are not denying the existence of problems beyond their clients' control. Rather, they are assisting their clients in working on aspects of the problems that are within the clients' own ability to change. Clients can learn to communicate effectively and assertively and invite others to make changes, but their work needs to focus on what they want to change about themselves.

Examples of Blaming Others for Problems and Ways to Respond

- If the client states that her boss is unfair to her, the practitioner might help the client see her part of the problem as her inability to figure out what she can do to be treated more fairly.
- If clients state that the problem is the city's failure to adequately maintain their neighborhood, the practitioner might help the clients to see part of the problem as their lack of information about how to effectively lobby for services.

In both of the above examples, the practitioner is not denying that there is an external problem (the boss is unfair or the city is negligent), rather, s/he is inviting the client to think about an aspect of the problem that the client has control over and can do something constructive to solve.

- If the mother is upset because her son is doing poorly in school and wants to make him bring up his grades, the practitioner will accept this as a valid concern and work with the mother to figure out what she wants to change about herself. Maybe the mother focuses too much on what the child is not doing, or maybe she hasn't encouraged him, or hasn't discussed the problem with his teachers. It may be that the practitioner would want to work with the mother and son together or even with the whole family.

- If the client is a young single mother of three children who states that she doesn't have enough money for food and housing even though she works full time, the practitioner can support her desire for more income so that she can better provide for her family. Many of us might say that part of the problem is the unavailability of adequate low-cost housing and the fact that the minimum wage is too low to support a family. However, in working with this particular client, our focus would be on the problem of helping her secure adequate housing and food for her family.

HOMEWORK EXERCISE 11.2 | BLAMING OTHERS FOR PROBLEMS

Seeing problems that others have is much easier than identifying and working on our own part of the problem. Think of some problem that you have (or have had) that involves at least one other person. If you are like most of us, you might have blamed the other person for the problem. Striving to be as honest as possible, identify your part of the problem or the aspect of the problem that you are willing to consider addressing. What might you change to contribute to the solution to the problem?

One method that can help clients to accomplish the various tasks required to move from one stage to the next is *motivational interviewing* (Miller & Rollnick, 2002). This type of interviewing is particularly useful in the early stages of change. Motivational interviewing involves four skills: *rolling with resistance, identifying discrepancies, expressing empathy,* and *supporting self-efficacy*. Rolling with resistance and identifying discrepancies are often helpful when working with clients in the pre-contemplation stage of client change.

ROLLING WITH RESISTANCE

Clients in the pre-contemplation stage have often been considered resistant because they are not ready to deal with problems other people have identified as important. Pushing these clients to accept another person's view of the problem often strengthens their resolve to do it their own way. Rolling with resistance is a motivational interviewing strategy based on the assumption that clients have valid insights and ideas about their situation. With this technique, arguments for change are avoided. Instead, the practitioner expresses understanding of the client's viewpoint and asks the client what changes, if any, s/he wants to make.

Rather than directly opposing resistance, practitioners focus on accepting and understanding the client's point of view and indicating their willingness to work on the problem identified by the client. For clients in the pre-contemplation stage, the task may be deciding whether a particular situation is a problem or not. For example, when working with a neighborhood group that is being pushed to do something about the potholes in the street, the practitioner might say, "I understand that some people see the potholes as a problem that should be solved, and others of you seem discouraged and don't think anything can be accomplished. We could focus on either of those problems." With this statement, the practitioner demonstrates willingness to work on whatever the neighborhood chooses to focus on. When working with a teen who has been sent to the practitioner by his parents because he is not spending enough time studying, the practitioner might say, "I can see that you are having trouble deciding between hanging out with your friends and spending time studying. Sometimes it's hard to see the value of doing something that you don't particularly want to do. Is there any part of what is happening that is a problem you want to work on?" When working with a family who has been told they must make their 14-year-old child go to school every day, the practitioner might say, "It sounds like you are really struggling with making enough money to pay your bills. I can see how also trying to figure out a way to be at home in the morning when your daughter should be leaving for school seems like too much to do. Is there some aspect of the problems you are facing that you want to work on?"

HOMEWORK EXERCISE 11.3 | ROLLING WITH RESISTANCE

Think of a time in your own life when instead of rolling with resistance you pushed against resistance. For example, maybe your friend, partner, or spouse said, "I don't care how much money I owe. I am going to get this great new car." You responded by saying, "Maybe you should wait until you have gotten yourself out of debt before getting a new car." What are your guesses about what the other person might say? Often when you push against resistance, the other person pushes back by making his or her position even stronger. In the above example if you had said, "It sounds like you really want the new car but are also a bit concerned about how much money you owe." How do you think the other person might have responded to this statement?

Resistance often occurs when clients are required to see a practitioner and are resentful about being required to seek help in correcting a problem they have not identified. Rolling with resistance with involuntary clients involves exploring their willingness to consider other problems. These clients are in the pre-contemplation stage for the problem requiring the referral, but they may be ready to work on another problem they themselves define. For example, if Child Protective Services requires that a mother see a practitioner to learn new systems of parenting, she might be angry at the system that is forcing her to see a practitioner. This anger might be expressed as resistance. When asked if there are any problems she would like to work on, she might say, "Get Child Protective Services out of my life." The practitioner could reach for agreement on the problem by saying, "So you have been unable to figure out a way to get Child Protective Services out of your life, and" (moving on to a general goal) "you want to figure out how to do that. Do I have that right?" Now instead of the client and practitioner pushing against each other, they can work together. The client will probably realize that she will need to learn some new parenting methods in order to achieve her goal of getting Child Protective Services out of her life.

Here is another example of exploring other problems with clients. An adolescent boy was referred to group counseling because his probation officer wanted him to stop shoplifting and cutting school. When the practitioner talked to the boy about the problems in his life, he said he was upset that a girl in his math class didn't want to go out with him. The practitioner agreed that not being able to get a date with a girl he liked was a problem. She suggested that they could focus on that problem. As the work proceeded, the boy realized that truancy and shoplifting were not effective ways to interest the girl. As he worked on achieving his goal, he also changed the behaviors that led to the referral.

HOMEWORK EXERCISE 11.4 | Rolling with Resistance through Exploring Other Problems

Think of a time in your life (or in the life of someone you know) when some person in authority defined a problem and said you had to work on it. How did you feel (or, if it happened to someone else, how would you have felt)? What level of readiness did you have to work on the problem? What level of motivation did you have? Would you have felt willing to work with a practitioner to solve this problem?

IDENTIFYING DISCREPANCIES

Identifying discrepancies is a motivational interviewing strategy that can be used with all stages of change, but it is particularly helpful when working with clients in the pre-contemplation and contemplation stages of readiness. Identifying discrepancies involves pointing out an incongruity between the client's present behavior and his or her broader goals and values. For example, an adolescent girl complained about being required to be in counseling after fighting a number of times in school. The practitioner pointed out the discrepancy by saying, "I know you've said that you hate coming here and think it is a waste of time. I understand that you think the principal has no right to make you see me just because you have been fighting in the halls. It sounds like you'd really like to stop coming to see me. If you really don't want to have to come here, what do you think has to change to make that happen?" The practitioner is accepting and acknowledging the client's frustration and pointing out that the client has the power to change the situation. Seeing the discrepancy between present behavior and what the client values may increase the client's motivation to consider making changes. The same kind of statement could be made with a family, group, or organization. With a family, the practitioner might say, "I know you think the agency had no right to put your child in foster care. What do you think will have to change for you to get your child back home?" With an organization, "I know that you have been complaining about having to attend these training meetings. What do you think would have to change to get your supervisor to decide that you have had enough training?"

HOMEWORK EXERCISE 11.5 | Identifying Discrepancies

Think of three examples from your own life or from someone else's life when there has been a discrepancy between the stated value, wish, or hope and the behaviors.

WORKING WITH CLIENTS IN THE CONTEMPLATION STAGE

Clients in the contemplation stage of readiness are aware there is a problem. They recognize the advantages of changing but are also aware of the costs involved with these changes. With these clients, it is important for the practitioner to state or restate the problems or challenges to be sure there is a clear understanding. The practitioner may need to discuss the client's perception of both the advantages and disadvantages of making a change. The client may see making a change as a future possibility but not something to commit to right now. In working with clients at this stage, practitioners need to support the client's feelings of ambivalence toward making a change, help clients gain a clearer understanding of what they want, and help them become aware of patterns and themes related to their problem.

EXPRESSING EMPATHY

Expressing empathy is important with clients at all stages of change. The expression of empathy provides acceptance that facilitates change and is described as an essential skill in motivational interviewing. As you learned in Chapter 4, respectfully and skillfully listening to understand clients is core to the empathic process. In Chapter 7 you learned many skills to express understanding or empathy. For the client in the contemplation stage, acceptance of the ambivalence that is a normal part of the human experience is particularly important. A statement like the following indicates empathy for the client: "I understand that you think it would improve your health if you gave up smoking, but giving up smoking feels almost impossible." The practitioner does not have to agree with the client or have the same values in order to demonstrate empathy.

| **HOMEWORK EXERCISE 11.6** | EXPRESSING EMPATHY THROUGH ACCEPTANCE OF AMBIVALENCE |

Read each of the following statements and write a possible response that would express empathic understanding of ambivalence.

1. "I know I should start saving money, but there are just so many things I want to buy for the kids."
2. "I really want to do well in school, but when I take time to finish all my assignments in the evening, I don't have any time left for my husband and children."
3. "I know I sometimes drink a bit too much, but I work hard and deserve some time to just relax with my friends."

There are two other skills that practitioners use with clients in the contemplation stage as well as in the preparation and action stages: *advanced reflecting* and *noticing patterns and themes.* With these skills the practitioner goes beyond what the client says to point out new possibilities or insights. It is important to have a good working relationship with the client and a solid understanding of his or her perspective before using advanced reflecting and noticing patterns and themes.

ADVANCED REFLECTING

Advanced reflecting is another way of expressing understanding. It is similar to what many call advanced empathy, additive empathy, or going beyond (Cournoyer, 2004; Ivey & Ivey, 2003; Murphy & Dillon, 2003). Although similar to reflecting when the practitioner shares his or her understanding of what the client has expressed, advanced reflecting goes beyond what has been expressed to what is beneath or behind the expressed message. When using advanced reflecting, the practitioner identifies values, meanings, feelings, and expectations related to the problem. In advanced reflecting, the practitioner considers what s/he knows about the client as well as the practitioner's experience, knowledge, observations, and feelings. Since practitioners might share what they *sense* is going on with the client rather than what they *know,* they often begin with "it seems like" to express the tentative nature of the comment.

Often practitioners will comment on feelings, meanings, and values that have only been implied in the clients' previous comments. These may be feelings that have been hinted at but not spoken, such as hurt, sadness, or fear that is felt along with the anger that was expressed. Think of a time in your life when what you expressed was anger, and what you felt was disappointment and anger. Sometimes advanced reflecting is used to give voice to something that is implied (Egan, 2007). For example, maybe your client is talking about leaving his present job because his wife thinks he could make more money in another position. As the practitioner, you hear little enthusiasm or motivation to leave his present job. You might say, "I wonder if getting another job is something your wife wants you to do, but you are quite ambivalent about." Advanced reflecting can be used to help clients recognize what they really value, want, or need in a situation. For example, "It sounds like you value living within your means and feel troubled about the amount of credit card debt you and your wife have accumulated."

One of the purposes of advanced reflecting is to invite the client to have insight, self-awareness, and/or deeper understanding of his or her situation. This understanding is helpful as the client thinks about his or her part in the problem. Sharing intuitive hunches with clients can help clients gain a different perspective or a new understanding of their problems. Advanced reflecting skills also help clients move from focusing on the problems and challenges they blame on others to focusing on the meaning of the challenges in their lives. With more understanding, clients may be able to move from the contemplation stage to the preparation stage.

Examples of Advanced Reflecting

- "It seems like you feel angry because you value communication and he doesn't." (moving from focusing on the client's husband to identifying what the client values)
- "It sounds like you feel angry because you expect clear directions from your boss. Without clear directions you feel afraid about making mistakes." (moving from focusing on the boss to focusing on the client's need for clear directions)
- "You value open communication and haven't found a way to invite other members of this group to share openly." (moving from focusing on what the client thinks is wrong with the other group members to focusing on what the client values)
- "I hear that you are frustrated and think this group isn't accomplishing enough. It seems like you really want this task group to do well." (moving from focusing on what the client is frustrated about to what the client wants)
- "It seems like several folks in this agency are feeling impatient because the needs of the growing Hispanic population are not being adequately addressed by the agency. It sounds like addressing the needs of the Hispanic population is

something many of you value and think is important." (moving from focusing on what is wrong with services at the agency to what the people in the agency value)

- "I'm wondering if you feel like you aren't getting much recognition at work and being valued for your contribution is important to your job satisfaction." (moving from what the people at work aren't giving the client to what the client wants)
- "I have a sense that the group really wants to deal with this issue, but you are afraid of hurting one another's feelings." (moving from what the group members are afraid of to what they want)
- "It seems like you folks in the neighborhood really want to get this problem solved but are feeling pretty discouraged right now because the process seems difficult." (moving from how hard the process is to what the people want)

As you read the above examples, you might think what the client wants, values, or expects should be obvious. Actually clients often begin the process by focusing on or blaming others and have not thought about what they want, value, or expect. Once they move to thinking about their own needs, they are in a much better position to figure out which problem to address.

HOMEWORK EXERCISE 11.7 | ADVANCED REFLECTING

Using the little bit of information provided in each of the following statements, indicate which statement is an advanced-reflecting statement and which statement shows reflecting feeling and content.

1a. Your family has been troubled and hasn't done fun things together ever since your dad moved out.

1b. You value the fun times you have had with your family and wish you did more fun things together now.

2a. In this group you seem frustrated because I haven't told you how I think this problem should be solved.

2b. My sense is that you are hoping that someone would give you the solution.

3a. I believe that you folks really wish this problem were solved.

3b. It seems like folks in the group are feeling a bit scared or hesitant to take the next steps in solving this problem.

4a. You expect your girlfriend to call you and are disappointed and worried when she doesn't call.

4b. When your girlfriend doesn't call you, you feel worried.

5a. As I understand it, your partner has gotten mad at you because you aren't spending as much time with him as you used to.

5b. You are feeling a lot of conflict because you value spending time with your partner and also think it is important to spend time on your studies so you will do well in school.

6a. I hear that the folks at this neighborhood meeting are feeling quite worried about the recent arrest of someone selling drugs in the neighborhood.

6b. You folks value living in a drug-free neighborhood and hope it will be possible to find a way to curb the sale of drugs around here.

NOTICING PATTERNS AND THEMES

Practitioners must listen for themes or patterns related to interacting, behaving, thinking, and/or feeling that run through the meeting or a series of meetings. Part of the practitioner role is to assist clients to see patterns or themes related to their problems so that they can move one step closer to the preparation stage.

Although themes and patterns are similar concepts, there are differences between them. A theme refers to an idea or point of view shared by several people, whereas a pattern refers to a consistent way of thinking, feeling, or behaving. Noticing themes is particularly important when working with families and groups of all sizes and types. Practitioners working with families are more objective than the family members, and this allows them to see themes that the family might have missed. For example, when working with a family the practitioner might say, "As I see it, high achievement is something that is important to everyone in this family. Some of you are most interested in school achievement and others are more focused on other types of achievement like getting into the high school band. The fact that not everyone in the family is working to achieve high grades seems to be a problem. Is that right?" With a group, the practitioner may choose to point out the similarities between group members. For example, "As I understand it, most of you want to get this project completed, but some folks are pushing to work more hours than other folks are willing to work. It seems like this is leading to conflicts in the group. Is that right?" Or there might be a theme between what was said at the beginning of a meeting and at the end. For example, "At the beginning of this meeting a few people mentioned being concerned about their children's safety in the playground, and now that we are finishing up it sounds like almost everyone feels concerned enough about the children's safety to consider working on this problem."

When pointing out patterns, the practitioner might comment on similarities between the client's words and nonverbal communication. For example, "When you were talking about your best friend moving away, I noticed your eyes tearing up. Maybe dealing with your feelings about your friend is something you might want to work on." The practitioner might notice that whenever the client gets into difficult situations, s/he tries to escape, run away, or use some self-defeating behavior. In suggesting this might be a pattern, the practitioner might say, "It seems like before meetings with your boss you scare yourself by thinking about things your boss might be critical about. Then when you meet with your boss, you are hesitant and don't explain things clearly because you are scared. Does that sound right?" Another example of a pattern is, "You like watching football games with your friends, but when you hang out with these friends it seems like it usually leads to drinking too much and feeling guilty later. Is that how you see it?" Since the client might not be ready to hear or accept the pattern as valid, the practitioner should be tentative in the tone of voice s/he uses and check out his or her understanding of the client's issues.

Noticing patterns sometimes requires the practitioner to identify discrepancies among things that the client has said or done. The practitioner might also notice a difference between words and nonverbal communication. For example, "I heard you say that you feel resolved about the fact that your husband has been unemployed for 6 months, but I noticed that your shoulders became tense when you said that. I wonder if the stress related to his unemployment is still bothering you." Working with a group, the practitioner might say, "I have noticed that when we get to the point of talking about who will go to the administrator with proposals, most people get very quiet and then John finally agrees to do it. Does that sound right to you folks?"

Examples of Noticing Patterns and Themes

- *Client:* This paper has a life of its own. I've created a monster with it. I want it to be perfect, but I can't seem to get it right. I see it as a separate entity that is totally burning me up. I'm creating my own anxiety.

  Practitioner: In previous meetings you have mentioned having high expectations of yourself and then feeling afraid that you can't meet your expectations. (noticing a pattern)

  Client: Yeah...This seems to be a major part of my life! It's really annoying and frustrating. I haven't been able to get past it.

- *Practitioner:* I have heard you mention getting very upset when you feel unappreciated by your mother, and you have also mentioned feeling unappreciated at work. Does this happen in other areas of your life? (noticing a pattern)

- *Practitioner:* Do you think there is a connection between your belief that you won't do well and the fact that you freeze up when taking exams? (noticing a possible pattern)

- *Practitioner:* Tonight I have heard several people talking together about the need to have more streetlights in this neighborhood. (noticing a theme)

- *Practitioner:* When Chanté brought up her fears about her mother's health, I noticed that everyone got quiet. I wonder if this is a topic that is a problem for several people in the group and might be hard to talk about. (noticing a possible theme)

- *Practitioner:* As I listen to you discuss the problems in the agency, it sounds like many of you have talked about improving the services to your clients. I wonder if this is something you are ready to work on. (noticing a theme)

HOMEWORK EXERCISE 11.8 | Noticing Patterns and Themes

Think about one self-defeating behavior that you recognize in yourself. Write down what you know about the pattern. For example, maybe you are trying to lose weight but when you go to the store you frequently buy cookies or other baked goods while telling yourself you are getting them for someone else and then end up eating too much of them yourself. Now think about any group that you are involved with and identify a theme in the group.

It is particularly powerful to relate the themes or patterns that clients experience in their day-to-day lives to what is happening between the practitioner and the client during their meetings. The practitioner might say, "It seems like your high expectations of yourself have led you to believe that you need to have all the answers when you come into a meeting with me," or "You have said that when you are afraid you have difficulty talking. It seems like that might have happened here when I asked you to describe your past substance abuse." Noticing themes or patterns as they occur in the relationship between the practitioner and client can have a great deal of impact.

WORKING WITH CLIENTS IN THE PREPARATION STAGE

Clients in the preparation stage are preparing to set goals and thinking about the steps necessary to achieve their goals. They may have already made some progress and have plans to make more progress. Goals can now be delineated more clearly, and the timing of beginning steps can be proposed. Generally people need to be at this stage before a major change is possible. Practitioners help clients at this stage by breaking the problem into smaller, more manageable parts and enhancing the clients' sense of self-efficacy by supporting their belief that they are capable of success in making the necessary changes.

PARTIALIZING

Clients in the preparation stage are ready to identify their role in problems and to begin setting goals. With these clients, it is important for the practitioner to state or restate the problems or challenges to be sure there is a clear understanding between the practitioner and the client. Often this communication will involve partializing, or breaking a complex problem into manageable parts. Because some problems can seem overwhelming, dividing the problem into smaller parts can make the problems seem more manageable. For example, if the client's problem is that she doesn't have enough money to pay the bills and feels scared, the practitioner might help the client see that the problem has several parts: the client has a minimum-wage job or is unemployed, the client's housing costs are too high, and/or the client is spending too much money on non-essential things. After dividing the problem into manageable parts, the practitioner may choose to work with the client to identify which difficulty should be addressed first. Sometimes it will be the problem that can be changed most easily and sometimes the problem that is causing the most pain to the client. Still other times it is the issue that will help solve other aspects of the problem. It is important to remember that the client's perception of what is manageable may be smaller than or different from what the practitioner might see as possible.

HOMEWORK EXERCISE 11.9 | PARTIALIZING

Think about some problem that you faced or a problem that someone you know has faced or is facing. Write out a plan in which you break the problem into several smaller, more manageable parts. You may want to challenge yourself to think of as many small parts as possible. It is important to generate these smaller parts of the problem since what seems like a manageable part to you may not seem so to others.

SUPPORTING SELF-EFFICACY

Another motivational interviewing skill that is particularly useful in the preparation phase is supporting self-efficacy. In Chapter 2 you learned about the value of empowerment. Self-efficacy involves believing in one's capacity to reach a goal. When supporting self-efficacy, practitioners encourage clients to acknowledge and believe in their ability to carry out and succeed with specific tasks. The general goal is to enhance clients' confidence and capability to cope with obstacles and to succeed in making changes. A statement that recognizes what the clients have already accomplished and identifies their strengths can support their belief in themselves. The skill of supporting self-efficacy is the same as the skill of identifying strengths that you learned in Chapter 7.

HOMEWORK EXERCISE 11.10 | SUPPORTING SELF-EFFICACY

Think of someone who believed in your ability to overcome your problems or who recognized your strengths and capacities. What influence did that person have on your life? If you can't think of an example in your life, think of an example from a family member or friend's life or even the life of someone you have read or heard about.

PROBLEM IDENTIFICATION

When helping clients identify problems, practitioners explore clients' strengths, environment, and general goals using all of the skills presented in this chapter as well as the previous chapters. If the client is an entire family, the practitioner might ask each person in the family what s/he likes best about the family (strengths), what s/he wants changed in the family (problems), what their neighborhood is like (environment), and how s/he would like the family to be (goals). The same type of questions could be asked about a larger system such as an agency or a neighborhood. For example, when working with a neighborhood, the practitioner might ask what the people in the neighborhood like best about the neighborhood (strengths), what they would like changed about the neighborhood (problems), what the surrounding areas are like (larger system or environment), and how they would like the neighborhood to be (goals). Identifying specific goals will be covered in Chapter 12.

Even though as a practitioner you may think there is a clear understanding of the problem, you need to state your understanding to be sure that you and the client are in agreement. Since stating problems is not something that is generally done in ordinary conversations, many beginning practitioners feel awkward when stating the problem. As you experienced with previous skills, this awkwardness goes away with practice. When the client is ready to identify the problem and to work toward solving it, the practitioner states the problem in terms of something the client has so far been unable to achieve.

Examples of Practitioner Statements that Move from Reflecting Feeling and Content to Identifying the Problem

- "The way you see your boss managing the business is frustrating to you, and you wish he'd get organized." (reflecting feeling and content)

    "You wish that you could talk directly to your boss." (advanced reflecting)

    "Your inability to make recommendations to your boss is frustrating to you." (identifying the problem)

- "You sound disappointed in your friend because she frequently asks you for money." (reflecting feeling and content)

    "You have noticed that you sometimes say 'yes' and later regret it." (noticing a pattern)

"When being asked for money by your friend, you are not happy with your inability to say 'no.'" (identifying the problem)

- "You feel unhappy because it seems like the people in your family don't listen to you." (reflecting feeling and content)

  "Having your family listen to you is very important to you. (advanced reflecting)

  "It seems like you haven't found a way to tell the folks in your family how important it is to you that they listen to you." (identifying the problem)

- "It sounds like some folks are disturbed because there hasn't been much openness in our group." (reflecting feelings and content)

  "I have heard several people say they wished for more openness in the group." (noticing a theme)

  "In this group it seems like folks have felt unable to be fully open with each other." (identifying the problem)

- "It seems like you are unhappy because the people in your family rarely spend time together." (reflecting feelings and content)

  "You really value spending time with your family." (advanced reflecting)

  "It seems like your family hasn't been able to figure out a way to spend more time together." (identifying the problem)

- "I understand that all of the people at this neighborhood meeting are feeling very disappointed that you didn't get any of the city's redevelopment money for your neighborhood." (reflecting feelings and content)

  "It sounds like most of you are interested in figuring out how to get a redevelopment grant." (noticing a theme)

  "It seems like you haven't been able to figure out how to successfully apply for the redevelopment money that is available." (identifying the problem)

Examples of Possible Problem Statements Related to Individuals, Families, Groups, and Neighborhoods

You have not been able to:

- Assert yourself when your rights are being violated.
- Listen to others without interrupting.
- Find a job with a salary above minimum wage.
- Express your anger and/or frustration without being abusive.
- Find time to spend with your children.
- Discipline your children without hitting them.
- Find a way to work, do well in school, and spend time with your family.
- Stop giving in to your child.
- Stop yourself from excessive drinking, eating, smoking, or spending money.
- Stop yourself from being overly critical and/or attacking others.
- Stop yelling and verbally attacking people when you are angry.
- Trust men/women/people.
- Stop criticizing yourself.

In your family you have not been able to:

- Communicate without yelling.
- Solve problems together.

- ○ Agree on appropriate rules.
- ○ Understand each other.
- ○ Find an adequate place to live.
- ○ Work together to reach goals.
- ○ Deal with the grief you feel.

In this group we have not been able to:

- ○ Trust each other with our feelings.
- ○ Treat each other respectfully.
- ○ Be honest about our thoughts about each other.
- ○ Support each other.
- ○ Clearly identify our goals.
- ○ Agree on a leadership plan.

In this neighborhood we have not been able to:

- ○ Reduce the crime rate.
- ○ Find a way to clean up the parks or get more playgrounds.
- ○ Work together to set goals.
- ○ Find a way to get the city to fill the potholes in the streets.
- ○ Figure out ways to accept the changes in the neighborhood from a racially homogenous neighborhood to a racially mixed neighborhood.
- ○ Find ways to effectively work with the school administration and teachers to improve the local schools.

HOMEWORK EXERCISE 11.11 | AGREEMENT ON PROBLEMS

Write at least four examples of other possible problems individuals, families, groups, or community associations might have to deal with.

ETHICAL CONSIDERATIONS IN PROBLEM IDENTIFICATION

The stages-of-change model and motivational interviewing both support essential ethical principles related to autonomy and self-determination (Ford, 2006). As a practitioner, it is important that you respect the rights of clients to make their own decisions about how they live their lives. Practitioners who believe clients have valid insights and ideas about their situation should demonstrate this belief by respecting the client's right to self-determination. Client decisions are influenced by culture, gender, age, and other factors that the practitioner may not fully understand. This right of autonomous self-determination should not be denied or interfered with by well-intentioned practitioners either through coercion or through undue influence. A practitioner's role is to support clients in the choices they make, even when the practitioner feels the client should make other choices. Ethically, practitioners should affirm the rights of clients to decide how to act as long as their behavior does not infringe upon the legal rights of others.

HOMEWORK EXERCISE 11.12 | PROBLEM IDENTIFICATION AND AUTONOMY AND SELF-DETERMINATION

Think of at least three times when you or someone you know was troubled about something and talked to another person about that concern. What if the other person said, "It seems to me your problem is...." That other person then follows up with, "What you really should do about that is...." The other person probably was trying to be helpful and was not in the role of practitioner.

Reflect on times when you have experienced this type of situation. How did you feel? What are your guesses about how the client might have felt and what the client might have thought if that kind of discussion happened between a practitioner and client? Do you think the client would have felt respected? Consider autonomy and self-determination. Would the client have thought the practitioner was respecting the client's autonomy and need for self-determination? If you had been the client, would you have continued working with the practitioner?

PRACTICE EXERCISE 6 | IDENTIFYING PROBLEMS AND CHALLENGES

Exercise Objectives
- To practice using skills that reach for agreement about problems or challenges.

Step 1: Preparation
Form groups of three people. Each person will have the opportunity to play the roles of client, practitioner, and peer supervisor. Each meeting will last about 10 minutes.

Client Role
- Think about a problem you can discuss with the practitioner.

Practitioner Role
- Although practitioners sometimes move to identifying problems in the first meeting, this task is often accomplished in subsequent meetings. Begin this and subsequent meetings as you would meetings after the first meeting. Review procedures for beginning a subsequent meeting in Chapter 6.
- Review the use of skills for identifying the problem: partializing, advanced reflecting, noticing patterns and themes, identifying discrepancies, rolling with resistance, and supporting self-efficacy.

Peer Supervisor Role
- Review the use of skills for identifying the problem: partializing, advanced reflecting, noticing patterns and themes, identifying discrepancies, rolling with resistance, supporting self-efficacy, and reaching agreement on problems.

- Prepare to record verbal responses of the practitioner and to keep track of the time.

Step 2: The Client Meeting
Client Role
- Tell your story, but stop talking after every few sentences to give the practitioner a chance to practice using his or her skills.

Practitioner Role
- Use all of the skills you have learned so far.
- Use any of the following skills as appropriate: partializing, advanced reflecting, noticing patterns and themes, identifying discrepancies, rolling with resistance, supporting self-efficacy, reaching agreement on problems.

Peer Supervisor Role
- Keep track of the time and tell the practitioner and client when 9 minutes are completed so the practitioner has time to close the meeting.
- Check off the beginning and ending skills used by the practitioner.
- Write down each practitioner statement and question. You may abbreviate, use a form of shorthand, or just write the first group of words in the statement, or you can tape record the interview and transcribe or listen to the tape.
- Check off inappropriate responses.

continued

PRACTICE EXERCISE 6 | IDENTIFYING PROBLEMS AND CHALLENGES *continued*

Step 3: Feedback

Client Role
- Describe how you experienced the practitioner.
- Identify any inappropriate responses.

Practitioner Role
- Evaluate her/his ability to reach agreement about the problems or challenges.
- Identify any inappropriate responses.

Peer Supervisor Role
- Give feedback to the practitioner from your notes on skills to reach agreement.
- Give feedback on inappropriate responses.
- Complete the evaluation form.
- Evaluate the practitioner's use of the core interpersonal qualities of warmth, empathy, and respect (all of the scales are in Appendix A).
- Record the feedback in the practitioner's book for future reference.

EVALUATION FORM: REACHING AGREEMENT ON THE PROBLEM

Name of Practitioner _____

Name of Peer Supervisor _____

Directions: Under each category (in italics) is a list of behaviors or skills. Give one check mark, worth one point, for each skill used by the practitioner.

Building Relationships

Beginning Subsequent Meetings

Give one point for each topic covered by the practitioner.

1. Asked client where s/he would like to begin.   _____
2. Summarized previous meeting.   _____
3. Identified tasks for this meeting.   _____
4. Asked client about progress.   _____
5. Asked client about homework.   _____
6. Asked client about problems.   _____
7. Made an observation about the previous meeting.   _____
8. Did a check-in.   _____

Closing Skills (for a meeting)

Give one point for each skill used by the practitioner.

1. Practitioner identified that the meeting(s) was about to end.   _____
2. Practitioner invited a summary of the meeting(s).   _____
3. Practitioner reviewed any tasks that the client agreed to complete.   _____
4. Practitioner discussed plans for future meetings.   _____
5. Practitioner invited client feedback about the work.   _____
6. Practitioner asked client about any final questions.   _____

Skills that Express Understanding

Give one point for each skill used by the practitioner.

1. Reflecting feelings   _____
2. Reflecting content   _____
3. Reflecting feelings and content   _____
4. Summarizing   _____

PRACTICE EXERCISE 6 | IDENTIFYING PROBLEMS AND CHALLENGES *continued*

5. Exploring meanings   _____
6. Identifying strengths   _____

Exploring

Questioning Skills

Give one point for each skill used by the practitioner.

1. Expressed understanding before asking questions.   _____
2. Asked open-ended questions when appropriate.   _____
3. Asked one question at a time.   _____
4. Asked closed-ended questions when appropriate.   _____
5. Asked questions about strengths.   _____

Person, Problem/Challenge, and Situation

Give one point for each topic discussed.

Problems or Challenges

Previous attempts to solve problem   _____
History of the problem(s)   _____
Severity or intensity of the problem(s)   _____

Person

Feelings about having the problem(s)   _____
Effects of the problem(s) on other areas   _____
(such as health, sleeping, ability to function at school or work)
Personal strengths   _____

Situation

Effects of the problem on other persons   _____
Available social support and strengths in environment   _____
Other demands and stresses in the situation/environment _____

Seeking Clarification

Give one point for each skill used by the practitioner.

1. Exploring the meaning of words and body language   _____
2. Exploring the basis of conclusions drawn by client   _____
3. Eliciting further clarifying information   _____
4. Allowing silence   _____

Defining the Focus

Reaching Agreement about Problems or Challenges

Give one point for each skill used by the practitioner. It rarely will be appropriate
to use all of these skills in one meeting.

1. Partializing   _____
2. Advanced reflecting   _____
3. Noticing patterns or themes   _____
4. Identifying discrepancies   _____
5. Rolling with resistance   _____

continued

PRACTICE EXERCISE 6 | IDENTIFYING PROBLEMS AND CHALLENGES *continued*

6. Supporting self-efficacy   _____
7. Stating agreement about problems or challenges   _____

Common Mistakes or Inappropriate Responses (subtract 1 point for each)   _____

(offering advice, reassuring, offering excuses, asking leading questions, dominating through teaching, labeling, interrogating)

Core Interpersonal Qualities

Using the scales in Appendix A, evaluate the appropriateness and effectiveness of the practitioner's expression of empathy, warmth, and respect. On the following lines write the scores, from 1 to 5, for warmth, empathy, and respect.

Score for warmth   _____
Score for empathy   _____
Score for respect   _____

EXPECTED COMPETENCIES

In this chapter you learned about identifying the client's key problems.

You should now be able to:

- Demonstrate how to help a client move from seeing the problem as belonging to someone else to something the client has the ability to change.
- Identify skills that can be used with clients in the pre-contemplation, contemplation, and preparation stages of change.

- Give examples of using the following skills: partializing, advanced reflecting, noticing patterns and themes, identifying discrepancies, rolling with resistance, supporting self-efficacy, and expressing empathy.
- Demonstrate the skills used to reach agreement on problems.

ESTABLISHING GOALS

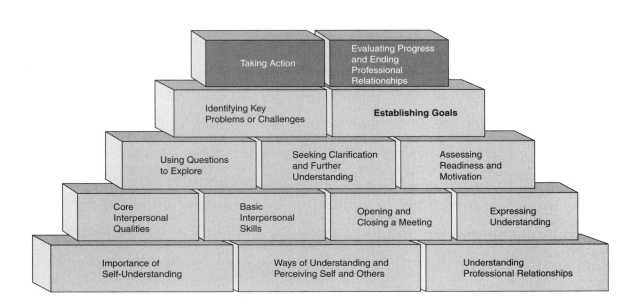

In this chapter, you will learn about the following topics:

Practitioner Tasks
- Helping clients to identify a general goal and move on to develop measurable, attainable, positive, and specific (MAPS) goals for each problem identified

Practitioner Skills
- Ability to use questions, summarize, and reflect to help the client define a measurable, attainable, positive, and specific goal

Client Attributes
- Willingness to think about their goals and to describe them clearly

After identifying the problems, practitioners help clients identify their goals. As in each previous phase of the work, the client's participation is critical to success. In this phase of the work, clients need to be willing to visualize and talk about the goal or goals they want to achieve. This chapter focuses on the process of reaching agreement about general and specific goals. Using all of the skills covered in the previous chapters, practitioners and clients come to an agreement on the primary goals for their work together.

IDENTIFYING GENERAL GOALS

Establishing goals is a crucial phase of the work done by the practitioner and client. Goals set the direction and focus of the work to be done. Clear goals are necessary in planning steps to be taken, reviewing and evaluating progress, and deciding when to end the relationship between the practitioner and client. In fact, setting goals is a task "that has received almost unanimous support" (Curtis, 2000, p. 194). Because many clients have had limited experience identifying or achieving goals, goal setting requires careful identification of the problems, thorough exploration of strengths and resources, and a focus on outcomes that will fit into the client's life.

Goals are what clients hope to achieve by working with the practitioner. They are the clients' vision of what life would be like if their problems were solved. The general goal may be the opposite of the problem. For example, if the problem is defined as "turning assignments in late," then the goal might be "turning assignments in on time." With a clear idea of the problem, clients can more easily identify their goals.

It is essential that goals be mutually established between practitioners and clients (Berg & Miller, 1992). Practitioners need to think about whether they are trying to direct clients toward certain goals or choosing goals for the clients. If the practitioner senses that s/he is working harder than the client, it is often because the practitioner has established a goal without adequate participation from the client.

Practitioners use many skills to help clients figure out their goals. Questions that seek clarification help clients figure out what goals they are motivated to achieve. In the solution-focused approach, for instance, clients are asked to describe what their life would be like if a miracle happened and the problems that led them to talk to a practitioner were solved (de Shazer & Molnar, 1984; Furman & Ahola, 1992; O'Hanlon & Weiner-Davis, 2003; Walter & Peller, 1992). To invite clients to think about goals, practitioners use open-ended questions that are focused on the future, such as the following:

- "At the end of our work together, what do you want your life to be like?"
- "When the problems that brought you here are solved, what do you want to be doing, feeling, or thinking?"
- "When we have finished our work together, what might other people see you doing that you aren't doing now?"
- "Tell me about your picture of what you want your family to be like."
- "Let's pretend that these problems are solved. What differences will you notice in your life (or in this group, or in this organization, or in this neighborhood)?"

Exception-finding questions can also be used to establish goals (de Shazer & Molnar, 1984; O'Hanlon & Weiner-Davis, 2003; Walter & Peller, 1992). Exception-finding questions explore times when the problem was not present. For example, "Think of a time when you didn't have this problem. What were you doing, feeling, or thinking at that time?" Even if clients can only think of a short period of time when the problem did not exist, a great deal of information can be gained about what the client's life is like when the problem is not present. This description of life without the problem may be what the client wants to establish as a goal. If clients can't identify a time when the problem was not present, it sometimes helps to ask about a time when the problem was smaller or less noticeable and to encourage the clients to think about what was happening that led to that decrease in the problem.

HOMEWORK EXERCISE 12.1 | General Goals

Review the list of examples of problem statements for individuals, families, groups, and neighborhoods on pages 155–156 and write a general goal for each problem in the list.

IDENTIFYING MEASURABLE, ATTAINABLE, POSITIVE, AND SPECIFIC (MAPS) GOALS

In some situations general goals are all that practitioners and clients develop. In other situations where there is more focus on evaluation of progress or outcomes, setting specific goals is important. To assess whether goals are achieved, clients must set goals that are measurable. Moving from general goals to Measurable, Attainable, Positive, and Specific (MAPS) goals often requires considerable work. MAPS goals need to be as clear and detailed as possible. For example, if the general goal is to use positive communication within the family, practitioners would ask a number of questions to move from the general goal to a MAPS goal. The following questions might be used:

- "Will you give me an example of what positive communication sounds like to you?"
- "When you have positive communication, what will you be doing that you aren't doing now?"
- "In what situations do you want to have more positive communication?"

As clients think about their answers to these questions, they often gain a clearer vision of their goal.

When clients are facing many problems, the practitioner may help them establish goals for each problem or may focus on establishing and working on one goal at a time. Working on one manageable goal can enhance the client's hope that other goals can be achieved. For example, a client may come in feeling depressed. Using the skills taught thus far, the practitioner determines that the depression began recently and is not part of a long-term pattern. The depressed mood seems to have developed in response to the death of the client's mother. Upon careful reflection, the practitioner finds that the problems leading to the depression can be partialized into worries about cleaning out and selling her mother's house, distributing the inheritance, and making arrangements for the care of a dependent sibling who had resided with her mother, as well as grief about her mother's death. After identifying the pieces of the overall problem, the practitioner and client will determine what aspect of the problem the client wishes to address first. After experiencing success in resolving one part of a multifaceted problem, clients usually feel more confident about their ability to address the remaining issues.

MEASURABLE AND SPECIFIC GOALS

The most helpful goals are those that are Measurable and Specific. Goals that are *measurable* and *specific* make it possible for clients and practitioners to evaluate whether the goals have been achieved. The client and practitioner can then acknowledge gains or changes that have been made. Setting measurable and specific goals also provides a clear direction or focus for the work. Clients and practitioners are more likely to be successful in creating solutions for problems if they have taken the time to figure out exactly what the goal is.

Some words that are commonly used in goal statements are not measurable and specific. Words such as "increase" and "more" are good starting points but not measurable until the practitioner obtains additional information. If the general goal is to get higher grades, the following questions can provide the information needed to make the goal measurable and specific:

- "Increase from what beginning point to what endpoint?"
- "How much do you want to raise your grades?"
- "When your grades are high enough to satisfy you, what grades will you be getting?"
- "How much more time do you plan to study?"

General goal statements also may include vague, non-specific words with unclear meanings. For example, a beginning practitioner set the following goal with an inner-city teenager: "I will increase my self-esteem." We have already discussed problems with the word "increase," but what about "self-esteem?" That sounds like the practitioner's language, not the teenager's, and self-esteem can be defined in many ways. If a word such as "self-esteem" is used, it is best to ask the client what s/he would be doing differently if s/he had a higher level of self-esteem. Another commonly used phrase is "improved communication." Again, each person's idea of what improved communication means is different, so the practitioner should ask the client for more specifics. For example, "When you begin communicating better, what will you be doing that you are not doing now?" Or, "What will improved communication sound like?" One of the authors remembers a wife who said that she wanted her husband to show her that he loved her. When asked, "What could your husband do to show you that he loved you?" the wife said, "He would get up on some Saturday mornings and take care of the kids and let me sleep in." The practitioner and the woman's husband were quite surprised by this reply. The wife explained that getting up on Saturday mornings was something her father used to do, and she thought it was very loving. Unfortunately, she had never shared this information with her husband, who was quite willing to get up every other Saturday and take care of the kids so she could sleep later.

HOMEWORK EXERCISE 12.2 | DEVELOPING MEASURABLE AND SPECIFIC GOALS

Underline the non-specific words in each of the following statements and rewrite each statement as a goal that is measurable and specific.

1. I will get a better grade this semester than last semester.
2. In this family we are going to talk to each other more than we used to.
3. In this group we will increase the number of times that we have 100% attendance.
4. At this agency we will reduce the turnover rate by adding some new benefits.
5. In this neighborhood we will have more get-togethers this year.
6. I am going to lose some weight.
7. In this family we are going to have some quiet times for everyone to work on projects
8. In this group we want most of our meetings to start on time.
9. In this organization we want to increase client satisfaction.

HOMEWORK EXERCISE 12.3 | VALUE OF MEASURABLE AND SPECIFIC GOALS

Suppose you are talking with three friends, and one tells you, "I sure wish I could go on a vacation." The second friend remarks, "Yes, I want to go someplace that is warm." The third friend says, "I am going to go to Florida the first week in April." Which friend do you think is most likely to achieve her goal? Why do you think that friend is most likely to achieve her goal?

Now think of goals that you have set in your life. Identify two goals that are general. "I'd like to exercise more" is an example of a general goal. Now write down two goals that are measurable and specific, such as "This week I will walk for half an hour each day." This goal is measurable and specific. To assess your progress at the end of each day, you would be able to answer "yes" or "no" to indicate whether you walked or not.

If your goals aren't measurable and specific enough so you can measure successful achievement of each goal, rewrite the goals to make them measurable and specific.

ATTAINABLE GOALS

Setting goals that are *attainable* seems obvious but it sometimes requires skillful work with the client. To be attainable, a goal needs to be something the client believes is possible to reach based on the available resources such as time, money, and people power. If the practitioner is working with a community that has very limited financial resources, an attainable goal might be to obtain a grant or to speak with a grant writer. A family who constantly fights might believe that they could achieve a goal, such as having dinner together once a week to talk about topics other than their problems. Research by Bandura and Schunk (1981) found that with clients who have had little success in achieving their goals, setting attainable small goals helped them sustain motivation. In our experience, establishing a series of attainable small goals helps clients experience success in goal achievement, feel more positive about their ability to achieve goals, and be motivated to continue the process of achieving goals. Practitioners can suggest beginning with a small goal that can be achieved in a reasonable period of time. After achieving that goal, the client can go on to set additional goals.

A challenge in establishing attainable goals is helping clients identify what seems possible to them. In order to effectively motivate action, goals need to be perceived as attainable. In Chapter 10 we looked at the ways in which capacity, resources, stress, and demands affect the level of motivation. Those same factors should be considered in relation to goal attainability. Attainable goals are ones that the client can achieve with the capacity and resources available.

Clients who participate in setting goals are more likely to believe the goals are achievable, and those who can clearly visualize the goals in concrete, specific, behavioral terms improve the most (Bandura & Cervone, 1983; Berg & Miller, 1992; Locke, Shaw, Saari, & Latham, 1981; Miller, 1987; Miller & Hester, 1989; Sanchez-Craig, 1980). When goals are attainable, clients have an increased sense of hope about the possibility of change.

Examples of Attainable Goals

If the practitioner is working with a 9-year-old child who is playing around during arithmetic and flunking arithmetic tests, the practitioner might want to help the child think of a goal that is attainable in the near future. Before setting any goals, it would be vital to determine that the child's problem did not result from skipping breakfast every day, family discord, physical problems, or a lack of basic skills. The first goal might be to get at least a C on the next quiz. If the child is not successful with this goal, further partializing of the goal may be necessary such as sitting still for five minutes while the teacher is giving instructions, studying for a 30-minute period at home five nights a week, or getting individual tutoring once a week for 4 weeks. After achieving the first small goal, another goal could be developed. With a young child, the practitioner probably would not work toward a long-term goal such as getting a B at the end of the semester. That goal is too far away to sustain motivation. When short-term, more easily attainable goals are used with children (and often with adults), the client and practitioner can celebrate each stage of the changes made toward reaching the larger goal.

HOMEWORK EXERCISE 12.4 | Attainable Goals

Think of a goal that you (or someone else) set that you consider unattainable. For example, people sometimes set goals such as losing 25 pounds before some important event that will happen in a month. Once you have identified an unattainable goal, write down how you felt about that goal. Discuss whether you achieved the goal and, if you did achieve it, how long you maintained it.

Positive Goals

Setting goals that are *positive* keeps the focus on what the client wants to do rather than focusing on what s/he doesn't want to do. Sometimes the initial statement of goals is to stop doing something, such as stop the fighting in this family, quit drinking, get rid of the drug dealers in this neighborhood, or stop the critical interactions in this task group. The problem with negative goals is that they invite people to focus on what they don't want to do rather that what they do want to do. If you are wondering whether it is true that negative goals invite focusing on the problem, try this experiment. Right this minute, stop thinking about pink elephants. Inevitably that direction leads to thinking about pink elephants. You have to think about them before you can stop thinking about them. If a person's goal is to stop doing something, s/he tends to think about doing that thing. A negative goal to stop a particular behavior creates a vacuum into which old behaviors inevitably return. A goal of not drinking for the next week is measurable, attainable, and specific but not positive. It is up to the practitioner to invite clients to think about what they want instead. Practitioners often use open-ended questions to invite clients to think in positive terms about what they want to start doing. The practitioner needs to ask the client, "What do you want to do instead of drinking?" This might lead to a goal such as, "When I feel like drinking, I will talk to someone that I know will be supportive," or "I will go to an AA meeting."

Examples of Questions Used to Develop Positive Goals
- "If one night at dinner you weren't fighting, what do you think you might be doing?"
- "If one day you felt the urge to drink but didn't drink, what would you do instead?"
- "What is your vision of what the neighborhood would be like without drug dealers?"
- "When you are concerned about how things are going in the group, how would you like to talk to each other about your concerns or hopes?"
- "If this agency was functioning in a way that you believe would be effective, what would people be doing that they aren't doing now?"

HOMEWORK EXERCISE 12.5 | POSITIVE GOALS

Change the following negative goals into positive goals. (*Hint:* Think about what the clients in the following examples might want to start doing.)

1. I will stop watching television when I am also reading my school assignments.
2. Our family will stop spending all weekend doing tasks.
3. In this group, we will stop interrupting each other.
4. In this agency, the employees will stop leaving early on Friday and coming in late on Monday.

Experiment with one negative goal and one positive goal from the following list for just one day. At the end of the day write down what you learned.

1. Today, I won't eat anything with sugar in it.
2. Today, I will eat at least three servings of fruit.
3. Today, I won't procrastinate on my reading assignments.
4. Today, I will read for at least two hours.
5. Today, I won't panic about the test.
6. Today, I will study at least two hours for the test.
7. Today, I won't say anything negative about anyone.
8. Today, I will say something positive to two people.

When goals are *m*easurable, *a*ttainable, *p*ositive, and *s*pecific, it is easier for clients to begin to create a vision of what life will be like when the goals are achieved. Having this clear vision increases their sense of hope. Sometimes it is helpful for practitioners to share their thoughts about clients' ability to achieve goals. The more strongly the clients believe in their ability to achieve the goals and in the practitioner's ability to help them, the more hope and confidence they will feel.

Example of Helping an Individual Move Toward Establishing a MAPS Goal

CLIENT: I'm so upset today that I can't even think. Last night my husband went to several bars and never came home. He hadn't had a drink for almost a year and now he's starting all over again.

PRACTITIONER: It sounds like you are really angry about him drinking again. (reflecting feelings and content)

CLIENT: Yes, I'm angry and hurt, too, really hurt. I've given up all kinds of things. I was willing to stay at home and be with him and help him stay away from drinking and now he has blown it.

PRACTITIONER: Since you made sacrifices to help him, it is particularly painful that he wasn't able to stay away from drinking. (reflecting feelings and content)

CLIENT: Right. I've been working hard to make our life together enjoyable so he would not want to go out and drink.

PRACTITIONER: I wonder if you are feeling resentful as well. It seems like you have put a lot effort into the relationship and now that he went out drinking you wonder if he is willing to do his part. (reflecting feelings and content)

CLIENT: I had made a life for myself without him because he drank so much, but when he said that if I would help him he knew that he would be able to quit drinking, I agreed. I thought we had an agreement. I have kept my end of the deal.

PRACTITIONER: It seems like the fact that he went out drinking is particularly hurtful because you thought things were going well, and you were doing what he had asked you to do. (advanced reflecting)

CLIENT: I've been told all alcoholics are con artists, and now I believe it.

PRACTITIONER: I can understand how betrayed you must feel since you believe that he conned you into thinking he really would change. (advanced reflecting)

CLIENT: I do feel conned. He seemed so sincere and so willing to be different. He even cried.

PRACTITIONER: It seems like you are also feeling confused. His behavior was so convincing, but he wasn't able to keep his promise. (reflecting feelings and content)

CLIENT: I am really confused. I was so sure that we were making progress.

PRACTITIONER: It sounds like you expect people to be able to keep their promises and the fact that your husband didn't do that is very troubling to you. (advanced reflecting)

CLIENT: Yes, that's what I expect. I have gone out of my way to help him.

PRACTITIONER: It seems like you feel particularly hurt because you expected that he would be able to use your help to resolve the problems he has with drinking. (advanced reflecting)

CLIENT: Yes, that was my expectation. I was awful to him this morning. I berated him terribly. I was so angry that I just couldn't stop myself from yelling.

PRACTITIONER: You seem disappointed in yourself for not being able to communicate with him without yelling. (identifying the problem)

CLIENT:	When I am angry, it is really hard for me to stop yelling. I don't want to act that way.
PRACTITIONER:	It sounds like you want to find a way to be able to restrain yourself from attacking or berating your husband. (agreement on general goal)
CLIENT:	Yes, I don't like myself when I act that way.
PRACTITIONER:	How would you like to respond to him when you are disappointed in how he has acted? (question to identify specific goal)
CLIENT:	I want to tell him about how I feel, the anger and disappointment, in a calm way.
PRACTITIONER:	What would you need to do so you could stay calm? (question to identify positives related to goal)
CLIENT:	I guess I could take a deep breath and count to 10.
PRACTITIONER:	That sounds like an achievable goal to me. So your goal is to take a breath and count to 10 before expressing how you feel in a calm way. Do I have that right? (MAPS goal)

Example of Helping a Family Move from a General Goal to a MAPS Goal

MOTHER:	In this family we just don't seem to talk in a nice way to each other. I'd like us to talk together rather than doing so much yelling and criticizing.
PRACTITIONER:	Do the rest of you agree that you would like to learn to talk to each other? (question related to attainability of goal)
BJ (DAUGHTER):	If Mom wasn't so mean, then we could do that.
JOHN (SON):	She's always telling us what to do.
PRACTITIONER:	I hear how frustrated you all have been. That's why I think it might be useful to focus on the goal of learning to talk with each other so that you might feel less frustrated and angry with each other. Are you willing to work on learning to talk differently with each other? (question related to attainability and positive aspects of goal)
BJ:	Yes, that would be good, but I'm not sure how to do it.
JOHN:	I guess it's worth a try.
PRACTITIONER:	Let's think about what it would be like if at dinner tonight nobody yelled or criticized each other. What would you be doing instead? (question related to positive aspects of goal)
JOHN:	Mom and Dad would ask me what I did after school rather than jumping on me about my grades, and no one would interrupt what I was trying to say.
PRACTITIONER:	Okay, and what might you do, John? (question related to positive aspects of goal)
JOHN:	Maybe instead of picking on BJ, I would ask her about what she did after school.
PRACTITIONER:	John, since you don't like people interrupting, would you be willing to listen to BJ and not interrupt her? (question related to attainability and positive aspects of goal)
JOHN:	Well, I guess so.
PRACTITIONER:	BJ, if John asked you about what you did after school, what would you do? (question related to specific positive aspects of goal)
BJ:	I'd sure be surprised, but I guess maybe I would tell him about the project I am working on.
PRACTITIONER:	Mom and Dad, when you notice John and BJ talking with each other instead of picking on each other, what might you do? (question related to specific positive aspects of goal)
DAD:	I think I would begin to relax. I usually feel tense at dinner, like any minute I am going to have to break up a fight or send them to their rooms.
PRACTITIONER:	Okay, let me summarize what I understand you want your family dinners to be like. You want to be asking each other about what happened in your day. You want to be taking

turns talking and listening to each other. It sounded to me like you would also be talking about positive things rather than about concerns. Have I got that right? (summary) Everyone agrees.

PRACTITIONER: How many nights a week do you want to plan to all eat together? (question related to measurability of goal)

MOM: We have lots of things going on around dinnertime. I think three nights a week would be about all we could do.

PRACTITIONER: I know that you have busy lives. So your goal will be eating together three nights a week, and each of you will take turns talking, you will talk about positive things, and you will listen to each other. Does that sound okay to all of you? (agreement on MAPS goal) Everyone agrees.

HOMEWORK EXERCISE 12.6 | CREATING MEASURABLE, ATTAINABLE, POSITIVE, AND SPECIFIC (MAPS) GOALS

After reading each of the following general goals, write a question a practitioner could use as a step toward developing a possible MAPS goal and then write a possible MAPS goal.

1. As I understand it, your goal is to increase your self-confidence. (*Hint:* What might good self-confidence look like? What might you see in a person who had adequate self-confidence?)
2. You want to learn to appropriately discipline your children. (*Hint:* How have you seen other parents discipline in ways that you liked?)
3. You will attend AA meetings every day for 90 days. (*Hint:* Is this a good plan in order to reach what goal?)
4. You will attend 6 family therapy meetings. (*Hint:* In order to achieve what goal?)
5. You want to stop drinking. (*You can do the rest of these without any hints.*)
6. You would like your family to do something together that is fun instead of working all the time.
7. You want the people in this group to stop spending so much time talking about what is going on outside of the group.
8. This task group wants to stop spending so much time complaining.

As you become more skilled as a practitioner, you may decide to approach agreement on problems and goals differently. In some situations, it makes sense to establish goals for each problem at the beginning of the work. In other situations, it is better to set the first goal and achieve it before going on to set further goals. For example, working with a neighborhood that initially expresses the problem as, "This neighborhood is going downhill rapidly," you may come to an agreement on four problems the neighbors are most concerned about and ready to address. First, the neighbors have been unable to figure out how to influence the absentee landlords to clean up their properties. Second, the neighbors are unsure how to get the parks cleaned up and safe for their children. Third, the neighborhood doesn't have any adequate childcare services and the neighbors have been unable to come up with a way to get this gap resolved. Fourth, although the neighbors have been meeting together at the community center, they have not developed a structured organization and they believe this is important. As the practitioner, you could help them figure out which problem they wanted to work on first, move ahead to developing a general goal related to that problem, and finally develop MAPS goals related to that problem. When you achieved that goal, you could go back and select the next most important problem on which to begin. Another way to work with the neighborhood would be to develop general goals and then develop MAPS goals for each identified problem. One of the advantages of using this approach is that you begin with an overview of the whole project. As you are focusing on one goal, your work may also be related to another goal. Sometimes establishing all the goals in the beginning helps clients more clearly visualize what they want to achieve. However, with other clients, seeing the whole scope of the work can be discouraging.

Although having measurable, attainable, positive, and specific goals allows clients to develop a clear picture of their targets and also allows clients and practitioners to measure progress toward goal achievement, some practitioners prefer to work with more general goals. As you develop more experience as a practitioner, you will be able to decide when developing MAPS goals will be most helpful and when more general goals might be adequate.

HOMEWORK EXERCISE 12.7 | ESTABLISHING SEVERAL MAPS GOALS

Think of a goal that you have such as completing your degree or completing a course. If your goal is to complete a course, would you list all the related goals such as completing each assignment with a particular grade? Or would you focus on the immediate goal of finishing the next assignment with at least a particular grade? What are the advantages and disadvantages of each way of developing goals?

AGREEMENTS FOR WORK

After the goals are defined, many practitioners establish a written or verbal agreement that serves to bring together previous understandings between the practitioner and client. These agreements are sometimes called agreements for work because they set the stage for the work that the client and practitioner are planning to accomplish. Some practitioners use a commitment to treatment statement. This is a signed and witnessed statement that identifies the client's motivation and commitment to the treatment process and outlines core expectations, such as the client coming regularly to appointments (Rudd, Mandrusiak, & Joiner, 2006). The agreement usually includes a restatement of the agreed-upon goals. Although agreements for work should be upheld if possible, since they are developed collaboratively between the practitioner and client, they can be modified as long as the change is acceptable to all people involved (Garvin & Seabury, 1997).

HOMEWORK EXERCISE 12.8 | AGREEMENTS

Think of two agreements that you have made, such as agreements to do tasks. If the agreements were verbal, not written, did each person remember the agreement in the same way? If there were misunderstandings related to the agreement, how do you think the agreement could have been improved?

 DVD Example Check out the *Developing Helping Skills* DVD for a demonstration of identifying problems and establishing MAPS goals.

CASE | CASE, PART 4: THIRD MEETING WITH JILL

Below is a transcript of the meeting at which Jill and Sylvia worked on identifying the problem and defining goals. Read the transcript aloud, with group members playing Jill and Sylvia.

SYLVIA: Let me review my understanding of the problems we've talked about so far. You've been feeling really discouraged. You don't want to get up most days. It's been hard to have energy to do things. You've been depending on your friends and not being very happy about that. You've been pressuring yourself to "feel better." Are there things that I've missed about how you're feeling right now?

JILL: I guess I'm tired of feeling like I need other people like that. I've always been the kind of person who calls others if they're having a bad day, and I'm so tired of being on the other end of that, and I guess I just feel kind of blah. I can't concentrate while I'm at work. I'm tired. My friends have started harassing me about the fact that I'm not eating, and I don't really notice it because I don't feel hungry.

SYLVIA: It seems to me like there are several things that you want to work on. One thing you said was bothering you is that you aren't eating right and you think that might be part of why you don't have much energy.

JILL: Yes, I don't feel hungry and just don't push myself to eat. I have been losing weight, and I don't need to lose weight, so I know this is becoming a real problem.

SYLVIA: You seem to know what you should be eating and realize that you haven't been taking very good care of yourself recently. What goal would you like to set about taking care of yourself?

JILL: Oh boy, this is going to be hard, but I do want to start feeling better. I know I should get back to eating something nourishing every day and doing at least some exercising.

SYLVIA: Once we decide on the goals, we will develop steps to reach each goal so that you can reach your goals one step at a time. Does that sound more doable?

JILL: Okay. I used to eat right and exercise a lot, so I guess I can get back to that.

SYLVIA: Good thinking. You did it before so you can do it again. So just to be sure I have this right, your next goal is to eat something nourishing and get some exercise every day. I guess I have a couple of questions about that. How much seems like enough exercise?

JILL: Eventually I want to get back to going to the gym three times a week for an hour and walking on the other days for 10 or 15 minutes. Maybe to start let's make the goal 10 minutes of exercise every day.

SYLVIA: That sounds like a good plan to me. In terms of eating, do you want to eat enough so that you stop losing weight or get back to your old weight?

JILL: I think just eating enough so my weight stays the same. I am not underweight, but I shouldn't lose any more weight either.

SYLVIA: Okay, so you want to stay the same weight and exercise at least 10 minutes every day. So we have our first goal. Just for a minute think about what you want your life to be like.

JILL: I just want it to be like it was.

SYLVIA: Tell me more about how that picture looks to you.

JILL: Well, I used to be a morning person. And yeah, I'd have my days when I was tired, but once the curtains are open, I was up and ready to go. And I don't feel I'm like that anymore. I used to enjoy going to work. It wasn't ideal, but I enjoyed it. I used to like to go hiking in the mountains, fish, and go to the beach... but he was always there with me... and I don't feel like I can do that anymore because he's not there.

SYLVIA: So in the past there were a lot of things you liked to do and the thing that struck me when you were talking about it, that you had a lot of energy around, is the fact that you were a morning person and that it sounds like if you were more of a morning person again, you might get around to doing some of the other things you want to do. Does that fit for you?

JILL: Yeah. I feel like if you don't start your day off right, then the whole day is spent trying to make up for the bad start and it tires me out.

SYLVIA: It sounds like not getting up and getting going is a real problem and that you want another of our goals to be that you will experience yourself as a morning person again?

JILL: Yeah, that would be a lot better. At least then I'd have my time in the morning to feel good and if something happens later, I'd still have my morning.

SYLVIA: Tell me about what a good morning would be like for you.

JILL: Well, I have to be to work at 7:45, so I get up at about 5:50, I guess.

SYLVIA: Even these days?

JILL: Um, pretty close, because it takes me 20 minutes to get to work and I can't get myself ready fast enough and get my things together, so I usually get up around that time. Then I get in the shower, get dressed, try to pick out what I want to wear.

SYLVIA: And all that's still happening now even though you're not feeling real "up" in the morning?

JILL: Yeah, I mean I have to go to work. I can't miss and the kids don't understand if their teacher ditches school, and I have to put clothes on. I don't really think much about it.

SYLVIA: I'm glad to hear that you are able to push yourself to do what you think is important. It sounds like what you're wanting is to feel different during that time, because it sounds like you're actually accomplishing getting up. Is it that what you're experiencing is emotionally hard?

JILL: Yeah. I feel kind of like a robot; I just get up, go to work, and do what I have to do there, come home, grade my papers, and I go to bed. It's just not fun anymore.

SYLVIA: It shows a lot of strength on your part that you continue doing what you are supposed to do even though you don't feel like it. I'm wondering what needs to be different so your mornings go better for you.

JILL: *(pause)* I don't know. It's so hard because I used to wake up and he was next to me. That was half the fun, you know. We would talk about what we were going to do that day or whatever.

SYLVIA: I can hear that you are feeling sad and missing Seth. *(Sylvia pauses to give Jill time to think about how she is feeling.)* Are there other things that made your mornings go better for you?

JILL: Hmm. *(pause)* I used to enjoy sitting out on my patio with my cup of coffee and hanging out a little bit.

SYLVIA: Coffee on the patio sounds like a lovely way to start your day. What other things did you do to make your mornings go well?

JILL: That's the problem. Seth used to get up before me so I just needed to get myself dressed and sit down to have coffee with him. I don't know how I can do it all. Maybe that's why I feel so badly in the morning.

SYLVIA: So getting back to being a morning person who enjoys the morning means that you will have time to enjoy a cup of coffee and still get out the door to school on time. Sounds like a good goal to me. Does that sound right to you?

JILL: Yes, picturing that kind of morning makes me feel a little better.

(Later in the meeting)

SYLVIA: We are about out of time. I think we have accomplished a lot. We have set clear goals. This week will you think about steps to achieve those goals?

JILL: Yes.

SYLVIA: My suggestion is that we meet together weekly for the next 4 weeks. After 4 weeks we can evaluate where you are on each goal and decide how much longer we think we should continue meeting. Does that sound okay to you?

JILL: Yes I think that is a good plan.

SYLVIA: Okay, see you next week.

Questions
1. What skills did the practitioner use to help the client work toward defining the problem and setting goals?
2. Analyze the MAPS goals that the client and practitioner agreed on in this meeting. Discuss whether each goal is measurable, attainable, positive, and specific.

continued

CASE | **CASE, PART 4: THIRD MEETING WITH JILL** *continued*

3. What did the practitioner do well in the meeting?
4. Identify any inappropriate responses used by the practitioner.
5. What is your assessment of the client's level of motivation to reach this goal? Take into account motivation, capacity, and resources, and stress and demands in the client's life.
6. What barriers or obstacles do you think might occur as the client works toward achieving these goals?

7. Do a role play with one person playing Jill and another person the practitioner. Your goal is to identify another problem and MAPS goal.
8. Analyze your role play.
9. What skills did the practitioner use to help the client work toward defining the problem and setting a MAPS goal?
10. Analyze the MAPS goal that the client agreed on in this role play. Is it measurable, attainable, positive, and specific?

PRACTICE EXERCISE 7 | REACHING AGREEMENT ABOUT GENERAL GOALS AND MAPS GOALS

Exercise Objectives
- To practice using skills to reach agreement about general goals and to move from a general goal to a MAPS goal.

Step 1: Preparation
Form groups of three people. Each person will have the opportunity to play the roles of client, practitioner, and peer supervisor. Each meeting will last 15 minutes.

Client Role
- Prepare to summarize what you previously said about yourself, problems, and situations in previous practice meetings.

Practitioner Role
- Review the process of identifying problems, establishing general goals, and developing MAPS goals.

Peer Supervisor Role
- Review the process of identifying a problem, establishing a general goal, and then developing that goal into a MAPS goal.

Step 2: The Client Meeting

Client Role
- Summarize what was said in previous meetings about your problem or situation.

Practitioner
- Ask the client to summarize the information about the problem(s), his or her role in relation to the problem, and the situation discussed in previous practice exercises.
- Express understanding and use questions to explore and clarify in order to help the client move through the process of identifying a problem, establishing a general goal, and then developing that goal into a MAPS goal.

Peer Supervisor Role
- Keep track of the time and tell the practitioner and client when 14 minutes are completed so the practitioner has time to close the meeting.
- Check off the ending skills used by the practitioner.
- Write down each practitioner statement and question. You may abbreviate, use a form of shorthand, or just write the first group of words in the statement, or you can tape record the interview and transcribe or listen to the tape.

Step 3: Feedback

Client Role
- Describe how you experienced the practitioner.

PRACTICE EXERCISE 7 | REACHING AGREEMENT ABOUT GENERAL GOALS AND MAPS GOALS *continued*

Practitioner Role

- Evaluate the client's ability to reach agreement about the general goals and the MAPS goals.

Peer Supervisor Role

- Give feedback to the practitioner from your notes on skills in reaching agreement about the general and MAPS goals.

- Give feedback on inappropriate responses.
- Complete the evaluation form.
- Evaluate the practitioner's use of the core interpersonal skills of warmth, empathy, and respect. (All of the scales are in Appendix B.)
- Record the feedback in the practitioner's book for future reference.

EVALUATION FORM: REACHING AGREEMENT ON THE GENERAL GOAL AND MAPS GOAL

Name of Practitioner_____

Name of Peer Supervisor_____

Directions: Under each category (in italics) is a list of behaviors or skills. Give one check mark, worth one point, for each skill used by the practitioner.

Building Relationships

Closing Skills (for a meeting)

Give one point for each skill used by the practitioner.

1. Practitioner identified that the meeting was about to end. _____
2. Practitioner provided a summary of the meeting. _____
3. Practitioner reviewed any tasks that the client agreed to complete. _____
4. Practitioner discussed plans for future meetings. _____
5. Practitioner invited client feedback about the work. _____
6. Practitioner asked client about any final questions. _____

Skills that Express Understanding

Give one point for each skill used by the practitioner.

1. Reflecting feelings _____
2. Reflecting content _____
3. Reflecting feelings and content _____
4. Summarizing _____
5. Exploring meanings _____
6. Identifying strengths _____

Exploring

Questioning Skills

Give one point for each skill used by the practitioner.

1. Expressed understanding before asking questions. _____
2. Asked open-ended questions when appropriate. _____
3. Asked one question at a time. _____
4. Asked closed-ended questions when appropriate. _____
5. Asked questions about strengths. _____

continued

PRACTICE EXERCISE 7 | REACHING AGREEMENT ABOUT GENERAL GOALS AND MAPS GOALS *continued*

Seeking Clarification

Give one point for each skill used by the practitioner.

1. Exploring the meaning of words and body language   _____
2. Exploring the basis of conclusions drawn by client   _____
3. Eliciting further clarifying information   _____
4. Allowing silence   _____

Defining the Focus

Reaching Agreement about Problems or Challenges

Give one point for each skill used by the practitioner. It rarely will be appropriate to use all of these skills in one meeting.

1. Partializing   _____
2. Advanced reflecting   _____
3. Noticing patterns or themes   _____
4. Identifying discrepancies   _____
5. Rolling with resistance   _____
6. Supporting self-efficacy   _____
7. Stating agreement about problems or challenges   _____

Reaching Agreement about Goals

Give one point for each skill used by the practitioner.

1. Reaching agreement on a general goal   _____
2. Using questions to develop a MAPS goal   _____
3. Reaching agreement on MAPS goal   _____

Common Mistakes or Inappropriate Responses (subtract 1 point for each)   _____

(offering advice, reassuring, offering excuses, asking leading questions, dominating through teaching, labeling, interrogating)

Core Interpersonal Qualities

Using the scales in Appendix A, evaluate the appropriateness and effectiveness of the practitioner's expression of empathy, warmth, and respect. On the following lines write the scores, from 1 to 5, for warmth, empathy, and respect.

Score for warmth   _____
Score for empathy   _____
Score for respect   _____

EXPECTED COMPETENCIES

In this chapter, you have learned responses to assist clients in identifying their goals and establishing measurable, attainable, positive, and specific goals (MAPS).

You should now be able to:

- Give an example of a general goal and explain how it could be developed into a more specific MAPS goal.

- List five questions that could be used to invite a client to move from a general goal to a MAPS goal.

- Give examples of MAPS goals for an individual, family, and group.

- Be able to describe having reached a general goal and a MAPS goal.

- Demonstrate skills used to reach a MAPS goal.

Doing the Work, Evaluating, and Ending the Work

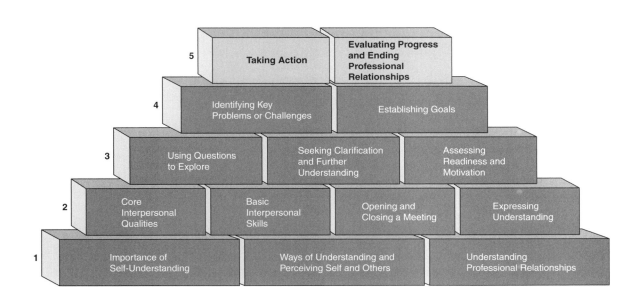

5 Taking Action | Evaluating Progress and Ending Professional Relationships

4 Identifying Key Problems or Challenges | Establishing Goals

3 Using Questions to Explore | Seeking Clarification and Further Understanding | Assessing Readiness and Motivation

2 Core Interpersonal Qualities | Basic Interpersonal Skills | Opening and Closing a Meeting | Expressing Understanding

1 Importance of Self-Understanding | Ways of Understanding and Perceiving Self and Others | Understanding Professional Relationships

The skills introduced in Chapters 13 and 14 will build the final layer on the foundation provided by the material in Chapters 1 through 12. Chapter 4 introduced the core interpersonal qualities you will use throughout your work with clients. Chapter 5 covered basic interpersonal skills and Chapter 6 described how to open and close a meeting. Chapter 7 outlined ways to demonstrate understanding, and Chapters 8 through 10 focused on exploring and assessing. Chapters 11 and 12 covered problem identification and goal-setting. In this final section, you will learn about the skills involved in *taking action* and the last phase of work with clients, *evaluation and ending*.

After the practitioner and clients have agreed upon MAPS goals, they are ready to take action to achieve the goals. Since professional relationships are purposeful, it is important to evaluate progress on a regular basis and end the relationship and the work when the goals are achieved. Doing the work draws upon all the skills discussed in previous chapters, along with some additional skills. As with the other phases of work, clients' strengths are an essential aspect of taking action, evaluating and ending. In this phase clients need to use their strengths and capacities in new ways to achieve their goals. They may have to give up old mindsets and behavior patterns and learn new ways of thinking and acting. They will also have to honestly evaluate what is working and what is not working.

TAKING ACTION

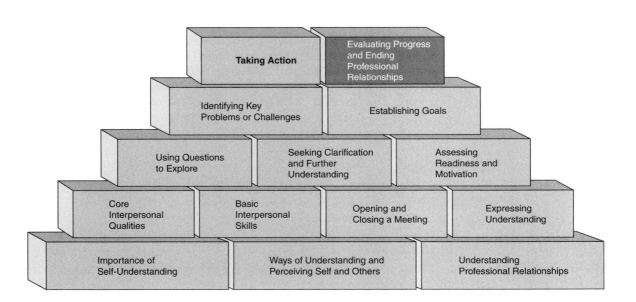

In this chapter you will learn about the following topics:

Practitioner Tasks
- Working with clients to design steps to achieve each goal and to facilitate the client's ability to take the necessary steps toward the goals

Practitioner Skills
- Teaching, directing, inviting a different perspective, identifying discrepancies, giving feedback, using self-disclosure, and focusing on improvements

Client Attributes
- Willingness to use strengths, capacities, and resources to move toward achievement of goals

The establishment of clear goals lays the foundation for the action phase of the work by providing direction and giving clients a clear picture of what they want to achieve. Generally, practitioners move from setting MAPS goals to asking clients to identify the action steps they think will be necessary to achieve a particular goal. Much of the work done by the client and the practitioner will consist of establishing and working on steps or tasks that are challenging for the client. Identifying the various steps gives clients a sense of hope as they begin to see a way to achieve their goals (Feldman, Rand, Shorey, & Snyder, 2002).

In this chapter you will learn five more skills (teaching, directing, inviting a different perspective, giving feedback, and using self-disclosure) that will be particularly valuable as you help clients take the steps necessary to achieve their goals. You will also learn new ways to use the skill of identifying discrepancies and a variation on identifying strengths called focusing on improvements. In the action phase of the work, you will continue to use all the skills you have learned so far, including the core skills of attending, observing, listening, and opening and closing a meeting. Skills related to expressing understanding and exploring are used in every meeting. The skills required for identifying the problem, such as rolling with resistance, advanced reflecting, noticing patterns and themes, partializing, and supporting self-efficacy, will also be useful in the action phase of work.

IDENTIFYING STEPS

Achieving a MAPS goal is a journey. Identifying the steps provides a road map for reaching the final destination or goal. Since many clients have not had the experience of planning to reach a goal, helping clients identify necessary steps can be an important learning experience. In addition, developing a plan for achieving a goal often enhances hope in the attainability of the goal.

Further Exploration of the Problem

Before identifying steps, further exploration may be needed to learn more specifics, including the frequency of the problem, where the problem occurs, who is involved, what are the immediate antecedents and consequences of the problem, and what meanings the client may be attributing to the problem. Practitioners may explore the situation or environment to discover what precipitates and maintains the problem. This exploration might cover areas such as family, neighborhood, school, agency, significant group and organizations, and general characteristics such as culture, race, and socioeconomic class. For example, a practitioner was working with a mother whose goal was to learn a new way to parent her 8-year-old child who was having behavior problems in school. In order to understand more about the mother's parenting style, the practitioner asked the mother to describe a typical morning with her son. The mother reported that she repeatedly told her son that it was time to get up, reminded him repeatedly to brush his teeth and get dressed, and informed him when it was time to go out to meet the bus. The son generally did not respond to his mother's reminders and missed the bus. The mother excused his behavior and drove him to school. Given this start to his day, what are your hunches about how he responded in school when asked to do something? How do you think this additional information about the family's typical morning routine might help the practitioner and client identify steps to solve the problem?

STEPS IDENTIFIED BY CLIENTS

In the past, practitioners have sometimes excluded clients from involvement in creating the action plan (Gollwitzer, 1999; Kottler, 2001). It is valuable to begin the process of identifying possible steps to achieving goals by asking what steps clients think will be necessary to reach their goals. Involving clients in every step of the process of problem-solving strengthens the working partnership between practitioner and client and makes problem-solving and goal achievement a collaborative process. Although clients may not possess fully formed ideas about what steps will be necessary, they know what has worked for them in the past and what has not worked. As in other phases of the work, collaboration is a key to success in this phase.

When a practitioner is working with a family or a group, every person needs to have a chance to suggest possible steps or tasks. Practitioners need to remember that at this point in the process the goal is simply to identify the steps to be taken. This is a brainstorming time. Assessing the usefulness, value, or possibility of each step will be done next. Since evaluating at this stage tends to limit creativity, practitioners often have to remind clients that the plan is to identify possible steps, not evaluate them or agree to do them.

Clients may have considerable information about what they need to do but need assistance in figuring out how to accomplish these tasks. Clients may generalize about the steps they have taken in the past by making comments such as, "I interviewed for a job," forgetting the many little steps that it took to get to the interview stage. It is the practitioner's job to be sure that the many discrete steps are delineated. Let's assume that your client, a mother, has the general goal of establishing a more positive relationship with her children. Her first MAPS goal is to develop a clear plan related to chores she expects the children to complete. Once the MAPS goal is established, the practitioner brainstorms with the mother about possible steps to reach the goal. To increase the likelihood of success, the practitioner might ask the mother about times when she has been successful with the children in the past. Together the practitioner and client determine the action steps the mother will take to achieve her MAPS goal. The first action step for the mother might be to draw up a list of chores the children are capable of completing. The next step might be for the mother to explain each chore to all of the children. Next, the mother would ask the children to pick three chores to complete from the list. If this is successful, subsequent steps might involve the mother determining what she will do if the children do not respond to her requests, how she will reward the children if they do respond, and how the tasks could be redistributed, if necessary, in a way that might be more successful. Assuming the client developed these steps with the practitioner in ways that were useful to her and that she successfully accomplished them, another MAPS goal would be developed that addressed other areas that would move her toward her overall general goal of having a more positive relationship with her children.

STEPS IDENTIFIED BY PRACTITIONERS

After clients identify steps, practitioners can suggest additional steps to help clients reach their goals. Practitioners may also ask clients which steps they expect to find particularly difficult. If a step seems too difficult at first, it will be important to break it down into smaller increments. Sometimes when working with more than one person (a couple, a family, or a group), steps suggested by one person as reasonable may seem very challenging to another person. In this situation, the practitioner helps the client break the step into a series of manageable smaller steps. By using this approach, clients learn something about the process of creating plans to achieve goals. Involving clients and practitioners in identifying steps to achieve goals is appropriate with individual clients of all ages, as well as with families, groups, and larger systems such as organizations and communities.

USING EXCEPTION-FINDING QUESTIONS TO IDENTIFY STEPS

In some situations, practitioners may use exception-finding questions, similar to those used in the goal-setting process (see Chapter 12), to help clients think about ways to solve problems. Using exception-finding questions, the practitioner asks the client to recall a time when the problem did not occur and to identify what s/he was doing at that time (De Jong & Berg, 1998; De Jong & Miller, 1995; McKeel, 1996). For example, in working with a family whose general goal is to have more fun together, the practitioner might ask them to think of a time when they had fun together and then ask each of them what s/he did to make that fun time possible. The family could then create a MAPS goal to plan one fun outing on a Saturday afternoon for two hours with the whole family and make a list of the action steps that would make that goal happen. A teen might have a goal of getting a 3.0 grade point average (GPA) for the next semester of high school. She might be asked to think of a time when she was able to keep up with homework assignments and get a 3.0 GPA. From this answer the client and practitioner could develop action steps. Using exception-finding questions, the practitioner helps clients discover their own unique ways of solving problems. Clients can use these past successes to help create the steps they will need to take to be successful in solving their current problems and reaching their goals.

Exception-finding questions can also help clients to identify strengths that can be used in problem-solving (Kottler, 2001). For example, a female client was a successful sales person because of her flexibility in quickly responding to the needs of customers. In her personal life, she tended to have relationship problems in part because she would rely on only one way of dealing with issues no matter what the circumstances were. When the practitioner asked her to think of situations in which she was more flexible, she quickly thought of her sales job. She was then able to see how she could use her flexibility to improve her personal relationships.

HOMEWORK EXERCISE 13.1 | IDENTIFYING STEPS

Think of a goal you would like to achieve (or have achieved). Next, take a few minutes to write down the steps you took to reach your goal. For example, you might use being accepted into college or graduate school as the goal. We know it took a lot of steps to

achieve that goal. You could use your goal of graduating from your program. Be sure that the steps you choose are ones that you have control over, such as "I will apply to five graduate schools" versus "I will be accepted into graduate school."

EVALUATING, ORGANIZING, AND PLANNING THE STEPS

Now that steps have been identified, the next part of the process is evaluating each step. If you truly invited brainstorming when identifying steps, you probably named some steps that will not work because they are impossible to achieve at this time or because they would be unacceptable to some person in the group. For example, when a practitioner was working with a couple who established the general goal of enhancing closeness in their relationship, one of the MAPS goals was to take a vacation together every year. The husband suggested biking to the West Coast as a possible vacation, despite the fact that this couple had not even taken a bike ride around the block recently. When evaluating this step, they agreed that someday they would like to bike to the West Coast, but for now, a more realistic step might be to bike together at least three times a week, weather permitting. Another client was discussing a power struggle between herself and her husband. The practitioner asked what small step might move her toward her general goal of a positive relationship with her husband. She said, "He could always agree with me." She and the practitioner both laughed and then went on to identify steps that were more realistic and possible for her to accomplish by herself.

After evaluating each possible step, the client and practitioner should organize the list of steps by prioritizing the steps to work on first, second, and so on. Sometimes clients want to start with the step that seems easiest to accomplish. Other clients prefer to begin by working on a step that seems most important or perhaps is causing the most discomfort. Some practitioners create a plan with the client that involves identifying all the steps and organizing them in order of which ones will be worked on first. When working with a task group or organization this method of creating an overall plan is particularly useful. When working with an individual, couple, or family, the practitioner may choose to use a more general approach of identifying some steps and/or asking clients at the beginning of each meeting what they want to work on or what their goal is for that meeting.

When planning for achieving steps, it is important that clients see the value of each step, have a solid plan for completing each step, and understand and agree to complete each step. This is easier when working with an individual than when working with more than one person. Even if you are just working with a couple or a parent and one child, a step may be acceptable to one person but not to another person. It is up to the practitioner to work with each person to find a step that will be acceptable to all. Sometimes this process may take considerable time, but it is important for all of the people involved to come to an agreement. In the process of discussing what step is acceptable to everyone in the couple, family, or group, they are learning how to work together collaboratively. As the practitioner it will be important for you to emphasize points of agreement, similar to noticing a theme, to reflect your understanding of what is important to each person, and to ask questions to invite each person to clearly identify what s/he wants or is willing to do.

It is essential to discuss with clients how they can use their strengths, capacities, and resources to complete each step. Practitioners might ask clients to think about other times when they faced new tasks. What did they do or tell themselves to help with accomplishing the task? If clients can't think of a new task or skill that they learned, the practitioner can suggest one, such as learning to ride a two-wheel bike, to drive a car, to read, to clean house, to cook, or to accomplish some other task.

Working together, the client and practitioner may identify additional incremental steps to achieve the more difficult or larger action steps. Creating small steps that can be successfully achieved helps clients gain a sense of confidence. For example, with a client whose goal was to effectively lead a group, the practitioner worked with the client to identify the various steps necessary to successfully conduct a group and talked about which tasks the client felt comfortable doing and what strengths the client had that could be used in leading a group. The practitioner and client then picked the first task to be accomplished. They selected a small task that the client felt ready to begin doing: to be active in a group by identifying when the group seemed to have come to a decision or was ready to move on to the next task. The practitioner and client discussed the value of this step in achieving the client's goal. In making a plan to complete the step, the practitioner asked the client what actions he thought would be necessary to achieve this step. Organizing and creating incremental steps helps ensure successful achievement of the MAPS goal. In addition, clients learn something about the process of creating plans to achieve goals—a skill that can be applied to many other situations in their lives.

HOMEWORK EXERCISE 13.2 | PLANNING AND ORGANIZING STEPS

For this homework assignment, all you need to do is list the steps from Homework Exercise 13-1 in order. Remember the various ways to order steps and select the one that you think would be best for this assignment.

SKILLS TO ENHANCE ACHIEVEMENT OF STEPS

As with previous phases of work, there are new skills that are particularly helpful in the action phase. Each of these skills can be used to help clients master a step in their plan. The new skills are: teaching, directing, inviting a different perspective, giving feedback, and using self-disclosure. You will learn a somewhat different use of identifying discrepancies and the importance of focusing on improvements. Besides these new skills, you will find that in the action phase you will continue to rely on the skills related to expressing understanding and exploring. At the end of this chapter, there is a summary of the skills useful in the action phase, their purposes, examples of when they might be used, and methods of using the skills.

TEACHING

As practitioners help clients to learn new behaviors through taking action steps, they may assume an educator role. In the role of educator, the practitioner is facilitating change by helping individuals, families, and groups to learn new methods, new ways of thinking, new behaviors, and new ways of acting (Minuchin, Colapinto, & Minuchin, 1998). Clients may need instruction or guidance in any number of areas such as learning appropriate ways to encourage their children, to contact potential employers, to approach community leaders, to communicate their needs effectively, or to conduct a meeting using parliamentary procedure. In groups with a focus on topics such as parenting skills, social skills, assertiveness skills, appropriately expressing feelings, making friends, or recovering from some difficult experience such as divorce or death, the practitioner often provides information and instruction (Sexton & Alexander, 2002). Teaching may occur in an organized class such as a class for parents who want to learn better ways to discipline their children, for teams who want to learn to work together more effectively, or for children who want to learn to make friends. Teaching may be appropriate at times when the practitioner realizes that new information might help clients achieve their goals.

Sometimes new information is essential to help clients take necessary steps. For example, working with the client who wanted to be an effective leader, the practitioner taught the client about effective leadership, suggested a class for the client to attend, and suggested reading a book on leadership. Working with families, practitioners often teach about problem-solving skills, communication skills, effective discipline methods, or parenting methods (Alexander, Robbins, & Sexton, 2000). Working with groups, practitioners might teach about accepting diversity, conflict resolution, decision making, or leadership styles.

In the role of educator, the practitioner might help clients understand what is considered normal in various contexts. For example, parents might need to learn what to expect from children at different ages. Patients in the hospital might need to learn what to anticipate as they recover. People in a grief group might need to learn the predictable stages of the grieving process, and participants in a neighborhood group might need to learn about the many ways to effectively lobby government officials.

As a practitioner who may know how to accomplish a particular step, it is easy to forget that the client may not know the necessary behaviors and may need to work with the practitioner to be ready to accomplish the step. In the case of the client who wanted to learn to lead a group, the client was hesitant about what to say to indicate that the group had come to a decision (action step). The practitioner suggested practicing in their meeting what he might say in a group to identify when a decision was made. This kind of practice is called *rehearsing or role-playing*. In the role of educator, practitioners sometimes help clients with difficult tasks by modeling new ways of acting and by inviting clients to rehearse or practice the behaviors that are challenging for them (Burlingame, MacKenzie, & Strauss, 2004; Mueser, Wallace, & Liberman, 1995). Rehearsing helps the client experience the action step so s/he will be more comfortable when it is time to actually make the change in a real-life situation. By practicing the action step, clients will be less anxious about it and be more likely to experience success. Role-playing with the practitioner and other group members is a common way to practice skills such as being assertive or being clear and direct about wants and needs with the boss, a teenager, a partner or spouse, and so on. In the role play, the practitioner can play the role of client and model a way of behaving or can play the role of the other person as clients try alternative ways of relating and communicating. For example, in a women's support group, one of the women was working on being more assertive at work. After discussing the situation, the practitioner suggested that the woman role-play the boss and pick a group member or the practitioner to act in an assertive way. After seeing appropriate assertive behavior modeled, another group member played the role of the boss while the woman tried acting in an assertive way. Whenever people are considering using a new behavior, practicing that behavior in a safe situation helps build their sense of confidence. With a neighborhood group that wants to talk to the mayor about improving the street lights in their neighborhood, the practitioner might decide to invite the participants to practice what they want to say before actually going to talk with the mayor.

Once clients have learned about and practiced the new behavior, it is important to explore their readiness to actually do the task. Using a solution-focused approach, the practitioner might ask the clients "On a scale of 1 to 10, with 10 being absolute certainty you can and will complete this task before our next appointment, what score would you give yourself right now?" If the score is below 8, the clients probably need more support or some other directions to feel more confident about successfully completing the action step. The practitioner and the clients together will need to identify the obstacles and decide what additional steps are needed. Of course, it will also be essential to discuss with clients how they can use their strengths, capacities, and resources to complete each task. Practitioners can help clients list strengths and resources they can use to accomplish the task. If clients have trouble thinking of strengths, the practitioner can ask them to think about strengths they used to complete some other task, such as learning to read or write, to garden, to repair a leaky faucet, and so on.

HOMEWORK EXERCISE 13.3 | Teaching

Think of a time when you needed to learn something from another person in order to achieve one of your goals. In what ways did the other person's teaching help you achieve your goal?

DIRECTING

In the action phase of work, there are times when it is appropriate for practitioners to be directive. Being directive involves asking clients to do something new or to go in a different direction. For example, in a meeting the practitioner may ask the client to go back to something that was said earlier, to talk more about a particular topic, or to try saying something differently—for example, using stronger words or a gentler tone. Directing is often used in role plays or during rehearsing. In a task group the practitioner might direct the members to go back and focus on a topic that needed further exploration.

Giving homework is another way of directing that involves asking clients to complete an activity between meetings (Allen, 2006; Kazantzis & Ronan, 2006). These directions usually involve completing a series of agreed-upon steps. When asking the client to respond to a specific direction, the practitioner should ask about the client's willingness and readiness to engage in the activity (Brodley, 2006). Scaling questions work well here to assess willingness and readiness. For example, "On a scale of 1 to 10, with 10 being 'I am definitely willing and feel ready to do this activity' and 1 being not at all ready to do this activity, what number would you give to yourself?"

Examples of Using Homework Assignments

- With an individual: "Between now and next week, will you make a list of all of the jobs that you think might interest you?"
- With a community group: "Between now and our next meeting, will each of you talk to two people in your neighborhood or church about this project?"
- With a family: "Between now and our next meeting, will each of you pay attention to something you like or appreciate about your family?"

Directing may be used when inviting clients to rehearse new behaviors. When asking clients to engage in a new activity, the practitioner may be encouraging the clients to explore an area of interest; to further explore their current situation, behavior or feeling; or to try out a new behavior. When directing action, the practitioner suggests that the client complete a specific action. The practitioner may offer guidance, feedback, and encouragement. Like role-play, practicing action steps helps the client successfully use these behaviors in real-life situations.

Examples of Directing

- With an individual: "Imagine you are talking to your supervisor now. Tell her what you want her to know."
- With a neighborhood group: "Will you take turns practicing what you are going to say to the police chief about the lack of patrol persons in this neighborhood?"

  - "Tonight several folks have expressed their frustration about how slowly this process is moving. Will some of the rest of you share your thoughts and feelings about the process we are using?"

- With a family: "During these meetings, I'd like you to talk about your own thoughts and feelings, so will you begin your sentence with 'I' rather than 'you'?"
- With a group: "I noticed you directing your comments to me. Would you be willing to talk directly to Herbert about your thoughts or feelings?"

  - "I'd like go back to the problem of some members not feeling heard."
  - "Let's stop for a minute and talk about how each of you feels about how this group is doing."

- ○ (Tyrone is a group member who has been looking at the floor and not talking during a group meeting.) "I would like the group to give Tyrone feedback about what they see him doing in group."
- ○ "LinLee, how did you feel about telling the group about your experiences in working with management? I imagine others have had similar experiences. Will someone else tell us about your experiences working with people who are in powerful positions?"

HOMEWORK EXERCISE 13.4 | DIRECTING

In the next couple of days pay attention to ways that people direct other people. Describe ways of directing that you think are effective and appropriate and ways of directing that you think are ineffective or inappropriate. Make a list of qualities and behaviors that are important when directing appropriately and effectively.

INVITING A DIFFERENT PERSPECTIVE

Sometimes clients have trouble taking action because their view of themselves, the world, situations, or other people is limiting their progress. Remember what you learned in Chapter 2 about constructs. Many times people have decided upon constructs that may have been appropriate when they were developed but inhibit their current growth and development. Sharing another perspective with clients invites them to view experiences, feelings, thoughts, behaviors, or situations in a new way. This skill is also referred to as reframing (Goldenthal, 1996). Many times clients can see aspects of their lives only from their own perspective, but the practitioner often sees things differently. This new perspective can motivate clients to make changes in their behaviors or thoughts, increasing their success in achieving their action steps and goals. Even when practitioners offer a different perspective, however, clients may not be willing to consider it. For example, one of the authors worked with a woman who often had problems trusting people. One night the man she was dating was not able to drive to her town to see her. A few days later he told her that he needed more time to decide if he wanted to move into a committed relationship. She reported that these two incidents meant that he was definitely seeing another woman. Offering a different perspective, the practitioner said, "He might have been telling you the truth about being busy one night and not being quite ready to make a commitment to you." In this case, the client did not want to change her view of the situation so the practitioner moved to expressing understanding.

Examples of Offering Alternative Perspectives

- About a decision: "I hear that you consider the decision of whether to leave your job and go to graduate school scary. Maybe it is also an exciting opportunity to make a change."
- About a feeling: "You said that you feel scared about talking to the mayor about the lighting in the neighborhood. I wonder if maybe part of that feeling is excitement about this new challenge."
- About an experience: "You said that you haven't learned anything from this group experience, but think about whether you have learned some important lessons about how to be a more effective group member."

- About a behavior: "Maybe his disruptive behavior in class is an indication that he is bored."
- About group dynamics: "Maybe the other members of the team are not resisting change but wanting more time to explore all the options before making a decision."
- About a conflict: "Another way of looking at this conflict is that it gives us an opportunity to practice accepting and understanding our differences."
- About self-concept: "I hear that you feel angry at yourself for being impatient with your daughter. Do you also feel good about the fact that now you are sometimes more patient with her?"
- About another person's behavior: "I understand that you see your wife as wanting to start a fight with you. Another way of looking at what she is doing is that she wants you to hear her position."
- About group performance: "It is disappointing that we didn't complete several of our goals. Maybe instead of criticizing ourselves for ending this project without completing all of our goals we should be celebrating everything that we did accomplish."
- About a new experience: "It sounds like you feel kind of scared about going to Spain for a semester and are worried about whether you will be safe there. For a minute, let's talk about what you think will be exciting and fun about being in Spain."

Practitioners sometimes use questions to invite clients to see things differently. Practitioners may challenge clients to evaluate whether their behaviors, thoughts, or feelings are effective in getting them what they want. Asking "how" questions often evokes responses in which the client is invited to reflect upon new or existing information. Questions can be used to invite clients to think about something they have avoided or to look at something from a different perspective.

Examples of Using Questions to Invite a New Perspective
- Individual client: "How do you think he felt when you refused to talk to him?"

  o "Is there another way of explaining his behavior?"

- Family: "How do the rest of you feel about your mother's decision to go back to work?"

  o "Just for a minute, would you think about this from your dad's point of view?"

- Task group: "How do the rest of you feel about Tom's wish to do this part of the project by himself?"

  o "What else might be going on that would explain Tom's need to do this part of the project alone?"

- A counseling group: "When Jose expressed his disappointment at thinking that Andrea got more attention from me than he did, did that feeling remind anyone else of how you have felt in other group situations or in your family?"

- An organization or community: "How does the group feel about Simone wanting to drop out of this project?"

HOMEWORK EXERCISE 13.5 | INVITING A DIFFERENT PERSPECTIVE

Tell a partner about your thoughts or views about a particular situation. Ask your partner to suggest a different way of looking at the situation. Now change roles and have your partner tell you about his or her thoughts about a particular situation. When s/he is finished, suggest another way of looking at the experience.

IDENTIFYING DISCREPANCIES

We first discussed identifying discrepancies in Chapter 11. Identifying discrepancies is similar to confrontation and is used during the action phase of work as a way to invite clients to see or think about something differently. The discrepancy usually involves a behavior that seems to be moving the client away from the stated goal and/or is preventing successful completion of the action step. Practitioners base these statements on discrepancies they have observed, heard, or surmised from the work with the client.

- The discrepancy may be between the client's stated goal and his behavior. For example, "You said that you wanted to talk more openly with your wife, and now I hear you saying that you are not willing to tell her about your concern about losing your job. Will you help me understand that?"
- The discrepancy may be between what the client is saying now and what she said in the past. For example, "Last week I heard you say that making a change was very important to you, and you planned action steps towards that goal. Now you are saying that you do not want to change."

The practitioner's intent is to invite the client to think about the discrepancy, so it is important to allow some time for the client to consider what has been said.

Discrepancies can include differences between:

What a client is saying or doing and what the practitioner is noticing.

- "I hear most of the members of the group saying that you agree with this plan, but I noticed that some of you are looking at the floor and seem un-comfortable. I wonder if maybe you are hesitant to express how you feel about this plan."
- "You're talking about being scared, but you're smiling."
- "I hear people in the group saying that they want everyone to have time to talk, but I notice that some group members are doing a lot more talking, while others are pretty quiet."

What the client is saying and what the practitioner heard the client say at another time.

- "This week in the meeting folks are indicating that cars driving too fast through the neighborhood isn't the problem, but in our last meeting several folks seemed ready to do something about cars speeding in areas near where your children often play. Help me understand what changed since last week."

- "I've heard you mention before that teaching is something that you really enjoy, but now you are talking about giving up your teaching job."
- "Last week I thought we had come to consensus about approaching the teacher, and now I hear that several of you are not willing to do that."

What the client is saying in the meeting and the client's actions outside the meeting.

- "All of you agreed that the problems in this neighborhood need to be solved. I understood that you were willing to talk to two neighbors about their view of the problems, but at this meeting only one person reported talking to her neighbors."
- "Part of your goal was to get better medical treatment, and yet you haven't approached your doctor with your concerns."
- "It seems that you want your wife to work but that you have difficulty doing your share of the housework when she does."

What the client says is important and his or her behavior.

- "When you said that you wanted your son to live at home, I noticed that you were shaking your head no. I wonder if maybe you aren't really sure about having him at home."
- "Last week the group said that they felt prepared to move ahead with plans to contact the absentee landlords, but now everyone seems hesitant to talk about moving ahead."
- "You have said you want your husband to express his feelings, but I notice that whenever he does you shrug your shoulders and turn away."

HOMEWORK EXERCISE 13.6 | IDENTIFYING DISCREPANCIES

Think about a discrepancy in your life, such as a discrepancy between a goal and your actions. Write down what you might say as a practitioner noticing this discrepancy. Think about other discrepancies that you know about, maybe in your family or in a group to which you belong. If you were a practitioner noticing this discrepancy, write down what you might say.

GIVING FEEDBACK

During the action phase of work when a solid working relationship has been established, additional skills and qualities may be used by the practitioner: giving feedback, immediacy, self-disclosure, and demonstrating genuineness. Giving feedback involves stating what the practitioner sees and hears. For example:

- "I notice that you are smiling."
- "I heard your voice crack when you said the word *daughter*."
- "I notice that your hands are clenched."
- "You look like you are about to cry."

When giving feedback, practitioners share an awareness of what clients are showing nonverbally or expressing in their tone of voice. Often, the information given to the client may be something of which the client has not been aware. Since practitioners cannot be sure how clients will receive feedback, it is important to follow up with a question such as "What are your thoughts and feelings about that feedback?" This is a time when it is particularly important to use your observation skills and to check for congruence between what the clients may have said they felt about the feedback and what they experienced. They may feel more troubled about the feedback than they are able to acknowledge.

Giving feedback in a group or family can be quite important, especially when the feedback is given by other members of the group. Rather than the practitioner giving feedback, s/he might ask other members of the family or group for their reactions. For example, the practitioner might say, "What have you noticed about Manuel's behavior during this discussion?" Since we so rarely receive truthful feedback, hearing this honest information is very valuable (Kottler, 1994).

Examples of Giving Feedback

- "Your voice got quiet when you said that your dad is quite ill."
- "All of you seem very quiet today." (to a family, a group, a team)
- "I've noticed that Maria and Thuy are the only people who have voiced an opinion." (to a team, a task group, a family)
- "I notice that several people in the group look at me frequently, even when you are talking to someone else in the group."
- "I think our team is beginning to agree; I see heads nodding."
- "I hear this side of the room saying they want to stop the discussion and the other side saying they want to continue."
- "As I look around the room, I am noticing that many folks are beginning to look tired. Maybe we should finish our meeting soon."

HOMEWORK EXERCISE 13.7 | GIVING FEEDBACK

Giving feedback is another skill that might feel awkward at first because it is probably something you have not done before. On three different occasions, think about what you might say if you were going to give feedback. Write down your ideas about what you could say to give feedback.

IMMEDIACY

Immediacy involves a particular type of feedback. Using the skill of immediacy, the practitioner focuses on what is happening in the moment. This skill generally involves commenting on what seems to be happening between the practitioner and the client (Egan, 2007). Giving the client feedback about how the practitioner is experiencing their relationship may help the client understand other relationship problems. For example, with a client who reports many problems maintaining relationships, the practitioner might say, "When you talk rapidly and don't identify what you want to focus on, I feel excluded, almost as if you do not want to maintain a relationship or connection with me." In a situation when a client who has been involved and focused and suddenly seems distant and withdrawn, the practitioner might say, "I noticed that you are looking away and aren't saying much." (giving feedback) "I wonder if I said or did something that is troubling to you" (immediacy).

HOMEWORK EXERCISE 13.8 | IMMEDIACY

In a relationship, think about what you might say if you were to comment on what you thought was happening between the two of you. For example, "I notice that as I am talking to you, you are glancing at the football game on television. I wonder if you are too distracted to talk with me." Write down what you might say.

SELF-DISCLOSURE

Practitioners use self-disclosure to share personal information, observations, and opinions with the client in order to give the client a different perspective or to offer an illustration or example of how a step may be accomplished. The information may be about the practitioner's personal experience or his or her experience of the client or other clients. There are three suggested guidelines to consider prior to using self-disclosure (Anderson & Mandell, 1989; Mahalik, VanOrmer, & Simi, 2000). First, the goal of disclosures should be to enhance or preserve the relationship. It is important that self-disclosures occur in relationships that are strong and well-developed (Myers & Hayes, 2006). For example, in a well-established relationship, the practitioner might say, "I am feeling concerned because it seems like our working relationship is strained. I wonder if there is a problem between us that you would be willing to discuss." Second, practitioners need to ensure that their personal needs do not take precedence over those of the client. The practitioner should not share anything about his or her personal life or problems that might invite the client to feel like s/he should take care of the practitioner. Third, disclosures must always be for the benefit of the client and be designed to keep the focus on the client. The practitioner might briefly say, "I have some understanding of the challenges you are facing dealing with your mother's illness, because I faced something similar several years ago."

Too much self-disclosure can be a way of subtly including values in interactions. When practitioners disclose decisions or life experiences they have had, clients may feel that they should make similar decisions. Examples might be a practitioner disclosing that she had an abortion, got a divorce, returned to work and put her young children into daycare, or had an affair. Each of these disclosures could imply that the practitioner is recommending similar behavior to a client whose values might be quite different.

Ethical concerns should also be considered when using self-disclosure. For example, a practitioner might use self-disclosure to relieve his or her own discomfort with the inequality of the relationship (Herron & Rouslin, 1984). In such a case, the practitioner chooses to tell the client something about his or her personal life in the same way that s/he might share with a friend. If self-disclosure is not carefully moderated, boundaries between the personal and professional become confused and the client's perceptions of the competence and empathy of the practitioner may be irrevocably damaged (Curtis, 1982). For example, a practitioner might have experienced a situation similar to the client's (a significant other with a substance abuse problem) and choose to reveal this to a client. If the purpose of the self-disclosure is to gain sympathy or support from the client, the relationship has crossed the line from professional to personal.

Kottler (2003) suggests a set of standards for practitioner self-disclosure. Prior to self-disclosing to a client, practitioners should ask themselves the following questions:

- What do I hope this will accomplish?
- Is there another way to make the same point?
- What do I risk by not sharing about myself?
- To what extent am I attempting to meet my own needs?
- Is this the right time to share this information?
- How can I say this most concisely?
- How will the client personalize what I share about myself?
- How can I put the focus back on the client? (p. 62)

Another challenging aspect of self-disclosure is how to respond when asked direct and often personal questions, particularly if these questions are asked early in the relationship with the client. Practitioners need to consider what led the client to ask the question. If the client, a middle-aged mother of four children who is living in poverty, asks the young, well-dressed female practitioner, "Do you have children?" what are your hunches about the client's reasons for asking this question? In our experience, this kind of question is often an indication that the client is afraid that the practitioner doesn't have enough life experience to understand her and her situation. Although there are different opinions about how to respond to such a question, we recommend that you keep the focus on the client and say something like, "I wonder if maybe you are concerned about whether I will be able to understand your situation. Will you tell me more about what it is like for you to be caring for four children?" Many personal questions are veiled concerns about not being understood.

Some personal questions a client might ask may be efforts to change the relationship from a professional relationship to a personal relationship. These are the kind of questions you might ask a friend over coffee, such as "Who are you going to vote for?", "What is your favorite type of music?", or "What do you think about (some sports team)?" Rather than answering the question, the practitioner needs to talk with the client about the nature of their relationship. The practitioner might say, "I am glad that you want to talk with someone about music. That is a great topic to introduce with someone you would like to make friends with, but it is important for us to stay focused on the goals we established. Since one of those goals involves making more friends, perhaps you would be willing to ask someone you would like to get to know better about their favorite type of music."

Another kind of personal question is actually a request for advice, such as "How do you think teenagers should be disciplined?" or "I notice you are married. What do you do when you are angry with your husband?" Once again the best policy is to explore the client's underlying concern. The practitioner might say, "Figuring out the most effective way to discipline teenagers is challenging. What have you tried that has worked?" or "What do you think might be worth a try?"

The use of self-disclosing statements by practitioners needs to be employed sparingly to keep the focus on the client (Meier & Davis, 2004). It is appropriate for practitioners to disclose their current feelings *only* if they are relevant to the immediate tasks or goals of the client. Self-disclosure of what the practitioner is experiencing in the present has a greater impact than reporting on experiences from the past. For example, a group practitioner might say, "I am feeling frustrated about what is going on in the group right this minute. It seems to me like we are avoiding dealing with the real problem. I wonder how other group members are feeling about what just happened."

GENUINENESS AND SELF-DISCLOSURE

As we discussed in Chapter 4, being genuine involves being natural and sincere rather than stiff, and being fully present rather than thinking about something else, such as what to say next. Genuineness also involves sharing feelings about what is happening in the work with the client. Using self-disclosure, practitioners may share their thoughts, feelings, and/or opinions about the immediate situation. For example, a practitioner might say, "I am having trouble paying attention to what you are saying because it seems like you are repeating the same things." In a team meeting, the practitioner might state, "I am feeling frustrated because it seems like only a few of us are doing most of the work." To a family, the practitioner could say, "I am amazed at how much you have accomplished in a short period of time."

As with the other core interpersonal qualities, you can evaluate the demonstration of genuineness using a scale.

Genuineness Evaluation Scale

Level 1: The practitioner appeared stiff, tense, distracted, and/or detached from the process most of the time, and responses were obviously not connected to the practitioner's feelings; flat affect.

Level 3: The practitioner appeared sincere and relaxed, but not clearly connected to or focused on the process.

Level 5: The practitioner appeared sincere, relaxed, focused on the client, and selectively shared personal reactions to the client's feelings, comments, and behavior.

HOMEWORK EXERCISE 13.9 | SELF-DISCLOSURE AND EXPRESSING GENUINENESS

Many people find it easy to share positive in-the-moment thoughts and feelings but more challenging to express negative in-the-moment thoughts and feelings. During groups, meetings, gatherings, or classes, write down what you might say if you were going to express your in-the-moment thoughts and feelings.

FOCUSING ON IMPROVEMENT

Focusing on improvement is similar to identifying strengths and helps clients see what they are doing well. Any progress should be noticed, reinforced, and fully explored. Practitioners might ask about the details related to the accomplishment. It is important to emphasize any positive steps, particularly those that the client might not be valuing. Clients sometimes criticize themselves for not doing enough instead of complimenting

TABLE 13.1 | SKILLS TO ENHANCE ACHIEVEMENT OF STEPS

Skill	Purpose	Examples	Specific Methods
Teaching	To help clients learn new methods, new ways of thinking, new behaviors, and new ways of acting.	• Ways to communicate needs in an appropriate way. • Better ways to discipline children.	• Providing information or explaining. • Demonstrating. • Rehearsing or role playing.
Directing	To invite clients to try something new or to go in a different direction.	• Asking a client to say something using "I" instead of "you" statements. • Suggesting a different approach to disciplining children.	• Making a suggestion. • Giving homework. • Giving direction in a role play.
Inviting a different perspective	To help clients view their experiences, feelings, thoughts, behaviors, or situation in a new way by sharing another perspective with them.	• Asking a client to consider her husband's inability to share his feelings as a lack of communication skills rather than a demonstration of his indifference to her.	• Offering an alternate view. • Asking questions to help clients consider another perspective.
Identifying discrepancies	To invite clients to see or think about something differently.	• One of the goals we identified is that you will spend time with your AA friends who support the way you want to live. Help me understand what happened that led you to go to a bar and eventually get drunk.	• Pointing out an incongruity between the client's present behavior and his or her broader goals and values.
Giving feedback	To give the client information s/he may not be aware of.	• "I noticed that when you started talking about seeing your father you clenched your jaw and made a fist."	• Describing to the client what the practitioner sees and hears (verbal and nonverbal).
Immediacy	To help the client understand his or her patterns of interpersonal behavior problems by examining the client's responses to the practitioner, the work process, or the client/practitioner relationship.	• Change in client behavior towards the practitioner. • Client pattern of avoiding eye contact with the practitioner.	• Discussing client reactions to the practitioner. • Statements about client behavior toward the practitioner.
Self-disclosure	To share personal information, observations, and opinions with the client in order to give another perspective.	• Practitioner comments on what s/he is experiencing with a group at the time.	• Statements about the practitioner's current thoughts or feelings or some experience of practitioner that is directly relevant to the client.

themselves for every small change. Practitioners, realizing how difficult change can be, should invite clients to celebrate each step in the process. For example, a practitioner might ask a family or a group, "What did each of you do to help make your time together go well?" Clients might be asked to focus on positives: "Between now and the next time we meet, I want you to find one aspect of your new behavior that went well and that you'd like to continue doing." Research has demonstrated that using this type of assignment correlates positively with improvement (Kazantzis & Ronan, 2006; Neimeyer & Feixas, 1990).

An important part of the action phase is the ongoing monitoring of progress. At regular intervals the practitioner and client should evaluate whether the client is satisfied with the progress. If little progress is being made, the problem may be related to the established goal or goals. Reconsidering whether the goals are attainable and highly valued is a useful practice. The practitioner and client could explore whether the client is really motivated and able to achieve the goals at this time. Maybe the goals are not attainable because they involve someone else changing, or maybe other stress in the client's life has limited his or her ability to move forward. Sometimes progress is being made but seems slow to the practitioner. In this situation, the practitioner may not understand all of the challenges the client experiences. Working with the client to create smaller steps or devoting more time to helping the client get ready to successfully complete tasks may be useful.

Examples of Focusing on Improvement
- With an individual:
  - "After talking to your boss, how did you feel about yourself?"

- With a family:
  - "Will each of you tell one person in the family about one thing he or she did last week that you liked?"
  - "Will you tell us about what you did that made things go a little bit better for the family this week?"

- With a group:
  - "Let's go around the circle and share one positive thing we noticed when we first met each other."

- With a team:
  - "We have been working together for a while now. How about if we take a minute to review what we have accomplished?"

HOMEWORK EXERCISE 13.10 | FOCUSING ON IMPROVEMENT

In a conversation with a fellow student, friend, or family member, spend 10 minutes listening, expressing understanding, and focusing on improvement. This will require you think about what the person is doing right. Remember that each small step in the direction of the person's goals is an improvement that deserves recognition.

EMPIRICALLY BASED PRACTICE

As practitioners assist clients in developing their action steps, the ways in which they use their professional knowledge to guide clients are based on many things, including the policies of their agency, their own practice experience, and theories of human behavior. In recent years there has been increasing interest in evidence-based practice based on research studies conducted to determine the most effective ways to respond to the various problems clients present. Most of these studies have focused on work with individuals (Castonguay & Beutler, 2006; Fonagy, Target, Cottrell, Phillips, & Kurtz, 2002). For example, there are many studies that support the importance of core interpersonal qualities in determining the outcome of work with individual clients. There are fewer research studies involving work with couples (Sexton, Alexander, & Mease, 2003), and even fewer on work with families (Roberts, Vernberg, & Jackson, 2000; Sexton, Alexander, & Mease, 2003). Little has been done to determine the most effective way to intervene when addressing the problems larger groups may present (Burlingame, Mackenzie, & Strauss, 2004).

After mastering the foundational skills in this book, you will want to go on to learn more about specific approaches or theories for working with individuals, families, groups, and organizations. As you learn about and evaluate the many possible approaches, it will be essential for you to consider which approaches have been empirically shown to be effective with specific types of client problems and situations. Keeping up with the latest research findings can enhance your understanding of how best to work with the particular issues your clients present.

 DVD Example Check out the *Devloping Helping Skills* DVD for a demonstration of taking action skills.

CASE | CASE, PART 5

Instructions: Refer to Part 4 of the class Example Case on pages 173–174 before working on Part 5.

1. Think about the case from the perspectives discussed in Chapter 2: constructivism, resilience, ecological, dual perspectives, strengths, and empowerment. Discuss how each perspective might be used to help you and your client during the action phase.

2. Select one goal and write out a basic plan for the beginning of the action phase of the work. Your plan should identify at least five steps and discuss three action phase skills that could be used. Do a role play with your group that continues the work into the action phase.

3. Evaluate the practitioner's work in the role-play.

4. What did the practitioner say to invite the client to identify steps s/he might take to reach the goal? Was this use of skills effective—that is, did it invite the client to work further to identify steps?

5. Did the practitioner use teaching? If so, what topics were covered? Did this use of skills seem helpful?

6. Did the practitioner invite a different perspective? If so, what did the practitioner say? If not, how might this skill have been used?

7. Did you notice any discrepancies between the client's statements and her reported behavior? If so, did the practitioner identify the discrepancies?

8. Did the practitioner use self-disclosure? If not, how might self-disclosure have been used?

9. In what ways did the practitioner focus on improvements? List specific responses used by the practitioner.

PRACTICE EXERCISE 8 | TAKING ACTION

Exercise Objectives
- To practice using skills related to action.

Step 1: Preparation
Form groups of three people. Each person will have the opportunity to play the roles of: client, practitioner, and peer supervisor. Each meeting will last 15 minutes.

Client Role
- Prepare to summarize the exploration of person, problem, and situation.

Practitioner Role
- Review the skills to invite action: teaching, directing, identifying discrepancies, inviting a different perspective, giving feedback, using self-disclosure, and focusing on improvements.

Peer Supervisor Role
- Review the skills to invite action.
- Prepare to keep track of the time.

Step 2: The Client Meeting

Client Role
- Summarize what was said in previous meetings about your problem and situation.

Practitioner Role
- Use all of the skills learned previously and those for inviting action.

Peer Supervisor Role
- Keep track of the time and tell the practitioner and client when 14 minutes are completed so the practitioner has time to close the meeting.
- Check off the beginning and ending skills used by the practitioner.
- Write down each practitioner statement and question. You may abbreviate, use a form of shorthand, or just write the first group of words in the statement, or you can tape record the interview and transcribe or listen to the tape.

Step 3: Feedback

Client Role
- Describe how you experienced the practitioner.

Practitioner Role
- Evaluate your use of the skills for taking action.
- In what ways did you help the client move toward his or her goals?

Peer Supervisor Role
- Give feedback to the practitioner from your notes on skills used for the action phase.
- Give feedback on inappropriate responses.
- Complete the evaluation form.
- Evaluate the practitioner's use of the core interpersonal qualities of warmth, empathy, respect, and genuineness. (The scales are in Appendix A.)
- Record the feedback in the practitioner's book for future reference.

Genuineness Evaluation Scale

Level 1: The practitioner appeared stiff, tense, distracted, and/or detached from the process most of the time, and responses were obviously not connected to the practitioner's feelings; flat affect.

Level 3: The practitioner appeared sincere and relaxed, but not clearly connected to or focused on the process.

Level 5: The practitioner appeared sincere, relaxed, focused on the client, and selectively shared personal reactions to the client's feelings, comments, and behavior.

EVALUATION FORM: ACTION SKILLS

Name of Practitioner_____

Name of Peer Supervisor_____

Directions: Under each category (in italics) is a list of behaviors or skills. Give one check mark, worth one point, for each skill used by the practitioner.

Building Relationships

continued

PRACTICE EXERCISE 8 | TAKING ACTION *continued*

Beginning Subsequent Meetings

Give one point for each topic covered by the practitioner.

1. Asked client where s/he would like to begin.   _____
2. Summarized previous meeting.   _____
3. Identified tasks for this meeting.   _____
4. Asked client about progress.   _____
5. Asked client about homework.   _____
6. Asked client about problems.   _____
7. Made an observation about the previous meeting.   _____
8. Did a check-in.   _____

Closing Skills (for a meeting)

Give one point for each skill used by the practitioner.

1. Practitioner identified that the meeting was about to end.   _____
2. Practitioner provided a summary of the meeting.   _____
3. Practitioner reviewed any tasks that the client agreed to complete. _____
4. Practitioner discussed plans for future meetings.   _____
5. Practitioner invited client feedback about the work.   _____
6. Practitioner asked client about any final questions.   _____

Skills that Express Understanding

Give one point for each skill used by the practitioner.

1. Reflecting feelings   _____
2. Reflecting content   _____
3. Reflecting feelings and content   _____
4. Summarizing   _____
5. Exploring meanings   _____
6. Identifying strengths   _____

Exploring

Questioning Skills

Give one point for each skill used by the practitioner.

1. Expressed understanding before asking questions.   _____
2. Asked open-ended questions when appropriate.   _____
3. Asked one question at a time.   _____
4. Asked closed-ended questions when appropriate.   _____
5. Asked questions about strengths.   _____

Seeking Clarification

Give one point for each skill used by the practitioner.

1. Exploring the meaning of words and body language   _____
2. Exploring the basis of conclusions drawn by client   _____
3. Eliciting further clarifying information   _____
4. Allowing silence   _____

Defining the Focus

Reaching Agreement about Problems or Challenges

Give one point for each skill used by the practitioner. It rarely will be appropriate to use all of these skills in one meeting.

PRACTICE EXERCISE 8 | TAKING ACTION *continued*

1. Partializing _____
2. Advanced reflecting _____
3. Noticing patterns or themes _____
4. Identifying discrepancies _____
5. Rolling with resistance _____
6. Supporting self-efficacy _____
7. Stating agreement about problems or challenges _____

Reaching Agreement about Goals

Give one point for each skill used by the practitioner.

1. Reaching agreement on a general goal _____
2. Using questions to develop a MAPS goal _____
3. Reaching agreement on MAPS goal _____

Taking Action

Give one point for each skill used by the practitioner. It rarely will be appropriate to use all of these skills in one meeting.

1. Skills related to identifying steps _____
2. Teaching _____
3. Directing _____
4. Inviting a different perspective _____
5. Identifying discrepancies _____
6. Giving feedback _____
7. Using self-disclosure _____
8. Focusing on improvements _____

Common Mistakes or Inappropriate Responses (subtract 1 point for each) _____

(offering advice, reassuring, offering excuses, asking leading questions, dominating through teaching, labeling, interrogating)

Core Interpersonal Qualities

Using the scales in Appendix A, evaluate the appropriateness and effectiveness of the practitioner's expression of empathy, warmth, respect, and genuineness. On the following lines write the scores, from 1 to 5, for warmth, empathy, respect, and genuineness.

Score for warmth _____
Score for empathy _____
Score for respect _____
Score for genuineness _____

Genuineness Evaluation Scale

Level 1: The practitioner appeared stiff, tense, distracted, and/or detached from the process most of the time, and responses were obviously not connected to the practitioner's feelings; flat affect.

Level 3: The practitioner appeared sincere and relaxed, but not clearly connected to or focused on the process.

Level 5: The practitioner appeared sincere, relaxed, focused on the client, and selectively shared personal reactions to the client's feelings, comments, and behavior.

EXPECTED COMPETENCIES

In this chapter you have learned about working with clients to create an action plan to achieve their identified goals. You have also learned the following skills that are useful in the action phase of your work with clients: identifying steps, teaching, directing, inviting a different perspective, identifying discrepancies, giving feedback, using self-disclosure, and focusing on improvements.

You should now be able to:

- Give an example of using exception-finding questions to help identify a step.
- Explain when and why practitioners might instruct their clients.
- Describe how a practitioner might invite clients to consider taking a new perspective on their experiences, behaviors, thoughts, feelings, or situations.

- Give an example of a statement identifying a discrepancy.
- Give two examples of how a practitioner might direct a client.
- Give an example of how you might give feedback to a client.
- Explain appropriate and inappropriate uses of self-disclosure by a practitioner.
- Identify several reasons for focusing on improvements.
- Demonstrate the skills related to the action phase.

EVALUATING PROGRESS AND ENDING PROFESSIONAL RELATIONSHIPS

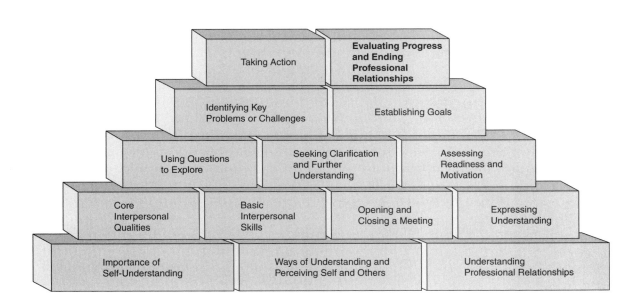

CHAPTER 14

205

In this chapter you will learn about the following topics:

Practitioner Tasks
- Working with clients to evaluate progress and end the relationship

Practitioner Skills
- Applying all the basic interpersonal skills that you have learned in order to evaluate and end the relationship

Client Attributes
- Willingness to share perceptions about the changes made, the progress of the work, and their thoughts and feelings related to ending the relationship

This final chapter covers important aspects of evaluating client progress and ending the relationship between clients and the practitioner. Once the practitioner and client have established clear goals, these goals provide a basis for evaluating progress and deciding when to end the professional relationship. Since professional relationships are purposeful, once the purpose or goal has been achieved, the relationship should end. The process of ending a relationship with a client will include preparing the client for ending, reviewing your work together, sharing feelings about ending, evaluating overall client progress, and supporting plans for continued growth. In keeping with the topic of evaluation, the chapter ends with a discussion of future professional development for practitioners.

EVALUATING PROGRESS

EVALUATION AS AN ONGOING PROCESS

Since evaluation should be continuous, throughout this book we have discussed evaluation in relation to each phase of work from beginning work with clients to expressing understanding, exploring, setting goals, and taking action. In this section we will review how evaluation fits into the earlier phases of work with clients.

Before the first meeting with a client, the practitioner should evaluate if additional information is needed and what level of expertise is likely to be necessary. During the exploration stage of the work, practitioners must evaluate whether they are obtaining the necessary information, if other people need to be involved, and if additional information about resources or challenges must be collected. Practitioners also need to evaluate whether they have the skills and abilities needed to work with a specific client. Some clients pose special challenges with which the practitioner may not be qualified to work. The practitioner's evaluation of his or her willingness to work with the client is also important. It is difficult to provide adequate services to clients if the practitioner cannot see the clients' strengths. In this case, the evaluation may lead to a referral. Of course, it is important for a practitioner to determine as early as possible whether s/he is qualified, willing, and able to work with a particular client. Sometimes this evaluation can be made based on the intake process, when preliminary information is provided before the practitioner begins meeting with the client.

During the exploring phase, the practitioner should evaluate whether s/he fully understands the problems, situation, and client. During the goal-setting phase of the work, practitioners need to evaluate whether they are accurately perceiving the goals that the client is motivated to achieve. In the action phase, the practitioner and client develop a plan for goal achievement that will provide a blueprint to evaluate progress.

After each meeting the practitioner should consider whether the work is leading to achievement of the identified goals. If the skills being used are not helping the client move forward, it is up to the practitioner to evaluate and decide what changes are needed. Maybe the practitioner has not really understood the client's situation or has chosen an inappropriate approach or method of working on the problem. As solution-focused therapists remind us, if what the practitioner is doing is not inviting progress toward goal achievement, the practitioner is obligated to evaluate and make a change (Kottler, 2001; O'Connell, 2005; Tohn & Oshlag, 2000). If progress is being made, it is important to highlight successes. An evaluation that emphasizes progress is supportive to clients and gratifying to practitioners. Research has shown that self-efficacy is enhanced as clients succeed in solving the problems they have identified (Bodenheimer et al., 2002). As self-efficacy increases, so does the client's sense of empowerment. Therefore, taking time to evaluate and celebrate each success is crucial to clients' growth.

As a part of the evaluation process, practitioners should talk to clients about whether they are ready and motivated to achieve the identified goals. Sometimes clients set goals that they believe someone else wants them to achieve, even though they are not ready or motivated to work on these goals. At other times, clients set goals that are really wishes for a change. Some clients want to achieve the goals they set, but they do not have enough energy to move ahead because of the many stresses and demands in their lives. For example, a couple stated their goal as improving their marriage, but in reality, neither partner was committed to doing anything except attending weekly meetings with the practitioner. They always gave the practitioner many reasons for not focusing on their marriage between meetings. In the fifth meeting, the practitioner decided to evaluate with the couple whether they were ready to invest the time and energy required to improve their marriage or whether the many stresses they were facing made working on their marriage impossible at that time.

One of the most important times for evaluation occurs during the ending process. During the ending phase of the work, the practitioner needs to evaluate the entire process and identify what was most helpful, what did not work as effectively, what was learned, and what areas for growth were identified. Involving clients in this overall evaluation is important. The practitioner and client might begin this evaluation by talking about what problems the client had at the beginning of the helping process, followed by reviewing what has been accomplished. The practitioner may share his or her own assessment of progress and ask the client for a similar assessment. It is important that the practitioner share feelings of pleasure about the positive changes the client has made and recognize the client's efforts. The practitioner may also help the client identify areas for additional work and affirm his or her ability to solve these problems using the skills developed in their work together.

Ongoing evaluation can be conducted weekly to identify how well the clients think that they are being heard and to determine the strength of the relationship between the practitioner and the client. Some of this evaluation may be completed with paper-and-pencil questions, but it is also important for the practitioner to observe the way the client responds as a part of the evaluation process. The client's level of comfort and participation will be part of this type of evaluation. This evaluation can be accomplished during the meeting by asking the client how s/he feels about being here today, how s/he feels about what has been discussed so far, or what has been most helpful in today's meeting. Remember that a positive relationship between the practitioner and client will make it much easier for the client to work toward goal achievement.

HOMEWORK EXERCISE 14.1 | Ongoing Evaluation

Write down at least three ways that you do ongoing evaluation of your activities or your progress toward goals. How is ongoing evaluation helpful to you?

Evaluation Using Scaling Questions

Evaluation should be an ongoing process that helps clients and practitioners know whether their work is effectively leading to goal achievement. Remember the previous discussion of scaling questions. Scaling questions are an excellent tool to use for evaluating progress (De Jong & Hopwood, 1996; Zalter & Fiske, 2005). Using scaling questions to evaluate progress, the practitioner asks clients to rate their progress on a scale of 1 to 10, where $1 =$ no progress and $10 =$ total achievement of the goal. If the client has a high score, s/he may feel ready to move on to another goal or to end the relationship. If the score is lower, the practitioner might ask the client what s/he could do before the next appointment to move up a little bit on the scale or the practitioner might work with the client to identify the steps needed to achieve the goal. The practitioner and client might also explore what has been helpful in achieving progress so far.

Examples of Evaluation
- "When we began working on reviewing the agency policies on providing services to elderly clients, we identified several goals. In our next meeting, let's review what we have accomplished in relation to each goal."
- "As you know, our final meeting will be three weeks from today. (reminding the client of when the relationship will end) Before our next meeting, will you think about what has been most helpful to you?"
- "Early on in this project we established clear goals. I think we should talk together about whether those goals have been achieved and decide if further work is necessary. Is that okay with you?"
- "On a scale of 1 to 10, with 10 being that you are completely satisfied with where you are in relation to the goals we set, what number would you give yourself?"
- "I remember that when we started working together you told me that folks in the family yelled at each other at almost every meal. You have come a long way since then. Let's spend a few minutes reviewing what you have accomplished since we began working together."

HOMEWORK EXERCISE 14.2 | Importance of Measuring Progress

Identify two goals that you set for yourself in the past: one goal that you achieved and one that you did not achieve. For each goal, think about what you did to keep yourself focused on achieving your goal. How did you measure your progress toward achieving the goal? Can you identify specific differences between the two goals in terms of the ways you stayed focused on the goal or monitored your progress?

It may be that you are so good at achieving goals that you move toward goals almost without consciously realizing what you are doing, but we often work with clients who are feeling incapable of achieving their goals. Helping clients monitor their progress will increase their confidence in their ability to achieve their goal and increase their motivation to take action needed to achieve their goals.

Think about programs such as Weight Watchers and Alcoholics Anonymous. Identify three things these organizations do to help participants stay focused and achieve their goals. Describe what they do to help people maintain their goals.

EVALUATION USING GOAL ATTAINMENT SCALING

Goal attainment scaling is another helpful evaluation system. Although goal attainment scaling was originally developed to monitor progress in work with patients in mental health programs (Kiresuk, Smith, & Cardillo, 1994), it has been used effectively in many other settings (Donnelly & Carswell, 2002; Rockwell, Howlett, Stadnyk, & Carver, 2003) and with systems of all sizes, from individuals to families to large organizations or neighborhoods (Compton, Galaway, & Cournoyer, 2005; Fisher & Hardie, 2002; Fleuridas, Leigh, Rosenthal, & Leigh, 1990; McLaren & Rodger, 2003; Robertson-Mjaanes, 2000). Using goal attainment scaling, the client and the practitioner create a 5-point scale or continuum that ranges from the most unfavorable outcome possible to the most favorable outcome that the client believes is possible. Each level of the scale should be measurable so the practitioner and client can determine where the client is on the scale. A scale is created for each goal. The client and practitioner can use the scale to identify the level of progress achieved either during the course of the work together or toward the end of the work. This scale includes the MAPS goal, or the expected outcome, as the midpoint. The following example shows how to use a goal attainment scale with an individual client, but goal attainment scales are also excellent evaluation tools to use with families, groups, and organizations.

Example: Goal Attainment Scale

For a client goal of obtaining employment, the practitioner would ask the client various questions as they worked together to establish a MAPS goal:

- "What kind of job do you feel you are qualified for?"
- "How many hours per week do you want to work?"
- "Is location important?"
- "What is the minimum salary you are willing to accept?"

For this example, the MAPS goal is a full-time job that pays minimum wage, is no more than 45 minutes from the client's home, and has one week of paid vacation per year. As the practitioner and client continue to work together to develop the goal attainment scale, the practitioner would ask questions such as the following:

- "What would it be like if you started moving backwards instead of making progress?" (This would establish the most unfavorable outcome thought possible.)
- "What if you almost achieved your goal, but not quite?" (This would establish the level of less than expected success.)
- "What will it be like when you are right on target for achieving your goal?" (The expected level of success is the MAPS goal.)
- "What do you think it will be like *when* you do a little better than achieving your MAPS goal?" (This establishes the greater than expected level of success. As a practitioner it is important that you carefully choose the words you use. What message would you be sending to your client if you asked, "What would it be like *if* you were able to achieve more than your goal?" The underlying message sent by using the word "when" is much more positive than the underlying message expressed by the word "if.")
- "What do you think it will be like when you achieve the most favorable result possible in the next six months?" (This question establishes the most favorable outcome the client believes is possible. It is important to state a time frame in this question because you want the client to be thinking about a time in the near future.)

Goal Attainment Scale

Most unfavorable outcome	Unemployed and about ready to give up the search.
Less than expected success	A part-time, minimum wage job with no benefits.
Expected outcome	(The MAPS goal) A full-time, minimum-wage job that is no more than 45 minutes from the client's home and has one week of paid vacation.
Greater than expected success	A full-time job that pays a dollar more than minimum wage, is no more than 45 minutes from the client's home, and has one week of paid vacation.
Most favorable outcome	A full-time job that pays two dollars more than minimum wage, is no more than 45 minutes from the client's home, and has one week of paid vacation.

As practitioners work with clients, they often set more than one MAPS goal. Using goal attainment scaling, each MAPS goal would become the expected outcome. The practitioner would then work with the client to establish the most unfavorable outcome, less than expected success, greater than expected success, and most favorable outcome. As you can imagine, it takes some time to develop a full goal attainment scale for several goals. However, this tool is very helpful as practitioners and clients evaluate progress, so it is worth taking the necessary time to create it. Since the goal attainment scale clearly shows not only the MAPS goal but also possible future goals, it helps clients visualize and begin to believe in the possibility of achieving even the most favorable outcome.

Example: Goal Attainment Scale for Three Goals

The problems identified by the client in this example were:

1. He was unemployed.
2. He was feeling so depressed that he stayed home most of the time.
3. He had no contact with his friends.

As the practitioner explored with the client what his life had been like when he wasn't depressed, the client identified that he was employed, had regular contact with friends, and regularly left the house to do things that he enjoyed.

EVALUATION FOR PROFESSIONAL DEVELOPMENT

Good practitioners are continually involved in evaluation of their work. As they work with clients, practitioners may elicit feedback about the things they said or did that were helpful as well as those that were not. As part of the final evaluation process, practitioners may invite clients to complete an evaluation form that asks about satisfaction with services, and/or the practitioner may decide to discuss satisfaction

	Unemployed	Lost Contact with Friends	Stays Home Most of the Time
Most unfavorable outcome	Unemployed and about ready to give up the search.	No contact with friends.	Only goes out if absolutely necessary.
Less than expected success	A part-time, minimum-wage job with no benefits.	Has reestablished contact with two friends that client talks to at least once a week.	Leaves home for necessary errands and tasks and goes out for a walk twice a week.
Expected outcome (MAPS goal)	A full-time, minimum-wage job that is no more than 45 minutes from the client's home and has one week of paid vacation.	Has reestablished contact with three friends that client talks to at least once a week and sees at least once a month.	Leaves home at least once a month for some pleasurable activity and goes out for a walk twice a week.
More than expected success	A full-time job that pays a dollar more than minimum wage, is no more than 45 minutes from the client's home, and has one week of paid vacation.	Has reestablished contact with four friends that client talks to at least once a week and sees at least once a month.	Leaves home at least once a month for some pleasurable activity and goes out for a walk three times a week.
Most favorable outcome	A full-time job that pays two dollars more than minimum wage, is no more than 45 minutes from the client's home, and has one week of paid vacation.	Has reestablished contact with four friends that client talks to at least once a week and sees at least twice a month.	Leaves home at least twice a month for some pleasurable activity and goes out for a walk three times a week.

HOMEWORK EXERCISE 14.3 | GOAL ATTAINMENT SCALE

Working with a partner, develop a goal attainment scale that includes three MAPS goals related to your life. Develop another goal attainment scale that includes three MAPS goals that you create for a family or group.

with the client face-to-face (Novick & Novick, 2006). Asking clients for feedback about their level of satisfaction with the work and what they identify as most helpful often gives practitioners important information for helping future clients.

ENDING PROFESSIONAL RELATIONSHIPS

Professional relationships end for a number of reasons. Sometimes clients know from the beginning of the process that their managed care provider has approved only a limited number of meetings or that they have only a certain amount of money for the service. Sometimes the practitioner may decide that the client would be better served with a referral to a different agency. Often clients achieve the results they want quickly and drop out of the helping process (Frank & Frank, 1991; Kazdin, 1995; Talmon, 1990). The client may choose not to continue the work for any number of other reasons: more pressing demands, illness, dissatisfaction with services, or moving to a different area (Gager, 2004). Some clients do not continue because they feel uncomfortable and believe that the practitioner did not understand them (Lever & Gmeiner, 2000). It is good practice to follow up when clients leave unexpectedly. Following up gives practitioners the opportunity to ask about the clients' decision to leave; to acknowledge the rights of clients to withdraw at any time; to offer to continue working with the clients in the future; and to possibly gain closure on the relationship. Ending because goals have been achieved or the clients are ready to move ahead on their own is generally the most rewarding outcome for clients and practitioners.

THE ENDING PROCESS

In many ways ending a professional relationship is similar to ending a meeting. As you remember from Chapter 6, there are six tasks for ending a meeting. The first task is for the practitioner to indicate that the meeting is about to end. In the ending process for a professional relationship, the practitioner identifies how many more meetings are remaining.

Second, at the end of a meeting the practitioner provides a summary of the meeting. In the ending process for a professional relationship, the practitioner and client summarize such things as what has been most important, what changes have been made, and what was most difficult. Reviewing and remembering the good and the difficult times in the process is important, even in brief professional relationships. During this review process, the client may want to thank the practitioner for his or her help.

Third, at the end of a meeting the practitioner reviews any tasks that the client agreed to complete before the next meeting. In the ending process for a professional relationship, the practitioner and the clients identify what tasks remain to be completed after the relationship has ended.

Fourth, at the end of a meeting the practitioner discusses plans for future meetings. In the ending process for a professional relationship, the practitioner and the clients discuss possible referrals and guidelines for returning to work with the practitioner.

Fifth, at the end of a meeting the practitioner invites client feedback about the meeting. In the ending process for a professional relationship, the practitioner invites feedback about the entirety of their work together.

Sixth, at the end of a meeting the practitioner asks the client about any final questions. This task is similar at the end of a professional relationship.

When the ending is planned, the practitioner should discuss this process thoroughly with the client. Even though the relationship is ending, practitioners often invite clients to return if they decide to be involved in the helping process at another time.

In talking to clients about ending the professional relationship, it is important to ask about their plans for maintaining the gains they have made, for pursuing continued growth, and for obtaining ongoing support. There are many ways that clients may continue to obtain support and to work on growth. The client may have friends, family, neighbors, church members, colleagues, and members of support groups who have been supportive and encouraging. Some clients move to other ways of sustaining their growth such as taking courses, becoming politically active, getting a new job, or joining a health club.

If clients have limited supportive relationships or are hesitant about their ability to continue on their own, they may feel scared, sad, or even angry, particularly if the ending process was not within their control but mandated by financial or insurance limitations. Sometimes the process of ending brings up old feelings of abandonment or loss for clients. They may suddenly say they are not ready to end the relationship with the practitioner after all. It is important to explore these feelings and to help clients realize that they have new skills to deal with their problems and that they can receive support from other relationships. Often clients can be encouraged to see this ending as an opportunity to prove to themselves that they can manage independently. With clients who are feeling hesitant about continuing on their own, it is particularly important to discuss available resources. Of course, clients always have the possibility of returning to the practitioner at some point in the future.

In a study on effects of ending support groups, Kacen (1999) studied group members' reactions and found that when participants experienced the group as cohesive and supportive, they felt temporary anxiety when the group ended. It is important to discuss normal feelings about ending supportive relationships. Often clients are pleased that they are ready to leave the group but are also ambivalent or scared about the prospect of no longer having the support of the group.

SHARING FEELINGS ABOUT ENDING

In long-term relationships the client and practitioner need to allow time to talk about their feelings about ending the relationship. They may be feeling happy and pleased about their achievements and ready to move on (Fortune, 1987). Just as it is important to note when goals are reached during the process of meeting with clients, it is even more valuable to allow time to celebrate what has been achieved and to recognize the strengths of all the individuals involved when the professional relationship is ending.

Time should be allowed to review accomplishments and to celebrate each change that has been made. Fortune, Pearlingi, and Rochelle (1992) found positive reactions about work accomplished were common. Clients reported feeling proud of their accomplishments and pleased to be ready to continue on their own. Practitioners were also positive about their clients' success and their own ability to be effective in helping clients.

Even though each practitioner/client relationship is unique, the ending of a relationship is a significant event and clients should have the opportunity to share their feelings about the ending. It is common to feel a sense of loss, sadness, fear, and even anger about ending, and practitioners should encourage clients to express their feelings. The practitioner might say, "We've spent a lot of time during this last meeting talking about your progress during our time together, but we haven't talked about our feelings about ending our relationship. What feelings do you have at this time?"

Practitioners also experience emotions as relationships end. Spending time together sharing emotions, talking about problems, setting goals, and evaluating progress often creates a strong bond that practitioners are also reluctant to lose. When appropriate, a practitioner might also share feelings about ending the relationship. For example, a practitioner might say, "I'm really going to miss our time together, and I feel sad when I think about it ending but happy that you are satisfied with your progress." When practitioners share their own feelings, the client may respond with additional feelings. Having the opportunity to share these feelings provides a sense of closure or completeness and opens the door to ending the relationship and saying goodbye.

Examples of Practitioner Statements that Provide Support and Share Feelings about Ending

- "This will be the last time that I see you. I hope the nursing home works out well for your father."
- "I am glad to hear that you have mended your relationship with your brother. I hope that over time you will become close friends and support each other."
- "I can see that you are really excited about the opportunities that your new job is going to provide for you."
- "Going to AA meetings seems to have been very helpful for you. I remember how scared you were about attending that first meeting, and now you are getting ready to sponsor and help someone else."

ENDINGS WITH GROUPS

Ending professional relationships with task groups, neighborhoods, organizations, and communities involves the same process as ending with individuals and families. First, it is important for the practitioner to talk about when the work will be completed or when the community or organization plans to continue the work without the assistance of the practitioner. Second, the practitioner needs to work with the organization or group to develop a thorough summary of what has been accomplished, as this will help to stabilize future changes. This discussion should lead to a review of agreed-upon tasks and future plans. Third, with large groups such as neighborhoods, organizations, and communities, it is essential that the practitioner work with the group to make plans for sustaining and building on the accomplishments. Scheduling a follow-up meeting at some time in the future is particularly helpful, as it gives the practitioner an opportunity to review the plans and provide support for continued development. Fourth, as part of any ending with a large group, there should be a system for evaluating the work accomplished and for giving feedback to the practitioner. Fifth and finally, celebrating the successes that have been achieved and recognizing individual and group efforts should be included in any ending.

Examples of Practitioner Statements for Ending a Professional Relationship

- "Before we say goodbye, let's talk about what you remember about our work together in this group."
- "I have enjoyed working with each of you and will miss seeing you, but I am confident that you folks will continue to use the parenting methods you learned in this group."
- "I have enjoyed working with your neighborhood group. I am pleased to see that many of you have moved into leadership positions in the group and are supporting each other as you move ahead with your plans."
- "Since next week will be our last meeting together, I think we should make a plan for how we will celebrate everything that you have achieved."
- "This is our last meeting. I hope you will call me and let me know how that job interview goes."
- "Let's take a few minutes to talk about resources that might be helpful to you in the future."
- "We have achieved a lot in our work together, but as you know everyone will face challenges throughout life. If something comes up in the future that you aren't able to solve on your own, I hope that you will feel comfortable calling me."

HOMEWORK EXERCISE 14.4 | ENDINGS

Think of a time when you ended an important relationship. How did you feel? What were some of the things that you needed to talk about before saying goodbye? Did you discuss the ending or changing of the relationship (for example, if your friend was moving a long distance away) or did you avoid talking about the possibly painful ending? What did you do that made the process easier or harder? Write down your ideas about how you can use what you know about ending relationships in your work as a practitioner.

Examples of Overall Process from Evaluating to Ending

- Discuss readiness to complete work together:
  - "Let's go over your goals and identify what we have completed and what we still need to work on." (You could use a scaling question related to each goal.)

- Evaluate progress:
  - "Let's review where you are related to your goals. On a scale of 1 to 10, with 10 being accomplishment of the goal we are working on, what score would you give yourself?" (Using goal attainment scaling would also be appropriate.)

- Evaluate the client's satisfaction with work completed:
  - "What are some of the things you liked about our work together?"
  - "Are there things that you were not satisfied with?"
  - "I'd like to hear any suggestions you have for improving our services."

- Identify when the meetings will end:
  - "We have decided to have two more meetings."
  - "As you remember, I will be leaving the agency at the end of next month."

- Share feelings about the work and the relationship:
  - "Would you tell me about when you were most uncomfortable in our work together?"
  - "I have enjoyed working with you."
  - "How are you feeling about the fact that our work together will be ending?"
  - "Sometimes ending a relationship like this one brings up memories of other relationships that ended. Is that happening for you?"

- Summarize accomplishments and review strengths:
  - "Let's talk about the challenges that brought you here and what you have accomplished."
  - "I am really pleased with all you were able to achieve. What are some of the things that you are most proud of accomplishing?"
  - "Some of your strengths I have noticed in our work together are . . ."
  - "What are your ideas about how you can use your strengths in the future?"

- Discuss plans for the future:
  - "Who are some of the people you might turn to for help if the going gets rough?"
  - "What are your ideas about things you can do to maintain the progress you have achieved? Let's review the tasks you are going to continue to work on."

CASE | **CASE, PART 6**

Based on your work with the class example case, put yourself in the role of practitioner and answer the following questions.

1. What are your plans for monitoring progress with the client?
2. What will you say to invite the client to give you feedback?
3. How will you and the client decide when to end your time together?
4. How might you prepare the client for the end of the professional relationship?

5. What could you do to help the client express his or her feelings about ending the relationship?
6. Write out at least five things that you might say as part of ending the relationship.
7. What issues and concerns in your own life arose as you worked with this client?
8. Do a role play with one person playing Jill and another person playing Sylvia. Role-play evaluating the goals, evaluating progress, and ending the work together. Use the evaluation form in your book to evaluate this final meeting.

PRACTICE EXERCISE 9 | EVALUATION AND ENDING

Exercise Objectives
- To practice ending the professional relationship with a client.

Step 1: Preparation
Form groups of three people. Each person will have the opportunity to play the roles of client, practitioner, and peer supervisor. Each meeting will last 15 minutes.

Client Role
- Prepare to discuss a problem.

Practitioner Role
- Review the skills of evaluating and ending with clients. (See evaluation form.)

Peer Supervisor Role
- Review the skills of evaluating and ending with clients. (See evaluation form.)
- Prepare to keep track of the time.

Step 2: The Client Meeting

Client Role
- Respond to practitioner.

Practitioner Role
- Use all of the skills learned previously and skills that are designed specifically for evaluating and ending with clients.

Peer Supervisor Role
- Keep track of the time and tell the practitioner and client when 14 minutes are completed so the practitioner has time to close the meeting.
- Check off the beginning skills used by the practitioner.

- Write down each practitioner statement and question. You may abbreviate, use a form of shorthand, or just write the first group of words in the statement, or you can tape record the interview and transcribe or listen to the tape.

Step 3: Feedback

Client Role
- Describe how you experienced the practitioner.

Practitioner Role
- Evaluate how well you worked with your client to evaluate his or her satisfaction and progress toward goal achievement.
- Evaluate how well you covered all the important topics related to ending a professional relationship (identified when the meeting will end, shared feelings about the relationship and work, summarized strengths and accomplishments, and discussed future plans).

Peer Supervisor Role
- Give feedback to the practitioner from your notes on the skills for evaluating and ending with clients.
- Give feedback on inappropriate responses.
- Complete the evaluation form.
- Evaluate the practitioner's use of the core interpersonal qualities of warmth, empathy, respect, and genuineness. (All of the scales are in Appendix A.)
- Record the feedback in the practitioner's textbook for future reference.

EVALUATION FORM: EVALUATING AND ENDING

Name of Practitioner_____

Name of Peer Supervisor_____

Directions: Under each category (in italics) is a list of behaviors or skills. Give one check mark, worth one point, for each skill used by the practitioner.

Building Relationships

continued

PRACTICE EXERCISE 9 | EVALUATION AND ENDING *continued*

Beginning Subsequent Meetings

Give one point for each topic covered by the practitioner.

1. Asked client where s/he would like to begin. _____
2. Summarized previous meeting. _____
3. Identified tasks for this meeting. _____
4. Asked client about progress. _____
5. Asked client about homework. _____
6. Asked client about problems. _____
7. Made an observation about the previous meeting. _____
8. Did a check-in. _____

Skills that Express Understanding

Give one point for each skill used by the practitioner.

1. Reflecting feelings _____
2. Reflecting content _____
3. Reflecting feelings and content _____
4. Summarizing _____
5. Exploring meanings _____
6. Identifying strengths _____

Exploring

Questioning Skills

Give one point for each skill used by the practitioner.

1. Expressed understanding before asking questions. _____
2. Asked open-ended questions when appropriate. _____
3. Asked one question at a time. _____
4. Asked closed-ended questions when appropriate. _____
5. Asked questions about strengths. _____

Seeking Clarification

Give one point for each skill used by the practitioner.

1. Exploring the meaning of words and body language. _____
2. Exploring the basis of conclusions drawn by client. _____
3. Eliciting further clarifying information. _____
4. Allowing silence. _____

Taking Action, Evaluating, and Ending

Evaluating and Ending

Give one point for each skill used by the practitioner.

1. Discussed readiness to complete work together. _____
2. Evaluated progress. _____
3. Evaluated client's satisfaction with work completed. _____
4. Identified when the meetings would end. _____
5. Shared feelings about the work and the relationship. _____
6. Summarized accomplishments and strengths. _____
7. Discussed plans for the future. _____

PRACTICE EXERCISE 9	Evaluation and Ending *continued*

Common Mistakes or Inappropriate Responses (subtract 1 point for each) _____
   (offering advice, reassuring, offering excuses, asking leading questions, dominating
   through teaching, labeling, interrogating)

Core Interpersonal Qualities

Using the scales in Appendix A, evaluate the appropriateness and effectiveness of
the practitioner's expressions of warmth, empathy, respect, and genuineness. On
the following lines write the scores, from 1 to 5, for warmth, empathy, respect,
and genuineness

Score for warmth _____
Score for empathy _____
Score for respect _____
Score for genuineness _____

 DVD Example Check out the *Developing Helping Skills* DVD for a demonstration of evaluating and ending.

PLANNING FOR FUTURE PROFESSIONAL DEVELOPMENT

In all professions there is an ethical obligation to evaluate your practice and to
continue to develop and enhance your skills (Ford, 2006; Orlinsky et al., 2005). Each
profession sets ethical guidelines for remaining current with best practices, being
involved in continuing education, and constructively evaluating your work. In most
states there are also legal obligations such as licensing requirements for ongoing
continuing education. Of particular importance is the development of multicultural
competence through increased self-awareness of one's own cultural values and biases,
sensitivity to other cultural perspectives, and learning how to incorporate this knowledge in selecting appropriate interventions for each client. Also, it is essential to
continue learning appropriate ways to work with people with a wide range of diversities
such as age, sexual orientation, gender, class, religion, and physical or mental ability.

Practitioners need to be involved in evaluation and growth throughout their
career. Besides self-evaluation and evaluation from clients, getting feedback from
peers and supervisors is very helpful. One way to get feedback is to assess your work
using the same system that you have learned using this book and to share with your
supervisor your self-assessment as well as your goals for improvement. To assist you
with that process we have included a complete evaluation form in Appendix B.

The best practitioners pursue ongoing professional development through several
methods. They develop self-knowledge by participating in personal counseling,
reflecting on their own values and ethics in their work with diverse clients, and/or
participating in lifelong learning to constantly keep abreast of new ideas, programs,
and resources. They also develop professionally through effective training in their
formal education, through high-quality supervision at training sites, and later from
peer consultation. At different times in your professional career, you may find yourself

focusing on one of these areas more than another, but each is important to your ultimate success. We hope that you will never forget your fundamental goal to be the very best practitioner you can be and that you will do whatever it takes to achieve your goal. Long-time practitioners usually find that they have become more eclectic in their approach to serving others in various venues. They note the importance of being flexible (changing the groups they work with), continuing to expand their knowledge (keeping abreast of new information about effective methods) and making time for good self-care (focusing on what makes them feel good).

Future challenges for practitioners are likely to include dealing creatively with decreased funding for all types of health care; adjusting to changing demographics of many cities (such as an aging population and more people of color), and keeping up to date on new research findings about what promotes effective change. We encourage your continued growth and development in this field.

CASE | CASE, PART 7

Jill tried several things before she began to feel better. She went back to exercising every day and stopped losing weight. She also began allowing herself time to enjoy her coffee in the morning, but reported that drinking coffee alone was okay but kind of lonely. She went out with her friends but found she didn't really enjoy herself or participate as much as she had in the past. She went for an all-day hike by herself but spent some of the time wishing she wasn't alone. In meeting 8, as she talked again about missing Seth's companionship, she told Sylvia that one of her friends had suggested getting a pet. Sylvia asked Jill how that sounded to her. As they explored Jill's feelings about having the responsibility of caring for a pet and what type of pet would suit her, Jill began to talk about the dog she had when she was growing up. She became more enthusiastic about the idea of adopting a dog "maybe from a shelter, since I need an adult dog so I don't have to be there all the time." Jill also talked about taking the dog to obedience training so the dog could come with her to school once in a while or she could take the dog to the nursing home to visit with the residents.

Sylvia had never seen Jill so excited and animated about anything they had talked about. She cautioned Jill to think carefully about it, but also encouraged her. By meeting 9, Jill reported having visited three local shelters and adopting a 3-year-old lab/border collie mix that she named Dreamer.

As they had agreed to meet one more time, Sylvia reminded Jill that their time together was nearly over.

At their final meeting, Sylvia summarized their meetings together and Jill remembered how she felt when she came to the first few meetings.

JILL: I know my life won't ever be perfect and sometimes things won't work out the way I want. I know that I will probably always give more to my friends than they will give back to me, but now I have Dreamer, who is always there beside me with a wagging tail and adoring eyes. We are signed up for Doggy Obedience classes and I am really looking forward to them since I can tell Dreamer is very smart. She can already sit on command and tries so hard to please me. I told my students about taking her hiking and it seems like it is a little easier to look forward to school now that I have something to talk to them about. I even make the stories about Dreamer a reward for them when they finish all their work. (*laughs*) I have to make up stories as I don't have that many real ones yet, but maybe by next year, I will. (*She looks serious again.*) Even better, I have something to get up for and to come home to at the end of the day.

Sylvia reminds Jill that she can return to talk if she feels the need to do so in the future, but Sylvia doesn't think she'll see Jill again for a long time, if ever.

Exercise

After reading how the real case ended, discuss your thoughts and feelings about the case as a whole.

EXPECTED COMPETENCIES

In this chapter, you have learned about evaluating progress and ending the professional relationship in an effective and supportive way.

You should now be able to:

- Design a goal attainment scale.
- State three reasons for lack of progress toward the MAPS goal.

- Give two examples of appropriate evaluation comments.
- Describe the six steps in the ending process.
- Demonstrate evaluating and ending a professional relationship.

Practice Evaluation Scales

Listening: Content and Process Evaluation Scale

Level 1: The practitioner did not summarize any of the major elements of content or describe anything about the client's way of speaking.

Level 3: The practitioner summarized *four elements* of content but did not describe anything about the client's way of speaking.

Level 5: The practitioner summarized all the major elements of content and accurately and fully described the client's way of speaking, including communication style, volume, and speed of delivery.

Empathy Evaluation Scale

Level 1: *Once during the meeting* the practitioner communicated an understanding of the client's experience and feelings with enough clarity that the client indicated agreement.

Level 3: *Three times during the meeting* the practitioner communicated an understanding of the client's experience with enough clarity that the client indicated agreement.

Level 5: *Five times during the meeting* the practitioner communicated an understanding of the client's experience with enough clarity that the client indicated agreement.

Warmth Evaluation Scale

Level 1: The practitioner communicated *little or no concern* for the client and appeared cold, detached, and/or mechanical.

Level 3: *At least half the time,* the practitioner communicated verbal and nonverbal expressions of concern and compassion that were appropriately suited to the unique needs of the client.

Level 5: The practitioner *consistently* communicated verbal and nonverbal expressions of concern and compassion that were appropriately suited to the unique needs of the client.

Respect Evaluation Scale

Level 1: The practitioner did not invite discussion of and/or recognize the client's strengths, resources, and/or capacities, and/or showed a lack of respect for the client's abilities such as helping or providing answers that the client did not ask for.

Level 3: *Once during the meeting,* the practitioner invited discussion of and/or recognized the client's strengths, resources, and/or capacities, and the practitioner did nothing that showed a lack of respect for the client's abilities such as helping or providing answers that the client did not ask for.

Level 5: *Three times during the meeting,* the practitioner invited discussion of and/or recognized the client's strengths, resources, and/or capacities, showed positive regard for the client, and did nothing that showed a lack of respect for the client's abilities such as helping or providing answers that the client did not ask for.

Genuineness Evaluation Scale

Level 1: The practitioner appeared stiff, tense, distracted, and/or detached from the process most of the time, and responses were obviously not connected to the practitioner's feelings; flat affect.

Level 3: The practitioner appeared sincere and relaxed, but not clearly connected to or focused on the process.

Level 5: The practitioner appeared sincere, relaxed, focused on the client, and selectively shared personal reactions to the client's feelings, comments, and behavior.

OVERALL EVALUATION FORM

Name of Practitioner_____

Name of Peer Supervisor_____

Directions: Under each category (in italics) is a list of behaviors or skills. Give one check mark, worth one point, for each skill used by the practitioner.

Building Relationships

Attending

Give one point for each behavior used by the practitioner.

1. Open and accessible body posture _____
2. Congruent facial expression _____
3. Slightly inclined toward the client _____
4. Regular eye contact unless inappropriate _____
5. No distracting behavior _____
6. Minimal encouragement _____

Observing

Give one point for each item accurately described by the practitioner.

1. Facial expression _____
2. Eye movement and eye contact _____
3. Body position and movement _____
4. Breathing patterns _____
5. Muscle tone _____
6. Gestures _____
7. Skin tone changes _____

Active Listening Skills Content and Process

Using the listening scale in Appendix A, evaluate the accuracy and completeness of the practitioner's ability to summarize what the client said and describe the client's way of speaking, including such things as speaking style, vocal tone and volume, and speed of delivery. On the following line write the score, from 1 to 5, for listening.   _____

Beginning Skills

Give one point for each topic covered by the practitioner.

1.   Introduce yourself and your role.   _____
2.   Seek introductions.   _____
3.   Identify where meeting will be held.   _____
4.   Identify how long meeting will last.   _____
5.   Describe the initial purpose of the meeting.   _____
6.   Explain some of the things you will do.   _____
7.   Outline the client's role.   _____
8.   Discuss ethical and agency policies.   _____
9.   Seek feedback from the client.   _____

Beginning Subsequent Meetings

Give one point for each topic covered by the practitioner.

1.   Asked client where s/he would like to begin.   _____
2.   Summarized previous meeting   _____
3.   Identified tasks for this meeting   _____
4.   Asked client about progress   _____
5.   Asked client about homework   _____
6.   Asked client about problems   _____
7.   Made an observation about the previous meeting   _____
8.   Did a check-in   _____

Closing Skills (for a meeting)

Give one point for each skill used by the practitioner.

1.   Identified that the meeting was about to end.   _____
2.   Provided a summary of the meeting.   _____
3.   Reviewed any tasks that the client agreed to complete.   _____
4.   Discussed plans for future meetings.   _____
5.   Invited client feedback about the work.   _____
6.   Asked client about any final questions.   _____

Skills that Express Understanding

Give one point for each skill used by the practitioner.

1.   Reflecting feelings   _____
2.   Reflecting content   _____
3.   Reflecting feelings and content   _____
4.   Summarizing   _____
5.   Exploring meanings   _____
6.   Identifying strengths   _____

Exploring

Questioning Skills

Give one point for each skill used by the practitioner.

1. Expressed understanding before asking questions.   _____
2. Asked open-ended questions when appropriate.   _____
3. Asked one question at a time.   _____
4. Asked closed-ended questions when appropriate.   _____
5. Asked questions about strengths.   _____

Person, Problem/Challenge, and Situation

Give one point for each topic discussed.

Problems or Challenges

Previous attempts to solve problem   _____
History of the problem(s)   _____
Severity or intensity of the problem(s)   _____

Person

Feelings about having the problem(s)   _____
Effects of the problem(s) on other areas   _____
(such as health, sleeping, ability to function at school or work)

Personal strengths   _____

Situation

Effect of the problem on other people   _____
Available social support and strengths in environment   _____
Other demands and stresses in the situation/environment   _____

Seeking Clarification

Give one point for each skill used by the practitioner.

1. Exploring the meaning of words and body language   _____
2. Exploring the basis of conclusions drawn by client   _____
3. Eliciting further clarifying information   _____
4. Allowing silence   _____

Defining the Focus

Reaching Agreement about Problems or Challenges

Give one point for each skill used by the practitioner. It rarely will be appropriate
to use all of these skills in one meeting.

1. Partializing   _____
2. Advanced reflecting   _____
3. Noticing patterns or themes   _____
4. Identifying discrepancies   _____
5. Rolling with resistance   _____
6. Supporting self-efficacy   _____
7. Stating agreement about problems or challenges   _____

Reaching Agreement about Goals

Give one point for each skill used by the practitioner.

1.   Reaching agreement on a general goals   _____
2.   Using questions to develop a MAPS goal   _____
3.   Reaching agreement on MAPS goal   _____

Taking Action, Evaluating, and Ending

Taking Action

Give one point for each skill used by the practitioner. (It rarely will be appropriate to use all of these skills in one meeting.)

1.   Identifying steps
2.   Teaching   _____
3.   Directing   _____
4.   Inviting a different perspective   _____
5.   Identifying discrepancies   _____
6.   Giving feedback   _____
7.   Using self-disclosure   _____
8.   Focusing on improvements   _____

Evaluating and Ending a Professional Relationship

Give one point for each skill used by the practitioner.

1.   Discussed readiness to complete work together.
2.   Evaluated progress.   _____
3.   Evaluated client's satisfaction with work completed.   _____
4.   Identified when the meetings would end.   _____
5.   Shared feelings about the work and the relationship.   _____
6.   Summarized accomplishments and strengths.   _____
7.   Discussed plans for the future.   _____

Common Mistakes or Inappropriate Responses (subtract 1 point for each)
(offering advice, reassuring, offering excuses, asking leading questions, dominating through teaching, labeling, interrogating)   _____

Core Interpersonal Qualities

Using the scales in Appendix A, evaluate the appropriateness and effectiveness of the practitioner's expression of warmth, empathy, respect, and genuineness. On the following lines write the scores, from 1 to 5, for warmth, empathy, respect, and genuineness.

Score for warmth   _____
Score for empathy   _____
Score for respect   _____
Score for genuineness   _____

REFERENCES

Ackerman, A. J., & Hilsenroth, M. J. (2001). A review of therapist characteristics and techniques negatively impacting the therapeutic alliance. *Psychotherapy, 38,* 171–185.

Alexander, J. J., Robbins, M. S., & Sexton, T. L. (2000). Family-based interventions with older at-risk youths: From promise to proof to practice. *Journal of Primary Prevention, 42,* 185–205.

Allen, D. M. (2006). Use of between-session homework in systems-oriented individual psychotherapy. *Journal of Psychotherapy Integration, 16,* 238–253.

Anderson, S. C., & Mandell, D. L. (1989). The use of self-disclosure by professional social workers. *Social Casework: The Journal of Contemporary Social Casework, 70,* 259–267.

Anderson, T., Ogles, B., & Weiss, A. (1999). Creative use of interpersonal skills in building a therapeutic alliance. *Journal of Constructivist Psychology, 12,* 313–330.

Appleby, G. A., & Anastas, J. W. (1998). *Not just a passing phase: Social work with gay, lesbian, and bisexual people.* New York: Columbia University Press.

Baez, R. (2003). *Teaching basic clinical skills: Assessment of a manual-based training program.*

Unpublished dissertation, Azusa Pacific University, Azusa, CA.

Bandura, A. (1989). Human agency in social cognitive theory. *American Psychologist, 44*(9), 1175–1184.

Bandura, A., & Cervone, D. (1983). Self-evaluative and self-efficacy mechanisms governing the motivational effects of goals systems. *Journal of Personality and Social Psychology, 45,* 1017–1028.

Bandura, A., & Schunk, D. H. (1981). Cultivating competence, self-efficacy, and intrinsic interest through proximal self-motivation. *Journal of Personality and Social Psychology, 41,* 586–598.

Banerjee, M. M., & Pyles, L. (2004). Spirituality: A source of resilience for African American women in the era of welfare reform. *Journal of Ethnic & Cultural Diversity in Social Work, 13,* 45–70.

Baucom, D. H., Shoham, V., Mueser, K. T., Daiuto, A. D., & Stickle, T. R. (1998). Empirically supported couple and family interventions for marital distress and adult mental health problems. *Journal of Consulting and Clinical Psychology, 66,* 53–88.

Baum, B. E., & Gray, J. J. (1992). Expert modeling, self-observation using videotape, and acquisition of basic therapy skills. *Professional*

Psychology: Research and Practice, 23, 220–225.

Beahrs, J. O., & Gutheil, T. G. (2001). Informed consent in psychotherapy. *The American Journal of Psychiatry, 158,* 4–10.

Bedi, R. P. (2006). Concept mapping the client's perspective on counseling alliance formation. *Journal of Counseling Psychology, 53,* 26.

Belcher, L., Kalichman, S., Topping, M., Smith, S., Emshoff, J., Norris, F., & Nurss, J. (1998). A randomized trial of a brief HIV risk reduction counseling intervention for women. *Journal of Consulting and Clinical Psychology, 66,* 858–861.

Belkin, G. S. (1984). *Introduction to counseling.* Dubuque, IA: Brown.

Bennet, L. A., Wolin, S. J., & Reiss, D. (1987). Couples at risk for transmission of alcoholism: Protective influences. *Family Process, 26,* 111–129.

Benson, C., Peet, C., Stephenson, N., Osterkamp, U., Boreham, A., Hatgis, C., Hofmeister, A., Despard, E., Papadopoulos, D., Kugelmann, R., Gulerce, A., & Malone, K. R. (2003). Self and subjectivity. In N. Stephenson, H. L. Radtke, R. J. Jorna, & H. J. Stam (Eds.), *Theoretical psychology: Critical contributions.* Toronto: Captus University.

Berg, I. K., & Miller, S. D. (1992). *Working with the problem drinker: A solution-focused approach.* New York: Norton.

Bernotavicz, F. (1994). A new paradigm for competency-based training. *Journal of Continuing Social Work Education. 6,* 3–9.

Beutler, L., Machado, P., & Allstetter-Neufelt, A. (1994). Therapist variables. In A. Bergin & S. Garfield (Eds.), *Handbook of psychotherapy and behavior change* (4th ed., pp. 229–269). Toronto: Wiley.

Beyeback, M., Morejon, A. R., Palenzuela, D. L., & Rodriguez-Arias, J. L. (1996). Research on the process of solution-focused therapy. In S. D. Miller, M. A. Hubbles, & B. L. K. Duncan (Eds.), *Handbook of solution-focused brief therapy* (pp. 251–271). San Francisco: Jossey-Bass.

Bodenheimer, T., Lorig, K., Holman, H., & Grumbach, K. (2002). Patient self-management of chronic disease in primary care. *JAMA 288,* 2469–2475.

Brave Heart, M. Y. H. (2003). The historical trauma response among natives and its relationship with substance abuse: A Lakota illustration. *Journal of Psychoactive Drugs, 35,* 7–13.

Brodley, B. T. (2006). Client-initiated homework in client-centered therapy. *Journal of Psychotherapy Integration, 16,* 140–161.

Brodsky, A. E. (1999). "Making it": The components and process of resilience among urban, African American, single mothers. *American Journal of Orthopsychiatry, 69,* 148–169.

Brueggemann, W. G. (2001). *The practice of macro social work* (2nd ed.). Belmont, CA: Brooks/Cole.

Bucky, S. F., Callan, J. E., & Stricker, G. (Eds.). (2005). *Ethical and legal issues for mental health professionals: A comprehensive handbook of principles and standards.* Binghamton, NY: Haworth Press.

Burlingame, G. M., MacKenzie, K. R., & Strauss, B. (2004). Small-group treatment: evidence for effectiveness and mechanisms of change. In M. J. Lambert (Ed.), *Bergin and Garfield's handbook of psychotherapy and behavior change* (pp. 647–696). New York: Wiley.

Burr, V. (1995). *An introduction to social constructivism.* London: Routledge.

Burr, V., Vutt, T., & Epting, F. (1997). Core construing: Self discovery or self invention? In G. J. Neimeyer & R. A. Neimeyer (Eds.). *Advances in personal construct psychology: Vol. 4* (pp. 39–62). Greenwich, CT: JAI Press.

Butler, W., & Powers, K. (1996). Solution-focused grief therapy. In S. D. Miller, M. A. Hubble, & B. L. Duncan (Eds.), *Handbook of solution-focused brief therapy* (pp. 228–250). San Francisco: Jossey-Bass.

Campbell, J. (2006). *Essentials of clinical supervision.* Hoboken, NJ: Wiley.

Carlson, T. D., Kirkpatrick, D., & Hecker, L. (2002). Religion, spirituality, and marriage and family therapy: A study of family therapists' beliefs about the appropriateness of addressing religious and spiritual issues in therapy. *American Journal of Family Therapy, 30,* 157–171.

Carter, B. (2003). Gender and child protection. *International Social Work, 46,* 555–557.

Carter, B., & McGoldrick, M. (Eds.). (1999). *The expanded family life cycle: Individual, family, and social perspectives* (3rd ed.). Boston: Allyn & Bacon.

Castonguay, L. G., & Beutler, L. E. (Eds.) (2006). *Principles of therapeutic change that work.* New York: Oxford University Press.

Chang, V. N. (1996). *I just lost myself: Psychological abuse of women in marriage.* Westport, CT: Praeger.

Chang, V. N., & Scott, S. T. (1999). *Basic interviewing skills: A workbook for practitioners.* Chicago: Nelson-Hall.

Cheavens, J. S., Feldman, D. B., Woodward, J. T., & Snyder, C. R. (2006). Hope in cognitive psychotherapies: On working with client strengths. *Journal of Cognitive Psychotherapy, 20,* 135–145.

Chestang, L. (1972). *Character development in a hostile environment.* Occasional Paper No. 3. Chicago: University of Chicago.

Cheung, Y. W., Mok, B. H., & Cheung, T.-S. (2005). Personal empowerment and life satisfaction among self-help group members in Hong Kong. *Small Group Research, 36,* 354–377.

Cho, H. J. (2005). Reviving the old sermon of medicine with the placebo effect. *Revista Brasileira de Psiquiatria, 27,* 336–340.

Christiansen, E. J., & Evans, W. P. (2005). Adolescent victimization: Testing models of resiliency by gender. *Journal of Early Adolescence, 25,* 298.

Clauss-Ehlers, C. S. (2004). Reinventing resilience: A model of culturally-focused resilient adaptation. *Community Diversity and Ethnic Minority Psychology, 5,* 65–75.

Colemena, M., & Ganong, L. (2002). Resilience and families. *Family Relations, 51,* 7–20.

Collins, D. (1990). Identifying dysfunctional counseling skill behaviors. *The Clinical Supervisor, 8* (1), 67–79.

Compton, B., Galaway, B., & Cournoyer, B. (2005). *Social work processes* (7th ed.). Belmont, CA: Thomson Learning.

Constantine, M. G., Lewis, E. L., Conner, L. C., & Sanchez, D. (2000). Addressing spiritual and religious issues in counseling African Americans: Implications for counselor training and practice. *Counseling and Values, 45*(1), 28–38.

Contarello, A. (2003). Body to body: Copresence in communication. In L. Fortunati, J. E. Katz, & R. Riccini (Eds.), *Mediating the human body: Technology, communication, and fashion* (pp. 123–131). Mahwah, NJ: Lawrence Erlbaum Associates.

Conyne, R. K., & Bemak, F. (2004). Teaching group work from an ecological perspective. *The Journal for Specialists in Group Work, 29,* 7–18.

Cottone, R. R., & Tarvydas, V. M. (2003). *Ethical and professional issues in counseling* (2nd ed.). Upper Saddle River, NJ: Prentice Hall.

Cournoyer, B. (2004). *The evidence-based social work skills book.* Belmont, CA: Wadsworth.

Cozolino, L. (2004). *The making of a therapist: A practical guide for the inner journey.* New York: Norton.

Curtis, J. M. (1982). The effect of therapist self-disclosure on patients' perceptions of empathy, competence, and trust in an analogue psychotherapeutic inter-action. *Psychotherapy: Theory, Research, Practice, Training, 19,* 54–62.

Curtis, R. C. (2000). Using goal-setting strategies to enrich the practicum and internship experiences of beginning counselors. *Journal of Humanistic Counseling Education and Development, 38*(4), 194–216.

Daniel, J. H., Roysircar, G., & Abeles, N. (2004). Individual and cultural diversity competency: Focus on the therapist. *Journal of Clinical Psychology, 60,* 755–770.

Davis, B. (2001). The restorative power of emotions in child protection services. *Child & Adolescent Social Work Journal, 18,* 437–454.

De Jong, P., & Berg, I. K. (1998). *Interviewing for solutions.* Pacific Grove, CA: Brooks/Cole.

De Jong, P., & Hopwood, L. E. (1996). Outcome research on treatment conducted at the brief family therapy center, 1992–1993. In S. D. Miller, M. A. Hubbles, & B. L. Duncan (Eds.), *Handbook of solution-focused brief therapy* (pp. 272–298). San Francisco: Jossey-Bass.

De Jong, P., & Miller, S. D. (1995). How to interview for client strengths. *Social Work, 40,* 729–736.

De Longis, A., & Holtzman, S. (2005). Coping in context: the role of stress, social support, and person-ality in coping. *Journal of Personality, 73,* 1633–1656.

De Shazer, S., & Molnar, A. (1984). Four useful interventions in family therapy. *Journal of Marital and Family Therapy, 10,* 297–304.

Dewees, C. H. (2006). An investigation of bereaved parents: Coping strat-egies and effects on the marital relationship. (Doctoral disserta-tion, St. Mary's University, 2006). *Dissertation Abstracts Interna-tional, 66,* 12-A.

Dishion, T. J., & Stormshak, E. A. (2007). *Intervening in children's lives: An ecological, family-centered approach to mental health care.* Washington, DC: American Psychological Association.

Dodd, P., & Gutierrez, L. (1990). Pre-paring students for the future: A power perspective on community practice. *Administration in Social Work, 14,* 63–78.

Donnelly, C., & Carswell, A. (2002). Individualized outcome measures: A review of the literature. *Cana-dian Journal of Occupational Therapy, 69,* 84–94.

Dore, M. M., & Alexander, L. B. (1996). Preserving families at risk of child abuse and neglect: The role of the helping alliance. *Child Abuse and Neglect, 20,* 349–361.

Dowden, C., & Andrews, D. A. (2000). Effective correctional treat-ment and violent reoffending: A meta-analysis. *Canadian Journal of Criminology, 42,* 449–467.

Dudley-Grant, G. R., Mendez, G. I., & Zinn, J. (2000). Strategies for anticipating and preventing psy-chological trauma of hurricanes through community education. *Professional Psychology: Research, and Practice, 31,* 387–392.

Egan, G. (2002). *The skilled helper: A problem-management approach to helping* (7th ed.). Pacific Grove, CA: Brooks/Cole.

Egan, G. (2007). *The skilled helper: A problem-management and opportunity-development approach to helping.* Belmont, CA: Brooks/Cole, Thomson Higher Education.

Farber, B. A., & Lane, J. S. (2002). Positive regard. In J. C. Norcross (Ed.), *Psychotherapy relationships that work: Therapist contributions and responsiveness to patients* (pp. 175–194). New York: Oxford Uni-versity Press.

Feldman, D., Rand, K., Shorey, H., & Snyder, C. (2002). Hopeful choices: A school counselor's guide to Hope Theory. *Professional School Counseling, 5,* 298–308.

Fisher, C. B. (2003). *Decoding the ethics code.* Thousand Oaks, CA: Sage Publications.

Fisher, K., & Hardie, R. J. (2002). Goal attainment scaling in evaluat-ing a multidisciplinary pain man-agement program. *Clinical Rehabilitation, 16,* 871–877.

Fishman, P., Taplin, S., Meyer, D., & Barlow, W. (2000). Cost-effective-ness of strategies to enhance mam-mography use. *Effective Clinical Practice, 4,* 213–220.

Fivush, R. (2004). Voice and silence: A feminist model of autobiographical memory. In J. M. Lucariello, J. A. Hudson, R. Fivush, & P. J. Bauer (Eds.), *The development of the mediated mind: Sociocultural context and cognitive development* (pp. 79–99). Mahwah, NJ: Law-rence Erlbaum Associates.

Flaskas, C. (2004). Thinking about the therapeutic relationship: Emerging themes in family therapy. *The Aus-tralian and New Zealand Journal of Family Therapy, 25,* 13–20.

Fleuridas, C., Leigh, G. K., Rosenthal, D. M., & Leigh, T. E. (1990). Family goal recording: An adapta-tion of goal attainment scaling for enhancing family therapy and assessment. *Journal of Marital and Family Therapy, 16*(4), 389–406.

Fonagy, P., Target, M., Cottrell, D., Phillips, J., & Kurtz, Z. (2002). *What works for whom? A critical review of treatments for children and adolescents.* New York: Guilford.

Ford, G. G. (2006). *Ethical reasoning for mental health professionals.* Thousand Oaks, CA: Sage.

Fortune, A. E. (1987). Grief only? Client and social worker reactions to termination. *Clinical Social Work Journal, 15,* 159–171.

Fortune, A. E., Pearlingi, B., & Rochelle, C. D. (1992). Reactions to termination of individual treat-ment. *Social Work, 37,* 171–178.

Frank, J. D., & Frank, J. B. (1991). *Persuasion and healing: A com-parative study of psychotherapy* (3rd ed.). Baltimore: Johns Hopkins University Press.

Friedman, N. (2005). Experiential lis-tening. *Journal of Humanistic Psy-chology, 45,* 217–238.

Furman, B., & Ahola, T. (1992). *Solu-tion talk: Hosting the therapeutic conversations.* New York: Norton.

Gabarino, J., Dubrow, N., Kostelny, K., & Pardo, C. (1992). *Children in danger.* San Francisco: Jossey-Bass.

Gager, F. P. (2004). Exploring relation-ships among termination status, therapy outcome, and client out-come. *Dissertation Abstracts Inter-national, 64,* 3522.

Garmezy, N., & Rutter, M. (1983). *Stress, coping and development in children.* New York: McGraw Hill.

Garvin, C., & Seabury, B. (1997). *Interpersonal practice in social work: Promoting competence and social justice.* Boston: Allyn & Bacon.

Gergen, K. J. (2006). Social construction as an ethics of infinitude: Reply to Brinkmann. *Journal of Humanistic Psychology, 46*, 119.

Germain, C. B., & Gitterman, A. (1995). Ecological perspective. In L. Beebe et al. (Eds.), *Encyclopedia of social work: Vol. 1* (19th ed., pp. 816–824). Washington, DC: NASW Press.

Gibson, L. (2006). Mirrored emotions. *University of Chicago Magazine, 98*(4), 34–39.

Gilbert, L. A., & Scher, M. (1999). *Gender and sex in counseling and psychotherapy.* Boston: Allyn & Bacon.

Goldenberg, H., & Goldenberg, I. (1998). *Counseling today's families.* Pacific Grove, CA: Brooks/Cole.

Goldenthal, P. (1996). *Doing contextual therapy: An integrated model for working with individuals, couples, and families.* New York: Norton.

Gollwitzer, P. M. (1999). Implementation intentions: Strong effects of simple plans. *American Psychologist, 54*, 493–503.

Gordon, K. A. (1995). Self-concept and motivational patterns of resilient African American high school students. *Journal of Black Psychology, 21*, 239–256.

Gregory, W. H. (2002). Resiliency in the Black family. *Dissertation Abstracts International, 62*, 4786.

Hagedorn, W. B. (2005). Counselor self-awareness and self-exploration of religious and spiritual beliefs: Know thyself. In C. S. Cashwell & Y. J. Scott, *Integrating spirituality and religion into counseling: A guide to competent practice* (pp. 63–84). Alexandria, VA: American Counseling Association.

Hammond, S. A. (1998). *The thin book of appreciative inquiry.* Bend, OR: Thin Book Publishing.

Hanna, F. J. (2002). Building hope for change. In F. J. Hanna (Ed.), *Therapy with difficult clients: Using the precursors model to awaken change.* Washington, DC: American Psychological Association.

Hardina, D. (2005). Ten characteristics of empowerment-oriented social service organizations. *Administration in Social Work, 29*, 23–42.

Harrison, S., Pollitt, C., Hunter, D. J., & Marnoch, G. (1990). No hiding place: On the discomforts of researching the contemporary policy process. *Journal of Social Policy, 19*, 169–190.

Haslam, D. R., & Harris, S. M. (2004). Informed consent documents of marriage and family therapists in private practice: A qualitative analysis. *American Journal of Family Therapy, 32*, 359–374.

Hayes, R. L., & Oppenheim, R. (1997). Constructivism: Reality is what you make it. In T. L. Sexton & B. L. Griffin, *Constructivist thinking in counseling practice, research, and training* (pp. 19–40). New York: Teachers College Press.

Hedges, L. E. (2000). *Facing the challenge of liability in psychotherapy.* Northvale, NJ: Jason Aronson, Inc.

Herron, W. G., & Rouslin, S. (1984). *Issues in psychotherapy.* Washington, DC: Oryn Publications.

Hill, C. E., & Lambert, M. J. (2004). Methodological issues in studying psychotherapy processes and outcomes. In M. J. Lambert (Ed.), *Psychotherapy and behavior change* (5th ed.). New York: Wiley.

Hill, C. E., & Lent, R. W. (2006). A narrative and meta-analytic review of helping skills training: Time to revive a dormant area of inquiry. *Psychotherapy: Theory, Research, Practice, Training, 43*, 154–172.

Hodge, D. R. (2005). Spiritual life-maps: A client-centered pictorial instrument for spiritual assessment, planning, and intervention. *Social Work, 50*, 197–206.

Hollister-Wagner, G. H., Foshee, V. A., & Jackson, C. (2001). Adolescent aggression: Models of resiliency. *Journal of Applied Social Psychology, 31*, 445.

Home, A. (1999). Group empowerment. In W. Shera & L. Wells (Eds.), *Empowerment practice in social work: Developing richer conceptual foundations* (pp. 234–245). Toronto: Canadian Scholars' Press.

Hopps, J. G., Pinderhughes, E., & Shankar, R. (1995). *The power to care: Clinical practice effectiveness with overwhelmed clients.* New York: Free Press.

Hosking, D. M. (2005). Bounded entities, constructive revisions, and radical re-constructions. *Cognition, Brain, Behavior, 9*, 609–622.

Hubble, M. A., & Miller, S. D. (2004). The client: Psychotherapy's missing link for promoting a positive psychology. In P. A. Linley & S. Joseph (Eds.), *Positive psychology in practice.* Hoboken, NJ: Wiley.

Ivey, A. E., & Ivey, M. B. (2003). *Intentional interviewing and counseling: Facilitating client development in a multicultural society* (5th ed.). Pacific Grove, CA: Brooks/Cole.

Jacobs, E. E., Masson, R. L., & Harvill, R. L. (1998). *Group counseling: Strategies and skills* (3rd ed.). Pacific Grove, CA: Brooks/Cole.

James, W. H. (2005). Biological and psychosocial determinants of male and female human sexual orientation. *Journal of Biosocial Science, 37*, 555–567.

Jones, A. C. (2003). Reconstructing the stepfamily: Old myths, new stories. *Social Work, 48*, 228–236.

Kacen, L. (1999). Anxiety levels, group characteristics, and members' behaviors in the termination stage of support groups for patients recovering from heart attacks. *Research on Social Work Practice, 9*, 656–672.

Karr, J. (1990). Goal attainment scaling in the treatment of children with behavior disorders. *School Social Work Journal, 15*, 14–20.

Katsavdakis, K. A., Gabbard, G. O., & Athey, G. I. (2004). Profiles of impaired health professionals. *Bulletin of the Menninger Clinic, 68*, 60–72.

Kazantzis, N., & Ronan, K. R. (2006). Can between-session (homework) activities be considered a common factor in psychotherapy? *Journal of Psychotherapy Integration, 16*, 115–127.

Kazdin, A. E. (1995). Scope of child and adolescent psychotherapy research: Limited sampling of dysfunctions, treatments, and client characteristics. *Journal of Child Clinical Psychology, 24*, 125–140.

Kear-Colwell, J., & Pollock, P. (1997). Motivation or confrontation: Which approach to the child sex offender? *Criminal Justice and Behavior, 24*, 20–33.

Keijsers, G. P. J., Schaap, C. P., & Hoogduin, C. A. L. (2000). The impact of interpersonal patient and therapist behavior on outcome in cognitive-behavior therapy.

Behavior Modification, 24, 264–297.

Kelly, G. A. (1991). *The psychology of personal constructs: Vol. 1. A theory of personality.* London: Routledge. (Original work published 1955).

Kendall, F. E. (2001). *Understanding white privilege.* Retrieved May 4, 2007, from http://www.cwsworkshop.org/resources/WhitePrivilege.html

Kim, B. S. K., Ng, G. F., & Ahn, A. J. (2005). Effects of client expectations for counseling success, client-counselor worldview match, and client strengths. *Journal of Counseling Psychology, 52,* 67–76.

Kiresuk, T. J., Smith, A., & Cardillo, J. E. (1994). *Goal attainment scaling: Applications, theory, and measurement.* Mahwah, NJ: Erlbaum.

Koerin, B. B., Harrigan, M. P., & Reeves, J. W. (1990). Facilitating the transition from student to social worker: Challenges of the younger student. *Journal of Social Work Education, 26* (2), 199–208.

Koocher, G. P., & Keith-Spiegel, P. (1998). *Ethics in psychology: Professional standards and cases.* New York: Oxford University Press.

Kottler, J. A. (1994). *Advanced group leadership.* Pacific Grove, CA: Brooks/Cole.

Kottler, J. A. (2001). *Making changes last.* Philadelphia: Brunner-Routledge.

Kottler, J. A. (2003). *On being a therapist* (3rd ed.). San Francisco: Jossey-Bass.

Kruger, J., & Dunning, D. (1999). Unskilled and unaware of it: How difficulties in recognizing one's own incompetence lead to inflated self-assessments. *Journal of Personality and Social Psychology, 77,* 1121–1134.

Krupnick, J. L., Sotsky, S. M., Simmens, S., Moyer, J., Elkin, I., Watkins, J., & Pilkonis, P. A. (1996). The role of the therapeutic alliance in psychotherapy and pharmacotherapy outcome: Findings in the National Institute of Mental Health Treatment of Depression Collaborative Research Program. *Journal of Consulting and Clinical Psychology, 64,* 532–539.

Lambert, M. J., & Barley, D. E. (2002). Research summary on the therapeutic relationship and psychotherapy outcome. In J. C. Norcross (Ed.), *Psychotherapy relationships that work: Therapist contributions and responsiveness to patients* (pp. 17–35). New York: Oxford University Press.

Lambert, M., & Bergin, A. (1994). The effectiveness of psychotherapy. In A. Bergin & S. Garfield (Eds.), *Handbook of psychotherapy and behavior change* (4th ed., pp. 143–189). Toronto: Wiley.

Lazarus, R. S., & Folkman, S. (1984). *Stress, appraisal, and coping.* New York: Springer.

Lee, J. A. (2001). *An empowerment approach to social work practice: Building the beloved community* (2nd ed.). New York: Columbia University Press.

Lever, H. & Gmeiner, A. (2000). Families leaving family therapy after one or two sessions: A multiple descriptive case study. *Contemporary Family Therapy, 22,* 39–65.

Lewin, K. (1952). Group decision and social change. In G. E. Swanson, T. N. Nowcomb, & E. L. Hartley (Eds.), *Readings in social psychology* (pp. 168–185). New York: Holt, Rinehart, and Winston.

Littrell, J., & Beck, E. (1999). Perceiving oppression: Relationships with resilience, self-esteem, depressive symptoms, and reliance on God in African American homeless men. *Journal of Sociology and Social Welfare, 26,* 137.

Locke, E. A., Shaw, K. N., Saari, L. M., & Latham, G. R. (1981). Goal setting and task performance: 1969–1980. *Psychological Bulletin, 90,* 125–152.

Lopez, S. J., & Magyar-Moe, J. L. (2006). A positive psychology that matters. *Counseling Psychologist, 34,* 323–330.

Lyons, M., Smuts, C., & Stephens, A. (2001). Participation, empowerment and sustainability: (How) do the links work? *Urban Studies, 38,* 1233.

Mahalik, J. R., VanOrmer, E. A., & Simi, N. L. (2000). Ethical issues in using self-disclosure in feminist therapy. In M. Brabeck (Ed.), *Practicing feminist ethics in psychology. Psychology of women book series* (pp. 189–201). Washington, DC: American Psychological Association.

Mahoney, M. J. (1986a). The tyranny of techniques. *Counseling and Values, 30,* 169–174.

Mahoney, M. J. (1986b). Authentic presence and compassionate wisdom: The art of Jim Bugental. *Journal of Humanistic Psychology, 36,* 58–66.

Mahoney, M. J. (2003). *Constructivist psychotherapy: A practical guide.* New York: Guilford.

Mascari, J. B., & Webber, J. M. (2006). Salting the slippery slope: What licensing violations tell us about preventing dangerous ethical situations. In G. R. Walz, J. C. Bleuer, & R. K. Yep (Eds.), *Vistas: Compelling perspectives on counseling 2006* (pp. 165–168). Alexandria, VA: American Counseling Association.

Masten, A., Best, K., & Garmezy, N. (1990). Resilience and development: Contributions from the study of children who overcame adversity. *Development and Psychopathology, 2,* 425–444.

McCullough, M. E., & Snyder, C. K. (2000). Classical sources of human strength: Revisiting an old home and building a new one. *Journal of Social and Clinical Psychology, 19,* 1–10.

McKeel, A. J. (1996). A clinician's guide to research on solution-focused brief therapy. In S. D. Miller, M. A. Hubbles, & B. L. Duncan, (Eds.), *Handbook of solution-focused brief therapy* (pp. 251–271). San Francisco: Jossey-Bass.

McLaren, C., & Rodger, S. (2003). Goal attainment scaling: Clinical implications for paediatric occupational therapy practice. *Australian Occupational Therapy Journal, 50,* 216–224.

Meier, W. M., & Davis, S. R. (2004). *The elements of counseling.* Belmont, CA: Brooks/Cole.

Melor, K., & Sigmund, E. (1975). Discounting. *Transactional Analysis Journal, 5,* 295–302.

Menen, S. (2004). *Manual-based clinical skills training: Developing relationship-centered clinical proficiency.* Unpublished dissertation, Azusa Pacific University, Azusa, CA.

Metcalf, L., Thomas, F., Duncan, B. L., Miller, S. D., & Hubble, M. A. (1996). What works in solution-focused brief therapy: A qualitative analysis of client and therapist perceptions. In S. D. Miller, M. A. Hubble, & B. L. Duncan (Eds.), *Handbook of solution-focused brief therapy* (pp. 335–350). San Francisco: Jossey-Bass.

Meyer, B., Pilkonis, P. A., Krupnick, J. L., Egan, M. K., Simmens, S. J., & Sotsky, S. M. (2002). Treatment expectancies, patient alliance, and outcome: Further analyses from the national institute of mental health treatment of depression collaborative research program. *Journal of Consulting and Clinical Psychology, 70*, 1051–1055.

Middlemiss, W. (2005). Prevention and intervention: Using resiliency-based multi-setting approaches and a process-orientation. *Child and Adolescent Social Work Journal, 22*, 85–103.

Miley, K., O'Melia, M., & DuBois, B. (2004). *Generalist social work practice: An empowering approach* (4th ed.). Boston: Pearson.

Miller, B. (2004). Feminist family therapy: Empowerment in social context. *Journal of Marital & Family Therapy, 30*, 391.

Miller, W. R. (1987). Motivation and treatment goals. *Drugs and Society, 1*, 131–151.

Miller, W. R., & Hester, R. K. (1989). Treating alcohol problems: Toward an informed eclecticism. In R. K. Hester & W. R. Miller (Eds.), *Handbook of alcoholism treatment approaches*. Elmsford, NY: Pergamon Press.

Miller, W. R., & Rollnick, S. (2002). *Motivational interviewing: Preparing people for change* (2nd ed.). New York: Guilford.

Minuchin, P., Colapinto, J., & Minuchin, S. (1998). *Working with families of the poor*. New York: Guilford.

Mohr, W. K. (2003). The substance of a support group. *Western Journal of Nursing Research, 25*, 676–692.

Morrow, D. F., & Messinger, L. (2006). *Sexual orientation and gender expression in social work practice: Working with gay, lesbian, bisexual, and transgender people*. New York: Columbia University Press.

Moursund, J. (1993). *The process of counseling and therapy*. Pacific Grove, CA: Brooks/Cole.

Mueser, K. T., Wallace, C. J., & Liberman, R. P. (1995). New developments in social skills training. *Behavior Change, 12*, 31–40.

Murphy, B. C., & Dillon, C. (2003). *Interviewing in action: Relationship, process, and change*. Pacific Grove, CA: Brooks/Cole.

Murphy, J. A., & Rawlings, E. I. (2002). A survey of clinical psychologists on treating lesbian, gay, and bisexual clients. *Professional Psychology: Research and Practice, 33*, 183–189.

Murphy, P. M., Cramer, D., & Lillie, F. J. (1984). The relationship between curative factors perceived by patients in psychotherapy of depression: An exploratory study. *British Journal of Medical Psychology, 57*, 187–192.

Myers, D., & Hayes, J. A. (2006). Effects of therapist general self-disclosure and countertransference disclosure on ratings of the therapist and the session. *Psychotherapy: Theory, Research, Practice, Training, 43*, 173–185.

Nash, J. (2005). Women in between: Globalization and the new enlightenment. *Signs, 31*, 145.

Neimeyer, R. A., & Feixas, G. (1990). The role of homework and skill acquisition in the outcome of group cognitive therapy for depression. *Behavior Therapy, 21*, 281–292.

Newton, T. (2006). Script, psychological life plans, and the learning cycle. *Transactional Analysis Journal, 36*, 186–195.

Nichols, M. P., & Schwartz, R. C. (2006). *Family therapy: Concepts and methods*. Boston: Allyn & Bacon.

Norcross, J. C. (April, 2007). *Psychotherapy relationships that work: Evidence-based practices*. Workshop presented for the Annual Conference of the California Psychological Association, Costa Mesa, CA.

Norcross, J. C., Ratzin, A. C., & Payne, D. (1989). Ringing in the New Year: The change process and reported outcomes of resolutions. *Addictive Behaviors, 14*, 205–212.

Novick, J., & Novick, K. K. (2006). *Good goodbyes: Knowing how to end in psychotherapy and psychoanalysis*. Lanham, MD: Jason Aronson.

O'Brien, M. (2005). Studying individual and family development: Linking theory and research. *Journal of Marriage and Family, 67*, 880–890.

O'Connell, B. (2005). *Solution-focused therapy*. London: Sage Publications.

O'Hanlon, B., & Weiner-Davis, M. (2003). *In search of solutions: A new direction in psychotherapy*. New York: Norton.

Okun, B. F. (2002). *Effective helping: Interviewing and counseling techniques* (6th ed.). Belmont, CA: Brooks/Cole.

Orlinsky, D., Grawe, K., & Parks, B. (1994). Process and outcome in psychotherapy: A review of reviews. *Psychotherapy, 21*, 431–438.

Orlinsky, D. E., Ronnestad, M. H., Gerin, P., Davis, J. D., Ambühl, H., Davis, M. L., Dazord, A., Willutzki, U., Aapro, N., Botermans, J., & Schröder, T. A. (2005). The development of psychotherapists. In D. E. Orlinsky & M. H. Ronnestad (Eds.), *How psychotherapists develop: A study of therapeutic work and professional growth* (pp. 3–13). Washington, DC: American Psychological Association.

Perkins, D. D., Crim, B., Silberman, P., & Brown, B. B. (2004). Community development as a response to community-level adversity: Ecological theory and research and strengths-based policy. In K. I. Maton, C. J. Schellenbach, B. J. Leadbeater, & A. L. Solarz, *Investing in children, youth, families, and communities: Strengths-based research and policy*. Washington, DC: American Psychological Association.

Peterson, C., & Seligman, M. E. P. (2004). *Character strengths and virtues: A handbook and classification*. New York: Oxford.

Pike, C., Bennett, R., & Chang, V. N. (2004). Measuring competency in the use of basic social work interviewing skills. *Advances in Social Work, 5*, 61–76.

Plant, E. A., Hyde, J. S., Keltner, D., & Devine, P. G. (2000). The gender stereotyping of emotions.

Psychology of Women Quarterly, 24, 81–92.

Pope, K. S., & Vasquez, M. J. T. (1998). *Ethics in psychotherapy and counseling: A practical guide* (2nd ed.). San Francisco: Jossey-Bass.

Prest, L.A., Russel, R., & D'souza, H. (1999). Spirituality and religion in training, practice and person development. *Journal of Family Therapy, 21*, 60–77.

Prochaska, J. O. (1999). How do people change, and how can we help many more people? In M. A. Hubble, B. L. Duncan, & S. D. Miller (Eds.), *The heart and soul of change.* Washington, DC: American Psychological Association.

Prochaska, J. O., Norcross, J. C., & DiClemente, C. C. (1994). *Changing for good.* New York: Morrow.

Proctor, E. K., & Davis, L. E. (1994). The challenge of racial difference: Skills for clinical practice. *Social Work, 39* (3), 314–323.

Rahman, Q., & Wilson, G. D. (2003). Born gay? The psychobiology of human sexual orientation. *Personality and Individual Differences, 38*, 1337–1382.

Rapp, R. C., Siegal, H. A., Li, L., & Saha, P. (1998). Predicting post-primary treatment service and drug use outcome: A multivariate analysis. *American Journal of Drug and Alcohol Abuse, 24*, 603–615.

Rappaport, J. (1981). Studies in empowerment: Introduction to the issue. *Prevention in Human Services, 3*, 1–7.

Rappaport, J. (1985). The power of empowerment language. *Social Policy, 16* (2), 15–21.

Raskin, J. D. (2001). On relativism in constructivist psychology. *Journal of Constructivist Psychology, 14*, 285–313.

Remley, T. P., & Herlihy, B., (2001). *Ethical, legal, and professional issues in counseling.* Upper Saddle River, NJ: Prentice Hall.

Roberts, M. C., Vernberg, E. M., & Jackson, Y. (2000). Psychotherapy with children and families. In C. R. Snyder & R. E. Ingram (Eds.), *Handbook of psychological change: Psychotherapy processes and practices for the 21st century* (pp. 500–519). Hoboken, NJ: Wiley.

Robertson-Mjaanes, S. L. (2000). An evaluation of goal attainment scaling as an intervention monitoring and outcome evaluation technique. *Dissertation Abstracts International, 60* (3), 272.

Rockwell, K., Howlett, S., Stadnyk, K., & Carver, D. (2003). Responsiveness of goal attainment scaling in a randomized controlled trial of comprehensive geriatric assessment. *Journal of Clinical Epidemiology, 56*, 736–743.

Rodger, K. B., & Rose, H. A. (2002). Risk and resilience factors among adolescents who experience marital transition. *Journal of Marriage and Family, 64*, 1024–1037.

Rogers, C. R. (1951). *Client centered therapy: Its current practice, theory, and implications.* Chicago: Houghton Mifflin.

Rogers, C. R. (1957). The necessary and sufficient conditions of therapeutic personality change. *Journal of Consulting Psychology, 21*, 95–103.

Rogers, C. R. (1958). The characteristics of a helping relationship. *Personnel and Guidance Journal, 37*, 6–16.

Rogers, C. R. (1961a). *On becoming a person.* Boston: Houghton-Mifflin.

Rogers, C. R. (1961b). The process equation of psychotherapy. *American Journal of Psychotherapy, 15*, 27–45.

Rose, S. M. (2005). Empowerment: The foundation for social work practice in mental health. In S. A. Kirk (Ed.), *Mental disorders in the social environment: Critical perspectives* (pp. 190–200). New York: Columbia University Press.

Rosenbaum, M., & Ronen, T. (1998). Clinical supervision from the standpoint of cognitive-behavior therapy. *Psychotherapy: Theory, Research and Practice, 35*, 220–230.

Roysircar, G. (2004). Cultural self-awareness assessment: Practice examples from psychology training. *Professional Psychology: Research and Practice, 35*, 658–666.

Rudd, M. D., Mandrusiak, M., & Joiner Jr., T. E. (2006). The case against no-suicide contracts: The commitment to treatment statement as a practice alternative. *Journal of Clinical Psychology, 62* (2), 243–251.

Rupert, P. A., & Morgan, D. J. (2005). Work setting and burnout among professional psychologists. *Professional Psychology: Research and Practice, 36*, 544–550.

Rutan, J. S., & Stone, W. N. (2001). Psychodynamic group psychotherapy (3rd ed.). New York: Guilford Press.

Safran, S. A., Heimberg, R. G., & Juster, H. R. (1997). Clients' expectancies and their relationship to pretreatment symptomatology and outcome of cognitive-behavioral group treatment for social phobia. *Journal of Consulting and Clinical Psychology, 65*, 694–698.

Saleebey, D. (2002a). The strengths perspective: Possibilities and problems. In D. Saleebey (Ed.), *The strengths perspective in social work practice* (3rd ed., pp. 264–283). Boston: Allyn & Bacon.

Saleebey, D. (2002b). Introduction: Power to the people. In D. Saleebey (Ed.), *The strengths perspective in social work practice* (3rd ed., pp. 1–22). Boston: Allyn & Bacon.

Saleebey, D. (2002c). The strengths approach to practice. In D. Saleebey (Ed.), *The strengths perspective in social work practice* (3rd ed., pp. 80–94). Boston: Allyn & Bacon.

Sanchez-Craig, M. (1980). Random assignment to abstinence or controlled drinking in a cognitive-behavioral program: Effects on drinking behavior. *Addictive Behavior, 5*, 35–39.

Sassaroli, S., & Ruggiero, G. M. (2005). The role of stress in the association between low self-esteem, perfectionism, and worry, and eating disorders. *International Journal of Eating Disorders, 37*, 135–141.

Seelau, S. M., & Seelau, E. P. (2005). Gender-role stereotypes and perceptions of heterosexual, gay, and lesbian domestic violence. *Journal of Family Violence, 20*, 363–371.

Seligman, L. (2004). *Technical and conceptual skills for mental health professionals.* Upper Saddle River, NJ: Pearson.

Sexton, T. L., & Alexander, J. F. (2002). Family-based empirically supported interventions. *The Counseling Psychologist, 30*, 238–261.

Sexton, T. L., Alexander, J. F., & Mease, A. C. (2003). Levels of evidence for the models and mechanisms of therapeutic change in family and couple therapy. In M. J. Lambert (Ed.), *Handbook of psychotherapy and behavior change* (5th ed., pp. 590–646). New York: Wiley.

Sexton, T. L., & Griffin, B. L. (1997). *Constructivist thinking in counseling practice, research, and training.* New York: Teachers College Press.

Shepard, D., & Morrow, G. (2003). Critical self monitoring. In J. A. Kottler and W. P. Jones (Eds.), *Doing better.* New York: Brunner/Routledge.

Sherman, M. D., & Thelan, H. M. (1998). Distress and professional impairment among psychologists in clinical practice. *Professional Psychology: Research and Practice, 29,* 79–85.

Shulman, L. (1992). *The skills of helping individuals, families, and groups.* Itasca, IL: F. E. Peacock.

Siegall, M., & Gardner, S. (2000). Contextual factors of psychological empowerment. *Personnel Review, 29,* 703–722.

Simon, B. (1994). *The empowerment tradition in American social work: A history.* New York: Columbia University Press.

Skovholt, T. M. (2001). *The resilient practitioner: Burnout prevention and self-care strategies for counselors, therapists, teachers, and health professionals.* Needham Heights, MA: Allyn & Bacon.

Smith, S. A., Thomas, S. A., & Jackson, A. C. (2004). An exploration of the therapeutic relationship and counseling outcomes in a problem gambling counseling service. *Journal of Social Work Practice, 18,* 99–112.

Snyder, C. R., & Lopez, S. J. (2001). *Handbook of positive change.* New York: Wiley.

Stam, H. J. (1998). Personal-construct theory and social constructivism: Difference and dialogue. *Journal of Constructivist Psychology, 11,* 187–203.

Steinglass, P., Bennet, L. A., & Wolin, J. (1987). *The alcoholic family.* New York: Basic Books.

Stone, G. L., & Vance, A. (1976). Instructions, modeling, and rehearsal: Implications for training.

Journal of Counseling Psychology, 23, 272–279.

Stular, S. (1998). Social construction of gender identity. *Druzbena konstrukcija spolne identitete, 35,* 441–454.

Talmon, M. (1990). *Single session therapy.* San Francisco: Jossey-Bass.

Tan, S. Y., & Dong, N. J. (1999). Psychotherapy with members of Asian American churches and spiritual traditions. In P. S. Richards & A. E. Bergin (Eds.), *Handbook of psychotherapy and religious diversity* (pp. 421–444). Washington, DC: American Psychological Association.

Thomas, S. E. G., Werner-Wilson, R. J., & Murphy, M. J. (2005). Influence of therapist and client behaviors on therapy alliance. *Contemporary Family Therapy: An International Journal, 27* (1), 19–35.

Thompson, R. A. (2006). The development of the person: Social understanding, relationships, conscience, self. In N. Eisenberg, W. Damon, & R. M. Lerner (Eds.) *Handbook of child psychology: Social, emotional, and personality development* (6th ed., pp. 24–98). Hoboken, NJ: Wiley.

Tohn, S. L., & Oshlag, J. A. (2000). *Crossing the bridge: Integrating solution focused therapy into clinical practice.* Sudbury, MA: Solutions Press.

Trevos, A. K., Quick, R. E., & Yanduli, V. (2000). Application of motivational interviewing to the adoption of water disinfection practices in Zambia. *Health Promotion International, 15,* 207–214.

Tseng, W. S. (2001). Culture and psychotherapy: An overview. In W. S. Tseng & J. Streltzer (Eds.), *Culture and psychotherapy: A guide to clinical practice* (pp. 3–12). Washington, DC: American Psychiatric Press.

Tully, C. T. (2000). *Lesbians, gays, and the empowerment perspective.* New York: Columbia University Press.

Ungar, M. (2002). A deeper, more social ecological social work practice. *Social Service Review, 76,* 480.

Ungar, M. (2004). A constructionist discourse on resilience: Multiple contexts, multiple realities among at-risk children and youth. *Youth & Camp Society, 35,* 341–365.

Van Buren, A. (2002). The relationship of verbal-nonverbal incongruence to communication mismatches in married couples. *North American Journal of Psychology, 4,* 21–36.

Vayda, E., & Bogo, M. (1991). A teaching model to unite classroom and field. *Journal of Social Work Education, 27,* 271–278.

Viederman, M. (1999). Presence and enactment as a vehicle of psychotherapeutic change. *Journal of Psychotherapy Practice and Research, 8,* 274–283.

Vinton, L., & Harrington, P. (1994). An evolution of the use of videotape in teaching empathy. *Journal of Teaching in Social Work, 9,* 71–84.

Vodde, R., & Gallant, J. P. (1995). Skill training as a place for self-exploration: A qualitative study of teaching social work methods from a postmodern perspective. *Journal of Teaching in Social Work, 11,* 119–137.

Walker Daniels, J., & Murphy, C. M. (1997). Stages and processes of change in batterers' treatment. *Cognitive and Behavioral Practice, 4,* 123–145.

Walter, J. L., & Peller, J. E. (1992). *Becoming solution-focused in brief therapy.* Philadelphia: Brunner/Mazel.

Wampold, B. E. (2001). *The great psychotherapy debate: Models, methods, and findings.* Mahwah, NJ: Lawrence Erlbaum Associates.

Watson, T. T. (2003). Resiliency: Mitigating effects of reciprocating social support on stress. *Dissertation Abstracts International: Section B: The Sciences and Engineering, 63* (8-B).

Weick, A. (1993). Reconstructing social work education. *Journal of Teaching in Social Work, 8,* 11–30.

Weick, A., & Chamberlain, R. (1996). Putting problems in their place: Further explorations in the strengths perspective. In D. Saleeby (Ed.), *The strengths perspective in social work practice* (2nd ed., pp. 39–48). White Plains, NY: Longman.

Weick, A., Rapp, C., Sullivan, W. P., & Kisthardt, W. (1989). A strengths perspective for social work practice. *Social Work, 34,* 350–354.

Westra, M. (1996). Active communication. Belmont, CA: Brooks/Cole.

Wiebe, L. M. (2002). Connection in the therapeutic relationship: Sharing a subjective world. *Dissertation Abstracts International, 62,* 5398.

Williams, E. N., Hurley, K., O'Brien, K., & de Gregorio, A. (2003). Development and validation of the Self-Awareness and Management Strategies (SAMS) scales for therapists. *Psychotherapy: Theory, Research, Practice, Training, 40,* 278–288.

Williams, E. N., Polster, D., Grizzard, M. B., Rockenbaugh, J., & Judge, A. B. (2003). What happens when therapists feel bored or anxious? A qualitative study of distracting self-awareness and therapists' management strategies. *Journal of Contemporary Psychotherapy, 33,* 5–18.

Williams, T. K., & Thornton, M. C. (1998). Social construction of ethnicity versus personal experience: The case of Afro-Amerasians. *Journal of Comparative Family Studies, 29,* 255.

Wolfer, T. A., & Scales, T. L. (2005). *Decision cases for advanced social work practice: Thinking like a social worker.* Belmont, CA: Thomson.

Wolin, S. (1999). A mindset of hope: Reaching today's youth. *The Community Circle of Caring Journal, 3* (3), 38–42.

Wolin, S. (2003). What is a strength? *Reclaiming Children and Youth, 12* (1), 18.

Wolkow, K. E., & Ferguson, H. B. (2001). Community factors in the development of resiliency: Considerations and future directions. *Community Mental Health Journal, 37,* 489–498.

Wolski, R. S. (2004). Reconceptualizing the individual: An ecological approach. *Dissertation Abstracts International, 64,* 2419.

Wong, Y. (2006). Strength-centered therapy: A social constructionist, virtues-based psychotherapy. *Psychotherapy, 43,* 133–146.

Wylie, M. S. (1996). Going for the cure. *The Family Therapy Networker, 20* (4), 21–37.

Yakin, J. A., & McMahon, S. D. (2003). Risk and resiliency: A test of a theoretical model for urban, African-American youth. *Journal of Prevention and Intervention in the Community, 26,* 5–19.

Yalom, I. D. (1995). *The theory and practice of group psychotherapy* (4th ed.). New York: Basic Books.

Zalter, B., & Fiske, H. (2005). Scaling in action. *Journal of Family Psychotherapy, 16,* 107–109.

Zimmerman, M. A. (1990). Toward a theory of learned hopefulness: A structural modal analysis of participation and empowerment. *Journal of Research in Personality, 24,* 71–86.

Zimmerman, M. A., & Arunkumar, R. (1994). Resilience research: Implications for schools and policy. *Social Policy Report, 8,* 1–20.

Zimmerman, M. A., Ramirez, J., Washienko, K. M., Walter, B., & Dryer, S. (1994). The encultural hypothesis: Exploring direct and protective effects among Native American youth. In H. I. McCubban, I. A. Thompson, & A. I. Thompson (Eds.), *Resiliency in ethnic minority families, Vol. 1: Native American families* (pp. 199–220). Madison, WI: University of Wisconsin Press.

Zimmerman, M. A., & Rappaport, J. (1988). Citizen participation, perceived control, and psychological empowerment. *American Journal of Community Psychology, 16,* 725–750.

INDEX